ERITREA

The Unfinished Revolution

ERITREA

The Unfinished Revolution

Richard Sherman

PRAEGER

PRAEGER SPECIAL STUDIES • PRAEGER SCIENTIFIC

Library of Congress Cataloging in Publication Data

Sherman, Richard.
   Eritrea, the unfinished revolution.

   Bibliography: p.
   Includes index.
   1. Eritrea--Politics and government. 2. National
liberation movements--Ethiopia--Eritrea. 3. Ethiopia--
Politics and government. I. Title.
DT395.5.S53   963'.5   79-24303
   ISBN 0-03-055921-9

DT
395.5
S53

Published in 1980 by Praeger Publishers
CBS Educational and Professional Publishing
A Division of CBS, Inc.
521 Fifth Avenue, New York, New York 10017 U.S.A.

0123456789   038   987654321

Printed in the United States of America

For Edith, Leo, and Gordon

In Memoriam

Foreword by
Basil Davidson

The problems of Eritrea, whether of its past, its present, or its future, are extraordinarily interesting for a whole number of reasons, and whether or not one is especially concerned with African questions. These problems are interesting for their human reference: the Eritreans with all their distinctive character and style, their ecology, their ethnic composition, their record of suffering oppression and of resisting oppression, their country and what (in spite of large and lengthy invasions) they have been able to make of their country. These problems, again, are interesting to the historian because they draw much of their substance from the very depths of the development of nationalism in the colonial and postcolonial world. They are interesting to the political scientist for their intractability, but also for their possible solutions that now stand to be examined. They are interesting to linguists, soil scientists, agronomists, and, not least on the list, plain observers of the drama of the human scene. They are old problems, not new ones; all that is new today are their possible solutions. How surprising must we therefore find it, in view of all this, that the world till yesterday, or even today, has preferred to ignore Eritrea or has simply known nothing about it.

Looking at only one aspect of the Eritrean question, the aspect of national identity and the natural drive for national independence, one is at once plunged into great African debates. If colonized African peoples have justly claimed and justly exercised the right to be free, and to build within colonial frontiers new nations of their own, resuming the development of their past history, then why should this right be denied to the Eritreans? They were colonized by the Italians, after all, in exactly the same way and in more or less exactly the same years as the rest of the continent was taken into colonial ownership and control. If they now find themselves formally within Ethiopia, that is not only a subsequent but also a similar development. Or if the colonial period proved to be, for other peoples, the "forcing bed" from which there duly flowered the harvests of modern nationalism— the nationalism by means of which colonized peoples could throw off their subjection and stand upon their own—then why should it be denied that the Eritreans, too, went through this same process, acquired a national consciousness during colonial rule, and came to feel the natural need for an assertion of their own identity? What today is so "special" about the Eritrean case except that they happen to be colonized by an African, not a European, power? Is an African oppression any different in principle from any other?

The passion of such debates, their intricacy and painfulness, are easy to comprehend, and easier still, if one wished for a further and related example, in the case of another Ethiopian colonial region, the Somali region of the Ogaden, seized by the Ethiopians at much the same moment as the British seized their chunk of Somalian territory and the Italians seized theirs. No one has ever seriously questioned that the vast majority of all the inhabitants of the Ogaden are and always have been Somalian—always, at least, since recorded history began, and that is a long time ago now. Yet the world has still stood by and supported or applauded the Ethiopian imperial rulers for taking the Ogaden, holding it as part of their imperial territory, administering it as a colony, and maintaining that hold and administration in the face of every Somalian demand for restitution. Now I am one of those Englishmen who thought and think it very just and right that England should give up her colonies. Yet the English, as a matter of historical fact, held India, for example, for almost twice as long as the Ethiopians have held the Ogaden. If the English should leave India, for example, what can justify the Ethiopians in not leaving the Ogaden? Once again, the same arguments can be applied with force to the case of Eritrea. A colony is no more justified in natural right because it is a new one than because it is an old one.

Yet it is one thing to apply arguments with force and another to understand the complexities of the situation to which they are applied: above all, in this context, is the situation in the Horn of Africa. And the counterarguments of those who deplore the formation of still more new nation-states, adding to the 50 or so into which Africa is now divided (and divided, please remember, as a direct result of the imperialist partition and the arbitrary frontiers that it drew), are not without a force of their own. Even if Eritrea could stand on its own, would it not do better to stand in federation with neighbors? If the Ogaden should be free to be Somalian, would its inhabitants not do well to welcome the blurring or effective removal of all the borders that surround them? If not, then why not? If so, then what is it that prevents a move toward desirable federal unities? The national question is not to be ignored, and woe betide those who try to ignore it; but must it therefore be surrendered to in all its divisiveness? Are there not better ways of structuring African independence than a mosaic of nation-states? Or, putting the same question in another way, If nationalism in Europe has led to huge wars and terrible disasters, what arguments can make us believe that nationalism may not do the same, as the divisive years pass by, in Africa as well?

More questions, more answers. I draw attention to them here for two reasons. First, because they help to show just why the Eritrean case deserves careful study and reflection, and, as I believe, active responses by those who study and reflect. Second, because

Richard Sherman sent me his book and asked me, if I found that I liked it, to write a foreword. I do like it, and I write this foreword happily, because Sherman has given us a guide to the Eritrean question—to the Eritrean questions—that is praiseworthy for its careful balance, prudence of judgment, and solid weight of information. It can have been no easy task to write in this way; and Sherman is to be thanked for doing it. Attractively modest, sympathetic, widely and well informed, this book will make its mark. To think this, as I do, it is not necessary to have agreed with all that Sherman writes or proposes. I do not myself agree with some of his conclusions, notably with his treatment of the recent Cuban record, for I find that he has the Cubans actively in direct support of the Ethiopians inside Eritrea some time after—according to my information—they had decided to pull out of that country, and did in fact pull out. But these are small matters of disagreement.

On the main issues, especially on the growth and development of Eritrean nationalism—and then on the development out of that nationalism of a movement of national liberation comparable, for example, with that of FRELIMO in Mozambique—he seems to me to be very soundly based. He is telling us things that we need to know if we are to form a sensible judgment not only on the Eritrean case but also on the wider scene in the Horn. His treatment of the Eritrean Liberation Front (ELF) is judicious; of the Eritrean Peoples Liberation Front (EPLF), fair and, in my view, right; while he rounds off his work with many other helpful insights and reflections on the nature of the political trends and influences now in play throughout the region. Read this book. You will be glad to have done so.

Preface

The purpose of this book is to describe and analyze the revolutionary process that has taken place in Eritrea, from its inception in 1961 until mid-1979, at which time this manuscript went to press.

The Eritrean revolution is an important, topical subject for investigation. I view the struggle as unique, in that it is the longest ongoing liberation movement in Africa, and possibly the least understood. Although various articles and monographs have attempted to deal with contemporary events in Eritrea, very little of this material has been of sound quality. In addition, much propaganda and counterpropaganda continue to obscure the fundamental issues.

In this book I will focus on the process of revolution in Eritrea. The Eritreans struggling against Ethiopia are organized into movement(s) based upon their analysis of socioeconomic conditions. In their attempt to radically alter Eritrea, the liberation movements have been guided by indigenous circumstances. While this might not make the movement(s) analyses correct, it undoubtedly makes them original.

This book began as a doctoral dissertation in politics at Brandeis University. The method I employed in writing both dissertation and book was primarily historical. In my description and analysis of the Eritrean revolution I have attempted to search for the social, political, and economic bases of the Ethio-Eritrean conflict. Two other studies of contemporary revolutionary movements served as models for my work. The first is Basil Davidson's The Liberation of Guinea. I am in debt to Davidson not only for his insights on revolution but also for certain patterns in organizing my data. Gerard Chaliand's Armed Struggle in Africa proved very useful for certain definitions; also helpful was his analysis of social structures.

Other literature, produced by the makers of revolutions themselves, was helpful in delineating my approach. Amilcar Cabral, particularly in Revolution in Guinea, sheds a great deal of light on a number of categories that are relevant to the Eritrean revolution. It should be noted, however, that Cabral was dealing with a European colonial power in Guinea-Bissau, whereas the Eritreans are opposed to an African (Ethiopian) colonizer. Works by V. I. Lenin and Mao Tse-tung, particularly those studied by members of the Eritrean movement, also provided insight into questions relating to revolution and nationalism.

Only two satisfactory book-length works in English on Eritrea are to be found, both of them historical pieces by Britons who played a part in administering Eritrea in the 1940s. The more recent and more analytic of the two is G. K. N. Trevaskis's Eritrea: A Colony in Transition (1960). Stephen H. Longrigg's A Short History of Eritrea (1945) is a more detailed history. Most of the works on Eritrea to come out of the Italian colonial period are subjective and paternalistic in nature. They give us a good picture of Italian colonialism but tell us little about the Eritrean people. The exception to this general direction is found in the works of Carlo Conti-Rossini, particularly in Storia d'Ethiopia (1929).

For contemporary material on Eritrea I have relied on a number of sources, including fieldwork and interviews. A number of the lengthy interviews I conducted both in the Sudan (December 1977) and Los Angeles provided much of the data for this book. The interview data provided a sense of perspective otherwise not attainable. A series of informal discussions and interviews with the Los Angeles Chapter of Eritreans for Liberation in North America (EFLNA) has also proved invaluable. Much primary source material was gathered through the study of literature issued by the Eritrean movements themselves, for example, the ELF's Eritrean Revolution magazine and the EPLF's Vanguard. These sources were supplemented by Western and African sources—such as, newsletters, bulletins, government documents, and radio broadcasts.

A brief note about my own perspectives and biases seems appropriate here. I have attempted to be as objective as possible in analyzing the data available to me. However, it will be evident throughout the book that my own sympathies tend toward the Eritrean movement. When I began researching materials for this work in 1976, I hoped and believed that some sort of reconciliation between Ethiopia and the Eritrean movement was possible. Three years later these hopes seem empty. I have come to believe that for the time being the interests of both the peoples of Eritrea and Ethiopia would be best served by the formal disassociation of Eritrea from Ethiopia.

I owe a great deal of thanks to a number of fine people who gave me assistance during the years in which this book was in process. Christopher Leu and Larry Littwin, under whom I studied at California State University, Northridge, were always supportive in any number of ways. Michael Lofchie, director of the African Studies Center at the University of California-Los Angeles, was kind enough to provide me with space at the center. My dissertation committee at Brandeis University—Ruth Schacter Morgenthau, Richard Lobban, and Robert Art—was patient and encouraging in reading rough drafts and providing constructive criticism. I would also like to acknowledge a great many individuals in the Sudan, Ethiopia, and Eritrea who gave of their time and knowledge so freely that I might gain invaluably from their experiences. Finally, I want to thank Susan Freedman, my wife, who has graciously accepted my obsession with Eritrea and the Horn of Africa. Her ability and willingness to share in this experience has been of immeasurable value.

Contents

LIST OF TABLES AND FIGURES

LIST OF MAPS

Introduction

It is my primary task in this work to undertake an analysis of the liberation fronts that have conducted revolutionary warfare in Eritrea. Initially, it is necessary to examine Eritrean precolonial and colonial background in some detail. Following the historical analysis are chapters dealing with internal political aspects of the struggle; a military analysis; social programming; prospects for an economically viable Eritrean state; and finally, some wider ramifications of the conflict.

I believe that it is important to emphasize that the Ethio-Eritrean conflict is a national liberation movement by an oppressed people, rather than a simple attempt at secession by a hard-core dissident faction. To qualify as a national entity, it is usually understood that a people must possess a separate history, a separate territory, a common language, and a common culture. The first chapter of the book deals with Eritrea's qualifications as such an entity.

While a systematic enumeration of both Ethiopian and Eritrean positions and grievances is presented in the first chapter, two cornerstones of Eritrean nationalism need brief mention here. These essential bases are, first, the common history of colonial occupation in Eritrea, with emphasis on the Italian period, 1896-1941, and, second, the increasingly repressive measures taken by the respective Ethiopian regimes in their attempts to stifle Eritrean national aspirations. I would contend that these two central experiences have given definition to an Eritrean national entity.

Colonialism, particularly Italian colonialism, gave some definition and scope to an Eritrean national entity. This is not to say that Italy formed any sort of homogeneous nation-state in colonial Eritrea. However, the Italian presence did serve to put Eritrea on common ground with numerous other African countries to emerge in a post-colonial world.

Eritrean national aspirations are unique because the former colony was federated on a nonequal basis with Ethiopia, rather than achieving outright independence. The treatment, or repression, visited upon the Eritrean people by Ethiopia became the decisive factor for the basis of a revolutionary liberation process in Eritrea. Ethiopian actions between 1952 and 1979, and particularly between 1974 and 1979, created a sense of unity among Eritreans that previously never existed: virtually all Eritreans want Ethiopia out of the former Italian colony. From the traumatic repression by Ethiopia emerged a series of increasingly well-defined political movements, and from each of these movements came a greater degree of actual revolutionary change in the pattern and structure of Eritrean life.

The Eritrean Peoples Liberation Front (EPLF) stresses the concept of a national democratic revolution. For this group, revolution is a process of societal change: toward an independent state where there is no exploitation of humanity by humanity. The revolution is national in that a number of Eritrean ethnic groups (nationalities) are in the process of creating an Eritrean national entity. It is democratic because it is a movement carried on by all patriotic forces—workers, peasants, and elements of the middle class, under the leadership of the proletariat.

For the Eritreans, a central concept in the process of revolution has been, and continues to be, that of national liberation. In defining national liberation I cite Amilcar Cabral, as quoted by Basil Davidson in The Liberation of Guinea. Cabral believed that national liberation meant not only the right of a people to rule itself but also the right of a people to regain its own history: "to liberate, that is, the means and process of development of its own productive forces." For Cabral, then, since the liberation of one's own productive forces

> calls for a profound mutation in the condition of those productive forces, we see that the phenomenon of national liberation is necessarily one of revolution.[1]

There are in Eritrea two major competing liberation groups: the Eritrean Liberation Front (ELF) and the EPLF. These groups are movements rather than formal political parties. Both fronts maintain that they are fighting for an independent, democratic Eritrea. Each has its strengths and weaknesses, concepts of political organization, political ideology, structures, and social programs, as well as competing personalities and power struggles. Many efforts have been made to unify these two forces into a unit capable of defeating the Ethiopian armed forces. In fact, the questions raised regarding unity are central to the course of the revolution. Divisions, whether of an ideological nature or petty and personal, loom as the key variable in the Eritrean revolution. The chapter of the book dealing with the political aspects of the situation will conclude with an analysis of the synchronization of the theory and the reality of Eritrean politics.

The military struggle of the Eritreans can only be viewed in close conjunction with the political aspects of the movement. The strategies and weapons employed by both the Eritreans and Ethiopians are thoroughly examined. Here again, internal divisions between Eritrean groups created conditions for an Eritrean civil war, pitting the ELF and EPLF against each other. Finally, in Eritrea, or elsewhere in Africa, can the revolutionary use of arms be viewed as the ultimate liberating force? What does liberation mean in Eritrea: simply the absence of Ethiopian colonial presence, or something more positive?

Accompanying the numerous Eritrean military victories of 1977 were a myriad of social programs set up in the liberated areas of the country. The variety and scope of these programs are unique not only for Eritrea but also for the entire Horn of Africa. The health-care program is particularly notable. Others underwent rapid development while the Eritreans occupied virtually all major towns.

If Eritrea were to achieve independence, what might the country's economic prospects be? Agriculture and livestock production have been the foundation of the country's economy in the past. What of the prospects for land reform and the adaptation of traditional land tenure systems to a more modern, cooperative mode of farming? Can light industry and commerce, largely de-emphasized in Ethiopian-ruled Eritrea, reemerge in the not-too-distant future? What of the country's mineral prospects, and the difficulties, political and technological, in exploiting them? Could all of these possibilities become a reality in a few short years, or would Eritrea be largely dependent on foreign aid to meet the basic needs of its population?

The wider ramifications of the Eritrean struggle are explored in the final chapter of the book. Although the Eritrean federation with Ethiopia was unique in post-World War II politics, the Organization of African Unity, to say nothing of the United Nations, treat, or ignore, the present conflict as if it were a purely internal Ethiopian matter. What, if any, significance would Eritrea's independence hold for other African countries?

The entire Horn of Africa, with its strategic proximity to Middle Eastern oil routes, underwent drastic political realignment during 1977/78. The Soviets are now heavily committed to backing the Ethiopian Dergue, or ruling council, that previously relied on the United States as its main source of military support. This has come about at the expense of Somalia, formerly the USSR's closest ally in all Africa. This radically altered state of affairs probably raises more questions than it answers, but certainly deserves investigation.

The Eritrean revolution is, indeed, unfinished. It is not at all certain that the revolution will lead to an independent Eritrean state. A long series of interrelated events will determine the results of the process that Eritrea and its people have undergone. The following chapters of this book are devoted to an examination of that process.

NOTE

1. Basil Davidson, The Liberation of Guine (Baltimore: Penguin, 1969).

ERITREA

The Unfinished Revolution

1
PRELUDE TO REVOLUTION

ERITREA: THE LAND AND ITS PEOPLE

Eritrea is located along 1,000 kilometers on the west coast of the Red Sea in northeast Africa. The name Eritrea is an Italian one, having been adopted from the Greek Erythraea, literally meaning "red." Positioned along this strategic body of water, Eritrea is bordered on the north and northwest by the Sudan, on the southeast by the Republic of Djibouti, and on the south by Ethiopia's Tigre Province. Eritrea's nearly 50,000 square miles are a variety of plateau highlands, deserts, bush country, and volcanic wilderness. The topography of Eritrea is composed of four varieties of land surface. These are the south-central core of the plateau highland, the Red Sea coastal plain, the hill country in the north and midwest, and the broad western plains.

The core of Eritrea is composed of the highland plateau, with altitudes ranging between 6,000 and 8,000 feet above sea level. The largest rivers emanating from the plateau are the Mareb (also known as the Gash), the Baraka, and the Anseba, all of which flow into the Sudan. With a few important exceptions, vegetation on the plateau is generally sparse. Rainfall here averages between 16 and 24 inches a year.[1] (See Map 1.)

On the east, this highland plateau descends sharply into the Red Sea coastal plain. The plain runs from 10 to 50 miles in width for the entire length of Eritrea's seacoast. The climate is extremely hot and humid here during the summer months; the coast is barren and treeless. Rainfall rarely exceeds ten inches a year and is often less.

The hill country to the north and west of the Eritrean plateau ranges in altitude from 2,500 to 4,500 feet above sea level. This area, approximately one-third of Eritrea, lacks both exact definition

1

MAP 1

Eritrea: Physical Regions

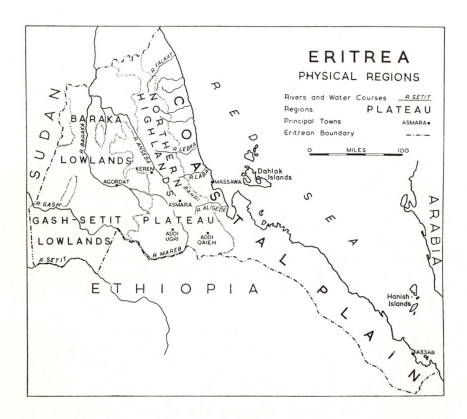

Source: G. K. N. Trevaskis, Eritrea: A Colony in Transition (London: Oxford University Press, 1960), p. 2.

and internal uniformity.[2] The hills are highest in the south, around Keren, and receive about 16 inches of rainfall per annum. As the altitude decreases, both the rainfall and vegetation become lighter.

The broad, western plains lie west and southwest of the River Baraka, and north of the River Setit (or Takazze, as it is known in Ethiopia). Here between the Rivers Gash and Setit, the soils are rich and dark, vegetation is thick, and during the rains the grass is plentiful. Rainfall for the western plains can be as little as 12 to 14 inches north of the Gash but usually reaches 20 to 25 inches in the Gash-Setit lowlands.

MAP 2

Eritrea: Social Groups

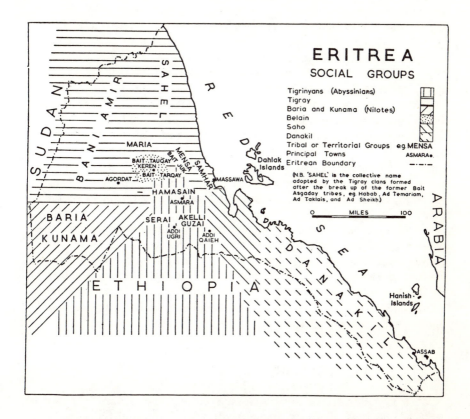

Source: G. K. N. Trevaskis, Eritrea: A Colony in Transition (London: Oxford University Press, 1960), p. 12.

The population of Eritrea has been variously estimated at between 2 million and 3.5 million people. No two sources are in agreement. An accurate census, difficult even under optimum conditions, has not been taken in the last ten years; the last meaningful census was conducted by the British in the early 1950s.

Eritrea has been described as being inhabited by a mosaic of diverse communities.[3] These peoples have varied origins and all have links with people outside Eritrea proper. Approximately one-half of the population is Christian, the other half being Muslim. There is also a small scattering of animists.

The Eritrean highlands, from Asmara southward, are inhabited by people who, before Italian colonialism, were culturally similar to their Tigrinya-speaking Ethiopian kinsmen. A great majority of the highlanders are Coptic Christians. For the most part, these people are settled agriculturalists and are organized in village communities, which are each composed of varying numbers of extended families. [4]

To the north and west of the central highlands, along much of the coastal plain, northern highlands and Baraka lowlands, are people who speak Tigre, the closest spoken derivative of the classical Ethiopic. Most of these people are Muslim and are predominantly pastoral nomads or seminomadic. The most notable exception would be the Keren area, where agriculture is widely practiced.

The southern portion of the coastal plain is sparsely inhabited by the Danakil, "a Moslem people who speak an Hamitic dialect called Afar." [5] The Danakil are organized as small clans and are highly mobile. One of the few permanent settlements in this part of Eritrea is the Red Sea port of Assab. Relatively few Danakil live in Eritrea; many more inhabit Ethiopia and Djibouti.

Three other groups of people should be mentioned briefly. Between the Danakil and the highland plateau live the Saho. These people are Muslims and the majority are pastoral nomads or seminomadic. In the Keren region live a number of small families known as Belain. Finally, in the Gash-Setit lowlands, are found the Baria and Kunama, offshoots of the Nilotic peoples inhabiting western Ethiopia and the southern Sudan. (See Map 2.)

PRE-AXUMITE BEGINNINGS

It is generally believed that Eritrea's earliest inhabitants were a Nilotic people, probably forest dwellers, who moved from the bush of the southeastern Sudan into the Gash-Setit lowlands. However, the first recorded history comes to us from the Egyptians, from as far back as 3000 B.C. [6] Most of this history relates to naval commerce between the pharoahs of Egypt and local chiefs on the Red Sea coast of Eritrea. In 1495 B.C. Egyptian vessels were welcomed by a local leader named Perehu. In exchange for their own merchandise they took fragrant woods, myrrh trees, ivory, gold, incense, skins, and some Eritrean slaves, as well. [7] It is also suggested that the Egyptians may have used Adulis as a port of landing and that the trading area extended as far inland as Hamasien, where present-day Asmara is located. [8]

From about 1500 to 1167 B.C., barter, including trading of slaves, flourished. From 1167 B.C. until almost 700 B.C., little documented history of Eritrea exists.

The earlier migrations of Milotic and Hamitic peoples into Eritrea were followed by a great Sabaean migratory wave. Many Sabaeans crossed the Red Sea from the Arabian peninsula when warfare forced numerous peasants, metal workers, masons, and artisans to migrate. They quickly moved on from the Dahlak Islands (off Massawa) to the plateau, where the climate and countryside resembled the South Arabian highlands from which they had come.

The Sabaeans revolutionized both the daily life and political organization of the Hamitic herdsmen. They brought the camel, the horse, the sheep, new plants and cultivation methods, the art of writing, and more advanced armaments. They also brought the nucleus of a ruling class and a knowledge of group life.[9]

During the Hellenistic conquest of Egypt, the Ptolemies occupied the Eritrean coast and kept it for centuries. They effectively forced the Sabaean immigrants inland to the plateau. Greek influence was strong in many ways, but none stronger than the language they introduced. It has already been noted that the name Eritrea is derived from the Greek Erythraea. More important, Greek was to become the language of the Axumite ruling class.[10]

AXUM

As the migrant Sabaeans (also known by the names Habashat and Agazian) moved to the highlands they began building towns and even dams. The best example of an early town was Cohaitu, on the eastern escarpment of the plateau. This civilization continued to spread throughout the Eritrean highlands and as early as the first century A.D. Axum became its center. It has been observed that "the Axum kingdom corresponded very little with the modern state of Ethiopia. It did not in its golden age, extend southwards beyond the limits of the present Tigre (province)."[11] Observations such as the above have led some to the thesis that Axumite civilization was "more of an Eritrean history than an Ethiopian one."[12]

Axumite power was in great part derived from the Sabaeans' political organization and from the wealth that they generated from trade flowing through the port of Adulis (now Zula). Their greatest commercial intercourse was with Egypt and the countries of the eastern Mediterranean, Red Sea, and Persian Gulf.[13]

G. K. N. Trevaskis in Eritrea: A Colony in Transition, notes that "though the first Axumite kings affected a Greek culture . . . and employed Greek as their official language, the Axumites remained for the most part wedded to the Semitic culture of their Sabaean ancestors."[14] Consistent with this Semitic-oriented culture was the development of the classical Ethiopic language, Ge'ez.

The conversion of Axum to Christianity dates from the fourth century A.D., when Syrian missionaries introduced a Monophysite doctrine to the Axumites. Correspondent to the introduction of Christianity, Axum attained its greatest power from the fourth to the sixth centuries. "From a region which was approximately coextensive with modern Eritrea and found the core of their empire, the Christian kings of Axum extended their power and influence far afield."[15] The Axumite kings moved westward into Nubia to conquer and destroy the civilization of Meroe. They also recrossed the Red Sea and subjugated South Arabia, on the pretext of protecting the Christians there from Jewish persecution.

However, after the sixth century, Axumite power declined as a direct consequence of the Arab invasion of Egypt.[16] This invasion forced the Beja tribes of eastern Egypt and the northern Sudan southward. In turn, these pushed their Beja kinsmen already in the northern highlands and Baraka lowlands on to the plateau. On the east, Axum found itself increasingly cut off from the sea by other tribes. This effectively halted the commerce upon which its wealth and power had been founded. By 750 A.D. the Red Sea coast was in the hands of the Bejas. Soon the Bejas pushed the Axumite ruling class southward. Axumite civilization had disintegrated.

THE "DARK AGES"

By comparison, the next four or five centuries in Eritrea were not an era of great accomplishment. Between the Nile and the Red Sea five independent Beja kingdoms were established. These five kingdoms were known as Naqis, Baqlin, Bazin, Jarin, and Qata. The Bazin were settled cultivators. The Baqlin were camel and cattle nomads. The other three kingdoms were involved in mining and the slave trade. One of the most infamous slave trading centers rose up on the Dahlak and Kabir island, off present-day Massawa. Dahlak Kabir existed as an independent island from the ninth century to the fourteenth century.[17]

With slave trading as the primary commercial enterprise, it comes as little surprise that these Beja kingdoms never lived with each other in peace. This constant warfare weakened the five kingdoms, ultimately leading to their disintegration, by the thirteenth century.

THE FOURTEENTH AND FIFTEENTH CENTURIES

There was very little change in the nature of Eritrean society until the plateau was invaded by peoples from the Ethiopian (southern) interior during the fourteenth and fifteenth centuries. The first wave was composed of Agaw from Lasta (presently Lalibela) who had set up the Zagwe dynasty in Ethiopia. They were followed by groups from Tigre who, with Agaw, took control of the Eritrean plateau from the crumbling Beja kingdoms.

The change from pastoral to agricultural life proceeded rapidly in the highlands. "Agriculture was characterized by infrequent moves of a whole community from land to land, which fresh forest clearance produced in abundance."[18] The social system came to be character-ized by the enda, or kinship group.

While the Ethiopian peoples controlled most of the highlands, they never effectively controlled the lowlands. They raided the low-lands regularly "but never remained to garrison them; they plundered but never governed."[19] As Trevaskis points out, the failure of the Ethiopians to control the people surrounding the plateau was to prove very costly: it would invite further intrusion from aliens far and near.[20] By the beginning of the sixteenth century the Fung, who had established a kingdom in central Sudan, were expanding eastward, gaining influence if not control, over the Gash-Setit and Baraka low-lands.

TURKS, PORTUGUESE, AND ISLAM

In the sixteenth century three new foreign powers made their presence felt in Eritrea. Their intervention was overlapping and often led to violence and bloodshed between them, to say nothing of the in-digenous peoples.

The Turks, under Selim I, sent their fleets into the Red Sea in 1517 and established initially feeble occupations at Massawa and Sua-kin (in the Sudan). In 1520, the Portuguese, accompanied by the his-torian Francesco Alvarez, also landed at Massawa. There followed years of warfare, on both land and sea, between these defenders of their respective faiths.

The third great power, and the one to leave the most lasting effect, came in the person of the Imam of Harrar, Ahmad bin Ibrahim, better known as Ahmad Gran (the left-handed). In 1530, from his base in Harrar in southeastern Somali-inhabited Ethiopia, he began to at-tack the Ethiopian plateau. Within four years he laid waste to all of the Christian highlands, including Tigre and Eritrea. He routinely devastated everything in sight and converted hundreds of thousands to Islam by force. Only by surrender and conversion could people save their lives.

Until 1541, conditions in Eritrea were unsettled under Ahmad Gran's rule; "guerrilla war never ceased though it never succeeded."[21] The Christian nobility survived only as a hunted band. Only the intervention of the Portuguese, at the request of the Ethiopian emperor, transformed the flow of events.

A Portuguese expedition, equipped and dispatched from the island of Goa, landed at Massawa in 1541, under the leadership of Christopher da Gama, son of Vasco da Gama. With 400 trained men under excellent arms, artillery, and eager followers from Eritrea and Tigre, the Portuguese helped to drive the Imam's forces from the plateau. The deciding factor was probably the death of Ahmad Gran himself. After he was killed in battle, "the Muslim forces dispersed, retreated, and disappeared."[22]

Although the Ottoman state was at the apex of its aggressive power, the Turks had taken no part in Gran's campaign. In 1557, with reinforcements to their garrison at Massawa, they strengthened their hold on Eritrea. From their coast base they proceeded to mount an assault on the Eritrean highlands. For nearly 20 years the Turks continued some form of occupation of the highlands. The Eritrean ruler (Bahr Negash, or Lord of the Seas) Issak remained in open revolt against the Turkish pasha.

Eventually both Issak and the pasha were killed in battle by the Ethiopian king, Malak Sagad. Ten years later, in 1589, an Eritrean chief, Walda Ezum struck an alliance with the new pasha, against the Ethiopian emperor's troops in Eritrea. The Turks were again defeated in the highlands and retreated to their heavily defended base at Harkiko, there resisting further Ethiopian advances. All efforts to drive the Turks into the sea were to no avail.

The Ethiopian king (or negus) consented to peace with the Turks. The Turks thus remained for three more centuries on the Eritrean coast, which would never again obey an Ethiopian ruler.[23] During their 300-year occupation of Massawa and the Red Sea coast, the Turks continued to enter into various alliances with the (respective) Bahr Negash.

BETWEEN TURKS AND EGYPTIANS

The events of the sixteenth century led to a more rapid evolution of society in Eritrea.[24] Agricultural clan-settlements had fixed residences, and definite land rights had been established. A static agricultural society was being formed. In addition, the social structure was being modified. Gran's bloody occupation had forced tremendous upheaval, and many people from central Ethiopia entered the Eritrean highlands seeking new homes.

New forms of land tenure were introduced. Fiefs were granted by the Ethiopian king of kings to both the Coptic clergy and royal favorites and other officials. The division between tenant and landholder became more appreciable. During this period the village superseded the enda (kinship organization) and, in turn, villages merged into districts.

During this period, Eritrea is identified as politically distinct from Ethiopia by a number of sources. When Portuguese explorers arrived in the seventeenth century they identified an area called "Medri Bahri," which was described as approximating modern Eritrea.[25] James Bruce of Kinnaird, the famous Scottish explorer, traveled through Eritrea in 1770 and noted both Ethiopia and Medri Bahri as separate political entities that were often at war with one another.[26]

Southern Eritrea, from the early eighteenth century, was politically aligned with the kingdom of Tigre, to the immediate south. On numerous occasions, they waged joint acts of resistance against the Amharas, or central Ethiopians, to the south. One such example was in opposition to Tewodros, the Ethiopian ruler who brought Eritrea under his control in 1860. Because Tewodros was holding several British subjects hostage, Sir Charles Napier was dispatched with 12,000 troops from India to challenge the Ethiopian negus.

Napier landed in Eritrea in January 1868. His first forces landed a few months earlier and set up an advanced base at Senafe. The British expedition received tremendous assistance from the Eritreans and Tigreans. For the first time since 1542 European troops were seen in Eritrea.[27] From Kassa of Tigre (later to be crowned as Yohannes IV) Napier received tactical advice, protection, and supplies. With Kassa's help, Napier easily defeated Tewodros at Magdala (Ethiopia) in April 1868. Tewodros shot himself when it was evident his forces would be defeated. The British abruptly departed, leaving a power vacuum among the Ethiopians. Four years later in 1872, Kassa of Tigre was crowned as Yohannes IV. As such, he was the first Tigrean king of kings since the restoration of the Solomonid dynasty in 1270.

THE WARS WITH EGYPT

Egyptian incursions into Eritrea had begun much earlier in the nineteenth century. The followers of Muhammed Ali first entered the Gash delta in 1823, and in 1840 established a standing camp that became the city of Kassala (on the present border between Eritrea and the Sudan). Their penetration continued with the occupation of the Baraka lowlands.

The opening of the Suez Canal in 1869 enhanced the importance of the Red Sea and the Horn of Africa. International trade and communications greatly increased the strategic significance of Eritrea.

The Egyptians quickly established themselves along the Red Sea and Somalian coasts and displaced the Turks at Massawa by 1872. Egyptian authority also extended to the coastal clans.[28] On the western side of the plateau the Egyptians had moved beyond the Baraka and Gash-Setit lowlands and were garrisoned at Keren, the key to the northern highlands.

Only the central highlands themselves were not in Egyptian hands. Life on the plateau was, in ways, very similar among the three highland provinces: Hamasien, Serai, and Akkele Guzai. Similarities existed in culture, religion, language, kinship, and inter-enda relationships. However, differences had emerged in the social order over the past century.[29] Hamasien lived under a hereditary governor. Sarae had witnessed endless struggles between powerful chiefs, even fiefs. Akkele Guzai was a region of small democratic elder-governed enda units, disunited and politically unambitious.

The Egyptian decision to advance to the plateau was largely influenced by Werner Munzinger, a Swiss national who joined the Egyptian service as governor of Massawa. Munzinger, as military strategist, vastly underestimated the forces of Yohannes, who was certainly prepared to keep the Egyptians from advancing further to the Christian plateau. In November 1875, Yohannes completely destroyed the Egyptian forces at Gundet. In March 1876, a more massive Egyptian force was again decimated at the battle of Gura. The threat of Egypt to the highlands had ended.

Yohannes sent his army north in 1879, defeated the Eritrean chiefs, and established his viceroy in two huts in the small village of Asmara.[30] Ethiopian forces, however, controlled the Eritrean high lands for a very short time, from 1880 to 1889.

During this period, Yohannes became preoccupied with repulsing the Mahdists threatening Ethiopia from the Sudan. Yohannes had designs on driving the Egyptians from Massawa and the coast. He was led to believe, by the British, that Massawa and Keren would both be his if he helped quell the Mahdist forces. To this effect, he signed a treaty with Britain and Egypt against the Mahdists in 1884. Although Yohannes carried out his end of the bargain, the British reneged on theirs. Instead of helping Yohannes to occupy Massawa, the British actively encouraged the Italians, in 1885, to seize the port city from the Egyptians.[31]

THE ITALIANS COME TO ERITREA

Great Britain has occupied Aden in 1839 and Perim Island (at the straits of Bab el Mandeb) in 1857; the French were busy occupying Somalian village ports, later to become the French Territory of the

Afar and Issas. In 1869, the Italian government, through the Ruba-
tino Shipping Company and their agent, Father Sapeto, purchased the
Eritrean port of Assab from the local sultan.[32] Assab and the surrounding areas were formally transferred to the Italian government
in 1882. These areas were explored and a treaty was negotiated with
the Shoan (Amhara) King Menelik, which established commercial links
between Shoa and Assab.

As noted above, the British encouraged the Italians to occupy
Massawa in 1885. This was done to develop an Italian influence in the
Red Sea as "a useful counter to the French, who were by this time
seated at Djibouti."[33]

The Italians began to bring the coastal people "under their protection," and to encroach on districts such as Saati and Dogali. The
Ethiopian (Tigrean) forces in Eritrea, under Ras Alula, put a temporary stop to any further advances by annihilating 480 Italian troops at
Dogali, in January 1887.

Yohannes had consistently denied the right of the Italian government to be at Massawa at all.[34] However, the Italians decided to play
off Menelik of Shoa against Yohannes in their drive for expansion in
Eritrea. Indeed, with Menelik coveting Yohannes's title of king of
kings for himself, the Italians had little trouble buying Menelik's
neutrality with gifts of arms. Menelik first signed a secret treaty of
neutrality with Italy in return for the option to purchase 5,000 Reming-
ton rifles.[35]

All of this served to put Yohannes in a most precarious position.
The Italians had every intention of mounting the plateau to the south.
Menelik was gaining strength due to his increasingly superior military
technology and his conquests throughout Ethiopia. On the western
flank, Yohannes was still committed to repulsing the Mahdist Dervishes. In dealing with the last of these threats, Yohannes was bat-
tling the Dervishes at Metemma when he was killed on March 9, 1889.
Menelik quickly seized power and was proclaimed King of Kings.

However, to genuinely secure the throne and be recognized as
emperor, he asked for an alliance with the Italians against his only
potential challengers, Yohannes's son Mengesha and Ras Alula, both
of Tigre. Consequently, Menelik and Count Antonelli signed the
Treaty of Uccialli at that village on May 2, 1889. The Italians received a great deal in return for this military alliance: the bill of sale
of the Medri Bahri, from this point to be known as Eritrea. In effect,
Menelik "traded" Eritrea and its inhabitants to the Italians to ensure
his title and crown.

Menelik had ceded lands on the highlands that included most of
Hamasien and Akkele Guzai. On January 1, 1890, a decree of the
king of Italy created the colony of Eritrea. The Italians lost no time
in establishing their capital at Asmara. A "strategic portion of the
Ethiopian empire" had been handed over to a European colonial power.

The Treaty of Uccialli soon led to a new series of problems between Menelik and the Italians: one based on interpretation. According to the Italian version of the treaty, Article 17 committed Menelik's Ethiopia to the status of an Italian protectorate. The Amharic version of the same article said that the Ethiopian government "might" use the Italian government as an intermediary in its relationships with European states. Menelik argued that he was required to do no more than inform the protecting power of his correspondence with foreign governments.[36] The Italians persisted in translating the "might" of Article 17 as "shall." By subsequently entering into direct negotiations with the French and the Russians, "the Emperor left the Italians in no doubt that he had the determination to suit his action to his arguments."[37]

During the first half of the next decade, both parties began military preparation to resolve their differences. The Italians had come to the Red Sea coast with visions of grandeur, which had been increasingly fed by the acquisition of Assab, then Massawa, and eventually all of Eritrea. They underestimated Menelik, however, in believing that they could just as easily possess Ethiopia.

In December 1894, the Italians advanced from Eritrea to the successful invasion of Tigre that overran the province and occupied it until March 1896. In December 1895, the Ethiopian army routed the Italians at Amba Alagi. This, however, was only a prelude to the Battle of Adowa, which began in the early morning hours of March 1, 1896. There, in what could be described as one of the most humiliating defeats in Italian history, Menelik decimated the forces of General Baratieri.

One major question surrounding the Battle of Adowa is why Menelik did not pursue his advantage in chasing the Italians from the highlands or even attempt to liberate the coast itself. In fact, Menelik did enter Eritrea and seize the fort at Adi Ugri. However, by March 18, 1896, Menelik was on his way back to Addis Ababa, leaving Mengesha and Alula in command in the north.

Menelik's failure to pursue the Italians has been explained in numerous ways, none of them entirely satisfactory. One theory posits that Menelik knew of the large reinforcement of men and material arriving from Italy. Another sees the possibility of the intervention of other European powers on the Italian side.[38] These, however, do not really address themselves to Menelik's priorities.

Menelik was committed to the conquest of southwestern portions of present-day Ethiopia and was thus prevented from continuing his battle against the Italians. Menelik desperately needed the Oromo and Sidamo lands in the southwest for two reasons. First, he found free land and labor in this region to feed and settle the famine-weary Amhara peoples. Second, this region supplied him with gold, ivory, and coffee—commodities that he could exchange for the much-needed European firearms.[39]

On October 26, 1896, Menelik signed the Addis Ababa Peace Treaty with Italy in which the latter renounced the Uccialli Treaty and paid war reparations to Ethiopia. The new treaty also established the present (larger) territory of Eritrea. If, in fact, Menelik did so desperately need to consolidate his holdings in the southwest, he did so at a very heavy price. By once again reaffirming Italian hegemony in Eritrea, he "left insecure Ethiopia's independence, and sowed the seeds of the current problems between the Eritreans and the Ethiopian government."[40]

Thus, as Richard Lobban has noted, the end of the nineteenth century

> saw the Turks replaced by the Italians in Eritrea and by
> the Mahdists in the Sudan. Eritrea was trapped between
> wider political powers. This sense of political entrapment
> sowed the seeds for present-day nationalism. Nationalism
> was figuratively pushed into shape from each of three sides
> of the geopolitical triangle which makes up the territory.
> Eritrea was at the periphery of three powers: Italy with
> the coastal base, the Mahdists from Omdurman, and Mene-
> lik in central Ethiopia.[41]

Trevaskis adds that as in most other colonial situations, Italy created an Eritrean territory "by an act of surgery: by severing its different peoples from those with whom their past had been linked and by grafting the amputated remnants to each other under the title of Eritrean."[42]

ITALIAN COLONIAL RULE IN ERITREA

Once Eritrea had been secured from Menelik, the policy of the Italian government became three pronged. First, Eritrea was to be developed for occupation of an Italian population. Second, natural production was to be encouraged. This was to include agricultural, livestock, and mineral production, but no manufacturing capabilities. Eritrea would serve, in part, to absorb Italian finished goods, in addition to providing raw materials for Italian industry. Third, Eritrea was to serve as a base for the projected African conquests. Italian administrative, social, and economic policies in Eritrea were reflective of their long-range goals.

The Italians divided the colony into seven administrative divisions or commissariati (Hamasien, Akkele Guzai, Serai, Keren,

Agordat, Massawa, and Assab). These, in turn, were subdivided into districts or _residenze_, which, in some cases, were further divided into subdistricts or _vice-residenze_. This administrative system served the Italian need for direct and close administration. [43] The Italians instituted no real system of local government. The result "was a lack of any authority intermediate between the village head and the government itself."[44] They did, however, establish municipalities in what were to become the seven principal towns: Asmara, Massawa, Keren, Decamare, Adi Ugri, Adi Caieh, and Assab.

During the Italian administration, the judiciary operated under four different types of law. The Italian penal code was applicable to all inhabitants of the colony. The Italian civil code served as law in civil matters where at least one Italian citizen was involved. Islamic law was applied when the contesting parties were Muslim. Finally, Eritrean customary law was enforced in civil cases between Eritreans.

Socially, the Italian occupation had a more far-reaching impact than it did politically. As second-class citizens, or more correctly, subjects, most Eritreans had little opportunity for political participation. But socially, the effects of 50 years of Italian colonialism touched the lives of many Eritreans.

Many people were brought into the production process, as cheap laborers, handling raw materials for Italian industry. Others were encouraged to serve in Italy's colonial army as low-paid mercenaries. Many traditional chiefs and ruling families were either eliminated or degraded. [45] Others, who more readily adapted to the new changes, took places offered them in minor-level administrative positions.

Social transformation occurred in all aspects of daily life in the colony's cities. Medical and veterinary services were highly developed. Secular education for Eritrean boys was provided through the fourth grade. The Italian language became the medium of communication. Electricity and running water were introduced in the cities. The local press and imported cinema brought not only new ideas but also new methods of introducing them.

Still, under Italian rule, the Eritreans were, at best, auxiliaries. And yet, despite this subordinate social and economic position, there was little or no Eritrean discontent. Food and consumer goods were always cheap and plentiful; taxation was at a token rate. Under this system of control, even co-optation, Eritreans "served their Italian masters as loyal laborers and soldiers";[46] they "remained content, docile, and obedient."[47] The Eritreans exhibited this passivity due to the fact that the Italians exploited the previously existing differences that existed along the lines of race, religion, region, and clan. This could appropriately be called a "divide-and-rule" policy on the part of the administration. Italian colonization also created relatively good economic opportunities for a large number of Eritreans.

These benefits tended to increase with the military mobilization of the late 1920s and early 1930s. And further, the Italians did not attempt any large-scale alteration of socioeconomic patterns in the rural areas, where most Eritreans resided. Unless a rural area was of some strategic or economic import, the Italians generally ignored it.

It was noted above that Eritrea's main economic function was to serve as a source of raw materials for metropolitan Italian industry. In addition, the process of building an economic infrastructure in the colony was to further Italian expansionist aims.

Italian agricultural policy was primarily concerned with the production of cash crops for the Italian home market. [48] Cotton, tropical fruits, sisal, and coffee were all grown for export to Italy. Very little was done to exploit the colony's potential wealth in livestock and its by-products. And nothing was done to encourage the production of grain or vegetables, for which Eritrea was dependent on imports. During the Italian occupation a large proportion of Eritrea's exports was made up of marine products, such as salt, pearls, mother-of-pearl, and fish.

The Italians also attempted to exploit Eritrea's numerous mineral resources. In various quantities, deposits of gold, iron ore, nickel, copper, manganese, and chromium, among others, had been explored. The colonial government put most of its effort into gold mining, on both the plateau and the Gash-Setit lowlands. In the 1930s, it began ambitious plans for gold mining in Gash-Setit, and by 1940 the industry showed promise of development. [49] However, due to the abrupt conclusion of Italian rule a year later, these plans were never carried to fruition.

A significant portion of the infrastructure developed by the Italians was a by-product of the Italian invasion of Ethiopia in 1935. A vast network of all-weather roads was constructed to facilitate Italian military mobility. A railway, running from Massawa, through Asmara, and on to Agordat, had been completed in 1922. The port of Massawa was enlarged and improved. Modern airports were built at Asmara and Gura. Telegraph and postal services were expanded and refined. All of this was only possible by the import of mechanical and construction material and an immense amount of Italian capital.

This military mobilization necessarily multiplied urban development in Eritrea. Between 1935 and 1941 military installations, public buildings, workshops, depots, warehouses, offices, shops, flats, villas, and encampments were rapidly built. During this period, the Italian population increased from 5,000 to 50,000. However, it has been pointed out that those who came from Italy during the war years were hardly the cream of Italian society: "Many of the lowest type were encouraged to leave their country for overseas." [50]

By 1940, Asmara had grown to a city with a population exceeding 100,000 with all modern services. Massawa, with more than

10,000 inhabitants was a fully equipped port and naval base; Assab was under intensive development as a second port. Decamare and Keren were rapidly expanding towns.

The Italians conquered Ethiopia, entering Addis Ababa in May 1936. A month later a decree revised the boundaries of Eritrea and Ethiopia for administrative purposes. Eritrea was now to include all of Tigre Province, virtually doubling the governorate in size and population. One observer stated that the new boundary "recognized, at least, what the Mareb frontier—that of before 1936, and since 1941— had ignored, the essential unity of the Tigreans."[51]

The advent of World War II was the beginning of the end for Italian rule in East Africa generally and Eritrea in particular. To counter Field Marshal Erwin Rommel's brilliant campaign in North Africa, British strategy called for weakening Germany's ally, Italy, by destroying its East African army before it could move northward to join with Rommel.[52]

British unified forces entered Eritrea in January 1941 from the Sudan, and by February British political officers had assumed the administration of western Eritrea. The British forces advanced toward Keren, where the only serious battle of the Eritrean campaign was fought. The heights of Keren were stormed and finally overcome on March 27. Less than a week later, on April 1, British troops entered Asmara. By April 8, with the fall of Massawa, all of Eritrea was under British occupation.[53] Fifty years of Italian rule thus came to an end.

BRITISH MILITARY ADMINISTRATION

The British, who would continue to occupy Eritrea for the next 11 years, initially utilized Eritrea as an allied military base from 1941 to 1943. The United States, in its war effort, also began using Eritrea as a supply depot and its ports as passageways for U.S. ships. The U.S. military constructed an aircraft assembly plant at the airport of Gura. They also established a naval base at Massawa and modernized the commercial harbor there.

During the period of British administration, political consciousness in Eritrea grew tremendously. Before discussing the various political movements that arose, a brief description of Eritrean life and its accompanying socioeconomic conditions is in order.

In terms of the administration of Eritrea, "the nature and obligations of an occupation administration are prescribed by international law, whereby its freedom both of policy and of method is severely limited."[54] The administration was a military one, with the chief administrator being identical to the British commander in chief. In effect, the British, operating under this rather strict interpretation, formed a caretaker or status quo administration in Eritrea. This necessarily disappointed many Eritreans who would have liked to think of the British as "liberators."

The British were committed to maintaining control over Eritrea to facilitate their effort in the war and during this period did little to alter the structure of Italian hegemony in Eritrea. During the first part of the occupation, disputes between Eritreans and Italians were still heard before Italian judges, applying Italian colonial law. The British took over the top administrative posts but needed Italian functionaries just below them to administer programs. Many incentives for increased agricultural production were given to Italian farmers. In some cases, following the legalistic construction of international law, the British actually appropriated some Eritrean-owned land and transferred it to Italian agriculturalists. After the war, British policy

> favored the Italian elements and the trade oriented Moslem communities . . . while it adversely affected Eritrean workers, urban elites, and clergy in urban centers.[55]

Nevertheless, the British did introduce certain reforms into the system they administered. They gradually removed the color bar and began an "Eritreanization" of subordinate administrative positions. They eventually introduced "Native Courts" to replace the residenti's courts. Eritrean Advisory Councils were set up in each division and in the principal towns. The education system was revitalized; books in Arabic, Tigrinya, and English were utilized in 60 new schools. A new public health service, with its network of hospitals and clinics, began to offer increased and better services to Eritreans residing in the cities and towns.

Under British administration during World War II, Eritrea experienced an economic boom. In addition to the aforementioned military projects that provided wage labor for Eritreans, the war had also created a scarcity of trade goods in the Middle East. By readjusting its economy, Eritrea provided goods to the Middle East that had formerly been imported from war-ravaged Europe.

With the favorable employment picture, and the creation of a domestic market with high purchasing power, Eritrea was provided with the stimulus for the development of a light industrial economy. Products manufactured during this period included soap, beer, matches, wine, hand tools, paint, leather goods, paper, and glue.

This boom did not continue much beyond the end of the war; few Eritrean industries could withstand revitalized European competition after 1945. More and more, Eritrea was pushed back to depending on its resources—livestock, agriculture, marine products, and minerals. Yet taken as a whole, the 1940s were years of considerable industrial growth. By 1950 the principal manufacturing industries, mining, transportation, and public utilities were responsible for employing 38,800 Eritreans and 19,800 Italians.[56] In addition, the number of livestock doubled between 1940 and 1946 and the export of agricultural goods began. The corollary to this economic development was, of course, the rise of political consciousness among Eritrean workers and, to a lesser degree, peasants.

A good deal of this new political consciousness can be traced to the increased degree of urbanization in Eritrea and the deteriorating economic conditions after the war ended. Approximately one-fifth of all Eritreans lived in towns or cities during the British occupation, and with the increase in unemployment, conditions were ripe for political activity. In Asmara, particularly, the British did little to change the Italian system, which, in turn, promoted discontent among much of the urbanized population. The rural population was unhappy about the occasional land appropriations and the higher taxes the British demanded of them. Under these conditions it was not surprising to find many Eritreans searching for an alternative political order.

It was precisely this situation that the Ethiopian government of Haile Selassie began to exploit. Ethiopia, for numerous reasons to be explored in a later section, felt that its claims on Eritrea were strong enough to warrant Eritrea in political union with Ethiopia. The Ethiopians initially believed that the British would do what they could to help them realize their claims but were sorely disappointed.

The Ethiopians then turned to the Coptic church, which was "the traditional bearer of Ethiopian nationalism." By 1942, every Coptic priest in Eritrea could have been considered a propagandist for unity with Ethiopia. At this time, however, most of the population remained politically apathetic in regard to these activities.[57]

An early separatist movement arose at about the same time in Akkele Guzai, the plateau district remotest from Asmara and the one that had suffered least from land appropriations. This, too, was a Christian-dominated movement. At one point, the separatists, with British "approval," proposed a union of Eritrea and Tigre as an autonomous state under British administration. One of the earliest leaders of the separatist movement was newspaper editor Woldeab Woldemariam.

The British, during the mid-1940s, held the view that

the best solution for Eritrea would be its partition between Ethiopia and the Sudan in such a way as to allow the Eritrean Abyssinians to join their kinsmen in Ethiopia and the

Moslem tribés of western Eritrea to be incorporated into the Sudan.[58]

This may be seen as a corollary to their "Greater Somalia" scheme. The problem with such a scheme was that there was no indication of what Muslim opinion was before 1946. Among many of the Tigre-speaking people, tremendous internal upheaval was taking place in the form of an emancipation struggle on the part of the serfs against their masters. One prominent movement leader, Ibrahim Sultan, called a meeting of all Moslem communities to consider the question of Eritrea's future in December 1946. Out of this meeting came the Muslim League, which opposed union with Ethiopia. The majority favored independence after a limited period under international trusteeship; none opted for partition of Eritrea.[59]

Up to this time the British administration had discouraged the formation of political parties. However, in September 1946, the Council of Foreign Ministers met and agreed that the Four Powers should decide the fate of Italy's former colonies. Should they fail, those decisions would be left to the General Assembly of the United Nations.

With Eritrea's future clearly on the line, the various political movements were converted into parties. The Muslim League was mentioned above. The Christian separatists organized themselves as the Liberal Progressive party. Unity with Ethiopia was embodied in the Unionist party under the guidance of Tedia Bairu. The Unionists were clearly the strongest organized group. But the opposition to unionism was substantial. Either out of despair, or at the prodding of the Ethiopians, some younger Unionists in Asmara began a series of terrorist attacks against selected leaders of the Muslim League and the Liberal Progressives. This was the beginning of a long string of terrorist attacks and counterattacks, leading to increased polarization based on religious persuasion, and continually fanned by Ethiopian, British, and Italian exploitation of the entire situation.

The Italian government, as well as the Italian colonial settlers, assumed

> that an independent Eritrea would look to Italy for economic
> assistance and also for political support against Ethiopian
> imperialism and would, moreover, allow the settlers to
> play a mediating role between the Moslem and Christian
> parties.[60]

Italy, with national pride never far from the surface, spoke in terms of its "civilizing mission" and guiding Eritrea to full maturity. Italy first pressed for a trusteeship, but when that looked unattainable, took up the independence banner.

The Italians had remained inactive until March 1947, when an Eritrean Old Soldiers' Association suddenly came into being, to provide cover for a pro-Italian political party. The Italians, in fact, owed thousands of Eritrean exsoldiers their paychecks and pension monies. It was only a short step to the formation of the Pro-Italy party. This party, although ostensibly Eritrean, received covert direction and lavish funds from local Italians. It slowly chipped away at Unionist support until the Unionists again resorted to terrorism, which reconverted virtually all of the previous Unionist supporters. So continued throughout the late 1940s the cycle of meddling, exploitation, violence, and polarization.

THE "DISPOSAL" OF ERITREA

The political rivalries within Eritrea were set against a backdrop of international bungling and indecision. The question of the "disposal" of Eritrea and the other Italian colonies first came up for discussion at the London Conference of the Council of Foreign Ministers in September 1945. The terms of the Italian Peace Treaty, which was debated for another year and a half, provided that Italy's colonies would be jointly disposed of by Britain, France, the United States, and the Soviet Union within one year of its coming into force. Thereafter, if the Four Powers could not agree by September 15, 1948, the matter would be turned over to the UN General Assembly. Considering the nature of postwar international politics, it comes as little surprise to find that the Four Powers could not agree upon an equitable solution.

There were two possible solutions, with numerous variations. Eritrea could become independent either immediately or after a period of trusteeship. Alternatively, it could be united partially or wholly with Ethiopia. Briefly (these claims will be explored in full later), the Ethiopians claimed that Eritrea was an integral part of their own country; that they needed Eritrea's access to the sea; and that Eritrea was the economic complement of Ethiopia.

For the Four Powers, the pros and cons of Eritrean independence or federation were much more complex. Eritrea was only one part of the larger problem of Somalia, Libya, and the Middle East itself. The British believed that the defense and political stability of the Middle East depended on the maintenance of their own influence.[61] Consequently, they proposed a "Greater Somali" scheme (to be administered by them) in addition to some sort of partition to Eritrea between Ethiopia and the Sudan. The United States initially proposed a form of collective trusteeship over Eritrea, an outlet to the sea for Ethiopia at Assab, and an independent Eritrean state after ten years.

The proposals and counterproposals continued until the Four Powers agreed to send a Commission of Investigation to Eritrea and the other territories to report on the wishes of the respective inhabitants. Needless to say, each political party in Eritrea claimed the support of the overwhelming majority of the population. For such a commission to evaluate accurately the will of the people concerned would, in any circumstances, have been a difficult task. Before the arrival of the commission in 1948, the British Administration in Eritrea implemented a plan that called for representatives from each clan and family to be elected and subsequently meet with commission members. The number of representatives elected was 3,336, and the commission's subsequent records reported that the Unionist representatives had the support of 44.8 percent of the population; the Muslim League representatives, 40.5 percent, the Liberal Progressives, 4.4 percent; and the Pro-Italy representatives, 9.2 percent.[62] In other words, the population was fairly evenly divided between supporters of union with Ethiopia and advocates of transition to independence. (The Muslim League and Liberal Progressive party, although committed to independence, had agreed to a trusteeship for ten years, should it be deemed necessary.) The population had divided its support largely in terms of geography and religion.

These findings were disputed by both the French and the Soviets who, for their own reasons, were eager to impose an Italian trusteeship on Eritrea. The Council of Foreign Ministers met to examine the commission's report in September 1948. Again, proposals and rebuttals were exchanged. It became apparent that agreement was impossible. On September 15, the Four Powers referred the entire matter to the United Nations.

One important consequence of the transfer of the problem to the United Nations was that Italy's power to influence a decision was greatly enhanced, not only as a member of the United Nations but also because of the sympathy Italy commanded from the Latin American states. The Italian settlers in Eritrea still hoped for a nominally independent Eritrea that would, in practice, be closely linked with Italy. What emerged as a result was a coalition of the Muslim League, the Liberal Progressive party, and the Pro-Italy party, which was known as the Independence Bloc and was pledged to the cause of immediate independence. Based on the Four Power Commission's report, the bloc could now claim a majority of followers in Eritrea; but the Italians would leave nothing to chance. Their government liaison officer in Asmara spent tremendous amounts of money bribing and co-opting would-be Unionists; "even among the staunchest Unionist communities the corrosive effect of Italian money became visible."[63]

In September 1949, the General Assembly decided that Libya should become independent immediately and that Somalia should be granted independence after a ten-year period of Italian trusteeship. However, it resolved to send its own commission to Eritrea to determine the wishes of the inhabitants. The commission included representatives of Norway, Guatemala, South Africa, Pakistan, and Burma.

The decisions on Libya and Somalia gave the Unionists cause for grave concern. The bloc had indicated that the commission would favor independence. Under these circumstances, terrorist violence by Unionists reached its apex. This violence was supplemented by a campaign of threats against the Italians and the Eritrean supporters of the bloc. Desertions from the bloc began to occur with regularity.

This was not, however, the only reason for the decline of the bloc. The serious splits in both the Muslim League and Liberal Progressive party caused the bloc to lose more than half of its members in early 1950. The splits were caused by the anti-Italian factions of each party; they were growing increasingly resentful of the bloc's close Italian connections. However, these two splinter groups had little in common with each other except their Italophobia. The newly formed Muslim League of the Western Province, because of internal feuding, ceased to be a politically relevant force. The rebel wing of the Liberal Progressives began, somewhat dejectedly, to seek some sort of alliance with the Unionists:

> In their eyes union with Ethiopia was only objectionable
> because of Ethiopia's Shoan hegemony. If some form of
> union could be devised which would leave the management
> of Eritrea's affairs in Eritrean hands and preserve Eri-
> trea's languages and customs, it would be incomparably
> more attractive than an Italian-sponsored independence. [64]

These rebels reorganized themselves as the Liberal Unionist party, working to establish a "conditional union" of Eritrea and Ethiopia. These events left the Unionist party in a much better position in which to receive and entertain the UN commission.

The UN commission arrived in Eritrea on February 14 and stayed until April 6, 1950. In attempting to ascertain the wishes of the Eritreans and in preparing a set of proposals to be presented to the General Assembly, the commission "conducted its inquiry in indifferent imitation of the representatives of the Four Powers."[65] Even worse, rather than employing any sort of systematic method of evaluation this commission usually made "casual observations of rival political gatherings at each center and addressed random questions to persons whose representative qualities it had no means of checking."[66] In addition, the members of the commission managed to develop a level of mutual hostility and, as a consequence, produced two separate reports and no less than three sets of proposals.

The Norwegian, South African, and Burmese delegates felt that only a minority of Eritreans favored independence. The Pakistani and Guatemalan delegates concluded that the majority of the population wanted independence. The latter two also accused the British Military Administration of preventing economic development as a means of furthering British dreams of partition. The three proposals, in their broadest forms, were (1) union with Ethiopia, (2) federation with Ethiopia, and (3) independence preceded by a ten-year trusteeship under UN administration.

Rather than clarifying the findings of the Big Four, the superficial inquiry of the UN commission simply added to them. The General Assembly, however, was in a better position to make some sort of decision as the alternatives had been narrowed down to the three solutions put before it. The proposed federal solution seemed, to the General Assembly, a nominal middle-of-the-road solution between the extremes of union with Ethiopia and independence. On December 2, 1950, the General Assembly adopted a resolution, Resolution 390A (V), by a vote of 46 to 10. The complete test of this resolution is found in Appendix A.

Resolution 390A (V) provided that Eritrea should "constitute an autonomous unit federated with Ethiopia under the sovereignty of the Ethiopian Crown." The Eritrean government was to have "legislative, executive, and judicial powers in the field of domestic affairs." The jurisdiction of the federal government was to include "defense, foreign and interstate commerce, and external and interstate communications including ports." An "Imperial Federal Council composed of equal numbers of Ethiopian and Eritrean representatives" was to be set up. There was to be a transition period not extending beyond September 15, 1952, during which the Eritrean government was to be organized and a constitution drawn up. The British administration was to organize an Eritrean administration and a representative assembly in conjunction with an appointed UN commissioner.

The appointed commissioner, Eduardo Anze Matienzo of Bolivia, arrived in Eritrea on February 9, 1951, to find that bandits, known as shifta, were paralyzing the country's government and economic life. In addition, political violence had not subsided, although it had slowed considerably. It took over a year for the UN administration, with Ethiopian government support, to reduce the banditry and political violence to manageable proportions. Only then could Anze Matienzo begin the task of consulting the Eritreans concerning a new constitution.

This was to be no easy task. Haile Selassie's representative at the constitutional discussions sought an arrangement that would ensure appointment of a reliable Unionist to every key position in the Eritrean government. The Unionists, Democratic Bloc (formerly the

MAP 3

Eritrea: As an Ethiopian Province

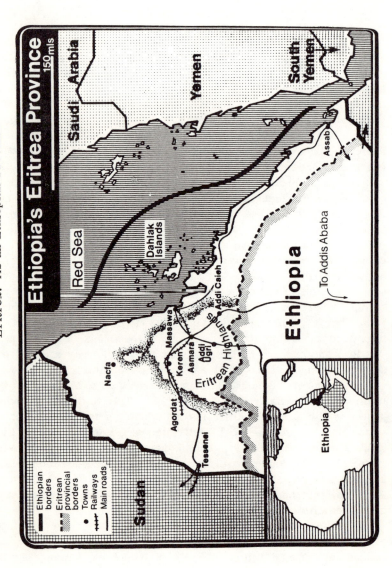

Source: Gemini News Services, Ltd.

MAP 4

The Horn of Africa

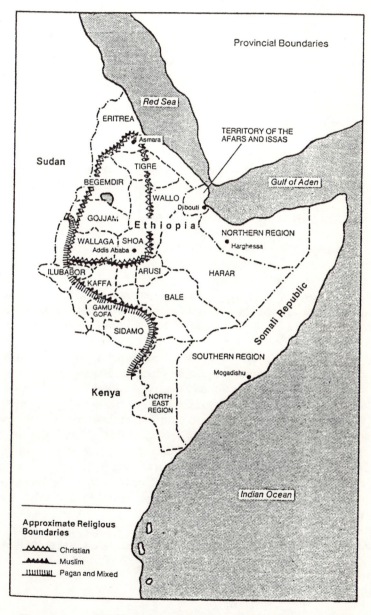

Source: c Conflicts in Africa. Adelphi Papers Number Ninety-three. (London: The International Institute for Strategic Studies, 1972). Reprinted by permission of the publisher.

Independence Bloc), and the Muslim League of the Western Province were also at odds with one another on a number of key issues. In fact, Anze Matienzo's draft constitution would probably never have been accepted if either the Unionists or the Democratic Bloc had enjoyed an overall majority.

Only a coalition, reflecting a compromise view, between the Unionists and the Muslim League of the Western Province eventually approved the constitution in the newly elected Assembly. Sixty-eight constituencies had been established, each with about 15,000 people and generally conforming with a recognizable social grouping. Elections took place in March 1952, with the 68 Assembly seats broken down as follows: the Unionists won 32; the Democratic Bloc, 18; the Muslim League of the Western Province, 15; with the remaining three divided between three splinter groups. [67]

As a result of this election, the once rebellious Muslim League of the Western Province found itself holding the balance between the Unionists and the bloc. Due to conflicting personalities and various intraparty pressures the league found it to its advantage to join the Unionists in a moderate compromise constitutional framework.

The new constitution provided that the Ethiopian government also be the federal government and that the emperor be represented in Eritrea by a governor-general. This federal representative was to promulgate legislation as well as render his opinion on any legislation that might involve "international responsibility." The emperor, however, was not given the power he wanted in appointing all executive officials. The legislature was a single Assembly with an elected president. The executive would be headed by a chief executive who would be elected by the Assembly and would appoint secretaries to head government departments. He was also to appoint judges who were to be free of legislative and executive control.

The new constitution seemingly protected the Eritrean government against undue Ethiopian control, and furthermore, in recognition of Eritrea's autonomous status, permitted it to have its own flag and official languages, Tigrinya and Arabic. As previously noted, the Assembly ratified the constitution on the strength of the new soon-to-govern coalition of Unionists and Muslim League of the Western Province representatives. Haile Selassie formally ratified the Federal Act on September 11. On the evening of September 15, 1952, the Union Jack was lowered in the center of Asmara and Eritrea passed on to its federated status with Ethiopia. (See Maps 3 and 4.)

FEDERATION WITH ETHIOPIA

Federation between Eritrea and Ethiopia lasted only ten years, ending in November 1962. Throughout the 11-year period from 1941 to 1952 the Ethiopian government contended that Eritrean autonomy was infeasible and that only complete union would serve the needs of both countries. During the period of federation, Haile Selassie, having previously failed to abort Eritrea's autonomy, set out to subvert, or undermine, the political, social, and economic order of the federated Eritrea. The reasons for this sabotage are only too numerous and are dealt with at length in the following section.

There are, however, several incongruities regarding the federal arrangement that deserve mention here. First, with Ethiopia being so much larger than Eritrea, it was difficult to see how any sort of balance would have been achieved in bridging potential conflicts between the two. Second, the two units were expected to coexist politically with radically different sociopolitical structures. Eritrea, its constitution "based on the principles of democratic government," stood in stark contrast with the authoritarianism of the Ethiopian monarchy. Third, there was no federal constitution to regulate clearly the relationship of governmental authority and responsibility of the two countries.

It was this omission, the lack of a binding federal constitution, that facilitated Haile Selassie in eroding the federal relationship, "through bribery, intimidation, and where necessary (as it often was) naked force."[68] During this ten-year period, the emperor did everything he could, through his representatives, to subvert the substance of both democracy and autonomy in Eritrea. The emperor could have hardly done such widespread damage without any assistance. In violating the Federal Act and interfering in the internal affairs of Eritrea, he utilized not only Ethiopian representatives but also co-opted members of the Eritrean bourgeoisie as well.

The parliamentary election of 1952 was at once the first and the last election to be held under the Eritrean constitution. Indeed, the constitution itself was "suspended" shortly thereafter. Tedla Bairu, the chief executive of Eritrea, resigned in mid-1955, due to excessive interference and pressure from the emperor's official representative in Eritrea. Newspaper editors began to be arrested without apparent cause; political commentary greatly decreased.

In 1956, the Eritrean Assembly was "temporarily suspended." Later in the year, a new parliamentary election took place, but this time with no organized political parties. In the same year, Amharic, the language of the Shoans, was made the national language of Eritrea. As a necessary corollary, Tigrinya and Arabic were eliminated as official languages. In December 1958, it was announced that the Eritrean Assembly had voted to discard the Eritrean flag and to fly only the federal, or Ethiopian, flag. In September 1959, after the chief executive and leaders of the Assembly had returned from a visit to Addis Ababa, the Assembly voted to replace their own laws and accept the Ethiopian penal code. In May 1960, the Assembly voted to change the name <u>Eritrean Government</u> to <u>Eritrean Administration</u>, with the chief executive becoming the chief of administration. Even the Eritrean seal was changed to read "Eritrean Administration under Haile Selassie I, Emperor of Ethiopia."

The emperor, however, did not limit his activities to the political arena. Eritrean workers had begun the formation of trade unions in the early 1950s. In December 1952, 11 years before labor unions were legalized in Ethiopia, the Eritrean General Union of Labor Syndicates was formed, under the direction of Woldeab Woldemariam. A short time later it was banned by the federal government. In response, the dock workers in Massawa and Assab staged a two-week strike. The strike ended in armed clashes between the Ethiopian army and the dock workers, who were supported by the Eritrean police. In February 1958, with the trade union movement very much "underground," a general strike in Asmara and Massawa lasted four days before being crushed by federal troops who killed or wounded at least 80 protesting workers and arrested hundreds more. [69]

During the period of federation more and more Eritreans entered the wage labor force. The federal government provided some money for schools and construction projects. However, the biggest new source of jobs was Kagnew Station, a U.S. communication facility on the outskirts of Asmara. Kagnew had been a British facility (Radio Marina) until, in 1952, the United States signed a 25-year lease with Haile Selassie for use of this base. Kagnew, among other functions to be considered later, provided thousands of jobs for Eritreans and poured additional money into the local economy.

Although Eritrean individuals, as well as groups, protested the constant erosion of Eritrea's autonomous federal status to the United Nations and the Ethiopian government, nothing was done to alter this course of events. In fact, little could be done; the very conditions of the federal agreement almost seemed to encourage Ethiopian encroachment into Eritrean affairs. As G. K. N. Trevaskis noted in 1960:

> With an Ethiopian Governor General and an Ethiopian garrison in the territory, with Ethiopian control of the broadcasting services, and with Eritrea dependent on Ethiopian financial aid, she has the means of paralysing any Eritrean Government and of putting an end to any semblance of Eritrean autonomy. [70]

By 1962 Haile Selassie was ready to move toward Ethiopia's unrealized ambition: full annexation of Eritrea and total abrogation of the federal status. Of course, any move to render the federation invalid and annex Eritrea violated the provision that stated that only the UN General Assembly has the power to alter or amend the Federal

Act.[71] Yet, on November 14, 1962, the federation of Eritrea and Ethiopia was declared null and void, with Eritrea becoming Ethiopia's fourteenth province.

Two versions, or interpretations, of the annexation process exist: one by decree, the other by vote. In either case, the Eritrean Assembly had, by this time, been so packed, bribed, and coerced that its unanimous acquiescence came as no shock. The erosion of the autonomous democratic decision-making process in Eritrea had come full circle. The only certain fact is that the overwhelming majority of Eritrean people had no voice in the matter. Their future had once again been determined by external forces. In spite of loud protests to the United Nations, annexation was a fait accompli.

G. K. N. Trevaskis ended his book, Eritrea: A Colony in Transition, by warning Ethiopia that it would be in Ethiopia's own interest, as well as Eritrea's, for the federal arrangement to survive in accord with UN Resolution 390A (V). However, he acknowledged that

> the temptation to subject Eritrea firmly under her [Ethiopia's] control will always be great. Should she try to do so, she will risk Eritrean discontent and eventual revolt, which, with foreign sympathy and support, might well disrupt both Eritrea and Ethiopia herself.[72]

THE ETHIOPIAN POSITION

The Haile Selassie government failed to heed G. K. N. Trevaskis's well-founded advice and consequently has, in fact, "disrupted both Eritrea and Ethiopia herself." From the Ethiopian viewpoint, the former emperor had a variety of defensible reasons for abrogating the federal agreement binding Eritrea and Ethiopia. A number of sources would support the Ethiopian claim that Eritrea is not historically a distinct entity; that historically and culturally it is a part of what Donald Levine has called "Greater Ethiopia."[73] Stephen Longrigg, in A Short History of Eritrea, maintains that Eritrea possesses "none of the qualities of geographical or cultural singleness which should entitle it to be a unit of territory or of government." He further believes that had the Italians not colonized Eritrea, that Eritrea "would be partly, as always before, the ill-governed or nongoverned northernmost province of Ethiopia."[74] In light of these statements, a systematic enumeration of Ethiopian claims to Eritrea is in order.

The Ethiopians feel that the union (not federated status) of Ethiopia and Eritrea constitutes a reintegration of two artificially separated entities. The complementary nature of Ethiopian and Eritrean economics and their geographic unity are commonly stressed themes.

Economically, the two countries have been interdependent. During Italian rule in Eritrea, Ethiopia became dependent on the port of Massawa and the storage and transport facilities based in Asmara. Eritrea, on the other hand, depended on Ethiopia for grain and raw materials. More than one-third of Ethiopia's industrial activity is located in Eritrea; Ethiopia's only oil refinery is at the port of Assab.

If the question of complementary economic factors is important, the Ethiopian need for an outlet to the sea is crucial. The Ethiopians argue that such an outlet has been long denied them by colonial encroachments onto Ethiopian territory. This point was, in fact, repeatedly made before the United Nations in that body's efforts to resolve the fate of Eritrea. Should Eritrea gain its independence, Ethiopia would be landlocked, its only access to the sea (besides the Eritrean ports of Massawa and Assab) via the newly established Republic of Djibouti.

Another aspect of unity, or reintegration, stressed by Ethiopian proponents, is that of ethnic affiliation. Their strongest case can be made in discussing the Eritrean plateau dwellers, who, like the people of neighboring Tigre Province, speak Tigrinya and are predominantly Coptic Christians. However, the Ethiopians often go even further in saying that most of the people of Ethiopia and Eritrea share the same values in addition to sharing the same social, religious, and cultural patterns of behavior.

There are yet other reasons for the Ethiopian incorporation of Eritrea as one of its 14 provinces. A central concern for hundreds of years has been the Ethiopian (Christian) fear of being "an island in a Moslem sea." The Ethiopian fear that the Red Sea will become an "Arab lake" is only intensified by the assistance that Eritrean revolutionaries have received from Arab countries. The Ethiopian government, speaking through the government-controlled press, regularly states that the present Eritrean war is Arab instigated, and that without Arab money there would be no fighting in Eritrea.

Historically, the Ethiopians have feared what they perceived to be a three-pronged Islamic threat. The Ethiopian highland core has traditionally resisted Islam and the associated Arab culture. Second, Ethiopia breaks the solid continuity of Islam from the Mediterranean Sea to the Indian Ocean. The third prong has to do with Islam itself: "its propensity to be militant and political with the jihad or holy war as its potent means."[75]

The Ethiopian government has been adamant in equating the Eritrean struggle with Pan-Arabism. The Ethiopians generally give the percentage of Muslims in Eritrea as 40, while more objective sources believe that Eritrea is about one-half Muslim, one-half Christian, with Muslims slightly in the majority.[76] By stating that the Muslims are a lower percentage than they really are, the Ethiopians attempt to make the Eritrean struggle appear as the isolated action of a dissident, Arab-supported minority.

Another argument put forth by the Ethiopians in justifying their incorporation of Eritrea is that for centuries Eritrea's Red Sea coast has been used by foreign powers as a base for invasion of the Ethiopian plateau. In a 70-year period, four foreign invasions were launched from Eritrea: Napier's successful expedition against Tewodros in 1868; the ill-fated Egyptian attempt of 1875; the Italian invasion and subsequent defeat at Adowa in 1896; and the Italian Fascist conquest of Ethiopia in 1935. Clearly, through Ethiopian eyes, alien (Arab or otherwise) rule in Eritrea constitutes a potential threat to Addis's sovereignty.

As a corollary to the base of aggression issues, the Ethiopians are concerned, as well, by the implications for their country of "fragmentation." Should Eritrea gain its independence, what would that imply for the Ogaden, or other dissident areas of the multiethnic polyglot called Ethiopia? As an Ethiopian concern, it is simply enumerated here and is discussed in full in the last chapter dealing with wider ramifications of the conflict.

Stephen Longrigg was quoted above in referring to "the ill-governed or non-governed northernmost province of Ethiopia." The question of political control can easily be turned against the Ethiopian government in refuting its claims to Eritrea. However, the government can also invoke its lack of centralized authority to support its position. Ethiopia has traditionally been an area of provincial dynasties; at many given points in the past it could be said to have been polycentric. Only occasionally did one dynasty succeed in controlling most of the others. Haile Selassie—and to a lesser degree, Menelik —only began to reverse this process. Historically, then, the case could be posited that Ethiopian central authority over Eritrea was not a relevant category in that throughout Ethiopian history there was no one real center exerting power over a vast periphery. Rather, the government might say, Eritrea was simply another one of a series of provincial dynasties in the larger context of a polycentric Ethiopia.

In any case, Haile Selassie's attempt to centralize political authority over his empire played a direct role in his abrogating the Ethio-Eritrean federal agreement. His highly autocratic imperial government simply could not tolerate the continued existence of a democratic Eritrea existing virtually within its own boundaries. This precedent might not only have encouraged a decentralizing trend within Ethiopia but, far more threatening to the emperor, the basis for a much more participatory, democratic political unit.

Finally, to cement their claims on Eritrea, the Ethiopians point to the alleged aspirations of the Eritrean people. The Ethiopians chose to believe that the Unionist party position in the late 1940s was a mandate for complete integration with the Ethiopian body politic. By incorporating Eritrea into Ethiopia in 1962 the Ethiopian government believed it was making its "historically valid demand good."[77]

In addition, the Ethiopians are quick to point out that "the democratically instituted Parliament of Eritrea voted overwhelmingly to abolish the federation in favor of complete unity with the motherland,
Ethiopia."[78]

THE ERITREAN POSITION

The Eritrean view of Ethiopia's claims to authority over their
country is in direct contradiction to that put forth by the Ethiopian
side. The present Ethio-Eritrean conflict is seen by virtually all
Eritreans not as a separatist war but as a national liberation movement against the latest in a series of colonial oppressions. A systematic examination of the Eritrean perspective is necessary for an
understanding of the present struggle. The relevant categories for
the Eritrean argument are: historical considerations, the lack of central authority, the colonial and national questions, ethnic differences,
economic exploitation, the UN role in the late federation, and the
abrogation of the federation itself.

A number of historical considerations were enumerated in detail
in previous sections. The most important or substantial of these, in
arguing the Eritrean position, would be the political implications of
Menelik's "Italian policy." Menelik's treaties and frontier demarcations with the Italians between 1889 and 1896, effectively establishing the political boundaries of Eritrea, "were not the work of hasty or
dictated treaties; they were free and formal acts of the Ethiopian
state."[79] These demarcations were to be the basis of future Eritrean
nationalist sentiments, which are discussed below.

Menelik, for various political and economic reasons, affirmed
Italian hegemony in Eritrea on three separate occasions: in the Uccialli Treaty on May 2, 1889; after the Battle of Adowa of March 1,
1896; and in the Addis Ababa Peace Treaty of October 26, 1896. In
doing so, the Eritreans believe, Ethiopia forfeited any claim that it
might have ever had to Eritrea. The effect of Menelik's actions in
allowing the Italians to colonize Eritrea was the de facto recognition
of the Medri Bahri as a political entity separate from Ethiopia.

The other historical consideration in refuting Ethiopian claims
to Eritrea is the lack of a centralized state in the region. The other
side of this argument was discussed in the previous section. The
statement that Eritrea has always been a part of Ethiopia, or that
Ethiopia has maintained control of Eritrea, is at least inaccurate.
The fall of the Axumite kingdom in the sixth century, contrary to
Ethiopian mythology, left few concrete economic, political, or social
links with the Beja and other systems that followed in Eritrea. From
the fall of Axum until the nineteenth century and the expansion of Eu-

ropean colonialism, there was no period when there existed an organized and centralized state controlling Eritrea.

Stephen Longrigg feels that there "is the certainty that much of
Eritrea was never Ethiopian." In referring to the sixteenth century
he states:

> Effective control (by the standards of an Ethiopian govern-
> ment) was thus maintained, it may be said, in the high-
> lands; some measure of authority admitted in the mountain
> and lowland areas nearest thereto; and no control beyond
> that. Turkish and later Egyptian government of Massawa
> continued, and was not seriously questioned, from the
> sixteenth century until the Italian occupation. [80]

A key issue for the Eritreans is that the current Eritrean struggle is viewed as a national liberation movement against both past and
present foreign colonial oppression. They point to a host of conditions
created by colonial domination—such as the absence of basic freedoms,
a dismal educational system, and an elitist socioeconomic structure.

Eritrea as a national unit did not begin to emerge until the advent of Italian colonial rule. By integrating the disparate regions of
Eritrea and establishing a centralized administrative system, Italy,
in fact, "brought forth Eritrea as a multi-national state with a definite
political and geographical identity."[81]

Richard Lobban finds it is usually agreed that a people must possess a separate history, a separate territory, a common language,
and a common culture to really qualify as a national entity. Historical and territorial considerations could certainly qualify Eritrea as a
national entity. The tricky question, Lobban notes, is that of Eritrean
national culture. Although there are a variety of ethnic groups in
Eritrea, and several (predominantly Semitic) languages are spoken,
a good case can be made for a national culture. Most Eritreans,
whether Christians or Muslims, have felt the burden of colonialism
from a series of oppressive masters. Lobban argues, as do the Eritreans, that

> this common tradition of colonial oppression has brought a
> variety of Eritrean language groups into a common national
> culture. This is not to say that ethnic differences do not
> exist, but that abuses from outsiders have synthesized and
> galvanized Eritrean nationalism more firmly than any Eri-
> trean politician could hope to have achieved through rhet-
> oric or slogans. [82]

One might go even further with this argument in suggesting that Eritrean nationalism is constantly growing, owing, in large part, to increasingly harsh treatment of Eritreans by the Ethiopian occupation army.

Lobban makes another point in regard to ethnicity. If ethnic heterogeneity is part of the composition of Ethiopia, the Sudan, and, for that matter, the United States, why should a multiethnic makeup disqualify the Eritrean nationality? In any analysis of African politics, this is a point well taken.

Since 1941, most Eritreans feel that they have simply traded one colonial administration for another. By virtue of Italy's defeat in World War II, any Eritrean anticolonial movement could not be directed against Italy. British presence in Eritrea was not technically colonial in nature. And, as Trevaskis has noted, even those Eritreans supporting union with Ethiopia (in the 1940s) recognized that foreign rule came in varying degrees:

> Fundamentally, the reason why they supported the Unionist
> Party was that they believed their interests would be better
> served under Ethiopian than under European colonial
> rule. [83]

It is important to reiterate the long history of animosity between the Eritreans and the Addis Ababa-based ruling (Amhara) Shoan dynasty. Referring to the Liberal Progressive party, of the 1940s, Trevaskis noted that "in their eyes union with Ethiopia was . . . objectionable because of Ethiopia's Shoan hegemony."[84] Other observers view Amhara hegemony as a fundamental grievance in the early years of the current Eritrean struggle:

> Their [Eritrean] participation is basically a protest at the
> inefficiency of the present [1971] autocratic regime domi-
> nated by the Amhara, who are rivals of long-standing and
> who are trying to enforce a national policy of Amharisation
> which is particularly galling to the more highly educated
> . . . Eritreans. [85]

Cultural imperialism, through Eritrean eyes, exists in both European and Ethiopian forms.

More objective, or economic, exploitation has been yet another grievance put forward by the Eritreans. A great deal of this economic exploitation can be seen in a colonial context. It was noted above that the Italians encouraged natural production in their colony: agricul-tural, livestock, and mineral production. However, in following clas-sical colonial form, no Eritrean manufacturing capabilities were encouraged. Eritrea served, in part, to absorb Italian finished product, in addition to providing raw materials for Italian industry.

The Eritrean economy has suffered a serious number of setbacks since the Italian occupation. It was hurt by the departure of first the Italian and then the British administration, followed by a gradual exodus of the civilian Italian population. The growth of Asmara was stunted, while smaller towns declined precipitously. Many Christian Eritreans migrated to parts of Ethiopia, where they found employment in trade and government service. [86]

The Eritrean economy continued to stagnate under Ethiopian union. Eritreans claim that they never received a proportionate share of Ethiopian development funds after 1962. Most rural Eritreans continued a life of bare subsistence. Aside from developing the port of Assab, which really benefits Addis Ababa the most, the Ethiopian government initiated no major agricultural or industrial projects in Eritrea:

> A number of dams, designed to relieve the chronic water shortage from which the province suffers and underwritten by international agencies, have been inexplicably shelved by the government, which argues that as Eritrea was already fairly advanced when it joined with Ethiopia the limited funds available should be used to bring the rest of the country up to its standards, rather than further accentuating regional imbalances. [87]

With regard to the legalistic issues surrounding the federation, the UN Resolution 390A (V) is a particularly sore point for many Eritreans, who feel the federation with Ethiopia was externally imposed upon them without any real evaluation of their own wishes. In fact, there was a great deal of confusion and division in Eritrea in the period preceding federation. In 1945 Stephen Longrigg stated:

> Those of the Coptic highlanders are deeply divided. . . .
> The idea of such unions [with Ethiopia] is opposed by most merchants who value principally security; by a majority of the chiefs; by all who value the progress made in Eritrea in the last half-century and contrast its present condition with that of northern Ethiopia; and by all ranks of the Muslims. It is untrue that the highlands, with a single voice or even with a clear majority, either demand or reject Ethiopian union. . . . "Demonstrations" in support of or opposition to anything at any time can, of course, be arranged with ease by anyone willing to pay for them. [88]

It has also been pointed out that the basis of the imposed federation was "unique" in postcolonial history. [89] In no case during the de-
colonization period (with the possible exception of Namibia) have historical, geographical (outlet to the sea), ethnic, and economic arguments been applied in deciding a colony's right to exist as a national
unit. Eritrea's status was given "special" attention, in large part
because of Ethiopian claims to the country.

The preceding argument leads into two other points that support
the Eritreans in their struggle for national liberation. The first is
that the United Nations had, de facto, recognized an Eritrean national
entity and its right to self-determination by agreeing to a federal relationship with Ethiopia rather than total amalgamation in 1952. [90]
Second, Eritrea was a self-contained colonial unit and therefore could
itself rely on the principle of the sanctity of colonial boundaries, which
are considered inviolate by the Organization of African Unity (OAU).

As outlined in a section above, the Federal Act itself was rid-
dled with important contradictions, thus dooming federation to failure
before it even went into effect. The incongruities regarding the size
and nature of government of the two countries could not be resolved.
The fatal weakness surfaced with the omission of a federal constitution
that would have clearly regulated the relationship of governmental responsibility and authority of the two countries. This omission allowed
the Haile Selassie government to undermine the decisions of the Eritrean government without any concern about violating a federal constitution.

Rather than attempting to ensure the viability of the federation,
the Ethiopian government "chose to make no significant concessions
to the uniqueness of the Eritrean situation." [91] Instead, the Ethiopians
undermined virtually every aspect of Eritrean politics and society,
and ultimately, on November 14, 1962, abrogated the federal agreement altogether. The Eritreans view the present Ethiopian occupation
as illegal, and "therefore, a form of colonial subjugation no different
than that of Italian or British colonialism." [92] They could not agree
more with international legal expert Tom Farer who believes that
breach of Resolution 390A (V) entitles Eritrea to seek review of the
original arrangement. [93]

The Eritreans believe that throughout the 1950s the bases of the
present conflict could have been resolved peacefully. Yet, the flow
of authority went in one direction only, rather than two. The constant
Ethiopian undermining of the federal agreement finally led to the abrogation of that agreement. Since 1962, both the United Nations and the
OAU (founded in 1963) have consistently refused to reevaluate the Eritrean position altogether, to say nothing of the federal agreement. In
light of these refusals for an international forum on the issue, the
Eritreans have sought "review of the original agreement" in the only
manner left available to them—armed struggle.

NOTES

1. Stephen H. Longrigg, A Short History of Eritrea (Oxford: Clarendon Press, 1945), p. 5.

2. Ibid., p. 7.

3. G. K. N. Trevaskis, Eritrea: A Colony in Transition (London: Oxford University Press, 1960), p. 17.

4. Ibid., p. 11.

5. Ibid., p. 14.

6. Araia Tseggai, "The Case for Eritrean National Independence," Black Scholar 7 (June 1976): 20.

7. Eritreans for Liberation in North America, "Notes on Eritrean History (Part I)," Liberation 5 (1976): 20-21.

8. Carlo Conti-Rossini, Storia d'Ethiopia (Milan: Officina D' Arte, Grafica A. Lucini, 1929), p. 50.

9. Longrigg, op. cit., p. 11.

10. For a more thorough discussion of Greek influence in the Red Sea area, see W. H. Schoff, Jr., Periplus of the Erythraean Sea (New York: Longmans, Green, 1912).

11. Longrigg, op. cit., p. 13.

12. Araia, op. cit., p. 21.

13. Trevaskis, op. cit., p. 5.

14. Ibid.

15. Ibid.

16. Ibid.

17. Eritreans for Liberation in North America, op. cit., p. 24.

18. Longrigg, op. cit., p. 34.

19. Trevaskis, op. cit., p. 6.

20. Ibid.

21. Ibid., pp. 47-48.

22. Ibid., p. 49.

23. Ibid., p. 54.

24. Ibid., p. 55.

25. Richard Lobban, "The Eritrean War: Issues and Implications," Canadian Journal of African Studies 10 (1976): 336.

26. For an extremely enlightening and detailed account of Bruce's travels in Eritrea and Ethiopia, see James Bruce, Travels to Discover the Source of the Nile (Edinburgh: G. G. J. and J. Robinson, 1790).

27. Longrigg, op. cit., p. 79.

28. Trevaskis, op. cit., p. 7.

29. Longrigg, op. cit., p. 102.

30. Herrick Warren and Anita Warren, "The U.S. Role in the Eritrean Conflict," Africa Today 23 (April-June 1976): 42.

31. Trevaskis, op. cit., p. 8; and Dilebo Getahun "Historical Origins and Development of the Eritrean Problem, 1889-1962," Current Bibliography on African Affairs 7 (Summer 1974): 226.

32. Longrigg, op. cit., p. 112.

33. Trevaskis, op. cit., p. 8.

34. Getahun, op. cit., p. 227.

35. Ibid., p. 228.

36. Trevaskis, op. cit., p. 9.

37. Ibid.

38. Getahun, op. cit., p. 234.

39. Ibid., pp. 235-36.

40. Ibid., p. 236.

41. Lobban, op. cit., p. 337.

42. Trevaskis, op. cit., pp. 10-11.

43. Ibid., p. 26.

44. Longrigg, op. cit., p. 135.

45. Getahun, op. cit., p. 237.

46. Ibid.

47. Trevaskis, op. cit., p. 29.

48. Ibid., p. 40.

49. Ibid., p. 41.

50. Longrigg, op. cit., p. 141.

51. Ibid., p. 142.

52. Araia, op. cit., p. 22.

53. For the fullest treatment of the military campaign see Arthur J. Barker, Eritrea, 1941 (London: Faber, 1966).

54. Longrigg, op. cit., p. 148.

55. Getahun, op. cit., p. 238.

56. Gebre Medhin Yordanos, "Eritrea: Background to Revolution," Monthly Review 28 (September 1976): 59.

57. Trevaskis, op. cit., p. 62.

58. Ibid., p. 69.

59. Ibid., p. 75.

60. Tom J. Farer, War Clouds on the Horn of Africa (Washington, D.C.: Carnegie Endowment for International Peace, 1976), p. 24.

61. Trevaskis, op. cit., p. 84.

62. Ibid., pp. 88-89.

63. Ibid., p. 95.

64. Ibid., p. 98.

65. Ibid., p. 99.

66. Ibid.

67. Trevaskis, op. cit., p. 120.

68. Farer, op. cit., p. 28.

69. Yordanos, op. cit., p. 59.

70. Trevaskis, op. cit., p. 130.

71. Araia, op. cit., p. 25.

72. Trevaskis, op. cit., p. 131.

73. Donald Levine, Greater Ethiopia (Chicago: University of Chicago Press, 1974).

74. Longrigg, op. cit., p. 3.

75. Mesfin Woldemariam, "Ethiopia and the Indian Ocean," in The Indian Ocean: Its Political, Economic and Military Importance, ed. A. J. Cottrell and R. M. Burrell (New York: Praeger, 1972), p. 183.

76. Trevaskis, op. cit., pp. 132-33.

77. U.S., Congress, House, Subcommittee on International Political and Military Affairs of the Committee on Foreign Affairs, U.S. Policy and Request for Sale of Arms to Ethiopia, Hearings, 94th Cong., 1st sess., March 5, 1975 (Washington, D.C.: Government Printing Office, 1975), p. 89.

78. Ibid.

79. Longrigg, op. cit., p. 169.

80. Ibid., p. 169.

81. Eritrean Peoples Liberation Front, National Democratic Programme of the Eritrean People's Liberation Front, 1977, Introduction, p. 5 (no publication information available).

82. Lobban, op. cit., p. 339.

83. Trevaskis, op. cit., p. 130.

84. Ibid., p. 98.

85. David Robinson, "War in Eritrea," Contemporary Review 219 (1971): 270.

86. John Markakis, Anatomy of a Traditional Polity (Oxford: Clarendon Press, 1974), p. 366.

87. Robinson, op. cit.

88. Longrigg, op. cit., pp. 170-71.

89. Araia, op. cit., p. 25.

90. Lobban, op. cit., p. 340.

91. Markakis, op. cit., p. 365.

92. Araia, op. cit.

93. Farer, op. cit., p. 137.

2
POLITICAL ASPECTS OF THE ERITREAN REVOLUTION

As the Eritrean liberation struggle entered its seventeenth year in September 1977, a number of important, if not dramatic, changes occurred within the movement. The early liberation movement was strongly nationalistic, but narrow, if not directionless in its political and organizational structure. Fifteen years later, the two major liberation forces, the Eritrean Liberation Front (ELF) and the Eritrean Peoples Liberation Front (EPLF) were well disciplined, highly motivated organizations with a much broader analysis of the Eritrean political process and the international political arena. No less a political analyst than Gerard Chaliand believes that "the EPLF is by far the most impressive revolutionary movement produced in Africa in the last two decades."[1]

In this chapter the political transformation of the Eritrean revolution is traced in detail. It will begin with an examination of the early liberation movement and the events leading to the split that produced the EPLF. An analysis of the Eritrean civil war between the ELF and EPLF will follow and in effect serve as an introduction for the redefinition of the Eritrean revolution by 1976. Next, there is a discussion of the ideological stance of the respective fronts. In conjunction with this section will be a discussion of the fronts' organizational structures because no analysis of the Eritrean revolution would be complete without addressing itself to the question of unity of the next movement, which has managed to elude the competing forces throughout a good part of the struggle. Finally, it is necessary to consider the relationship between the theory and reality of Eritrean politics: Do the political principles fit the concrete situation in Eritrea?

THE EARLY ERITREAN LIBERATION FRONT

Even before the complete abrogation of the Ethio-Eritrean federation by the Haile Selassie government, a number of Eritrean political notables left the country for self-imposed exile abroad. Most of these exiled leaders had experienced frustration at trying to work within the federated system. The Eritreans had retained very little power after 1952 and dissent was dealt with harshly by the Ethiopians. Most of the Eritrean leaders fleeing during the federation could be described as middle to upper class: merchants, landowners, wealthy intellectuals. Numbered among the above were men such as Woldeab Woldemariam of the Liberal Progressive party; Idris Mohammed Adum, former head of the Eritrean Assembly; Ibrahim Sultan Ali of the Muslim League; and Osman Saleh Sabbe, also of the Muslim League. A coalition was formed by these men in 1958 and came to be known as the Eritrean Liberation Movement (ELM), headquartered in Cairo.

(Unfortunately, little is known about these early or, for that matter, even later, leaders of the Eritrean movement. The same can be said for the present Ethiopian regime: the leaders tend to maintain a very low profile and do not dwell on details of their respective pasts. Part of the explanation may be attributed to the constant intrigue that traditionally has surrounded both Eritrean and Ethiopian political rulers. In the case of the present-day Eritrean movements, the leaders often seem to desire anonymity in order to focus attention on the efforts of the group rather than specific individuals. This pattern even carries over to Eritrean support groups abroad, such as the Eritreans for Liberation in North America.)

Woldeab, a newspaperman by profession, had previously served as a Liberal Progressive in the Eritrean parliament of the 1950s. He is considered the most respected national figure in Eritrea to this day. Osman Saleh Sabbe, the other early leader still visible as late as 1979, is reputed to have been a teacher from the area around Massawa. Contrary to Woldeab, Sabbe is held in contempt by much of the Eritrean population because he is perceived as a man without principles: an opportunist.

The ELM, strongly nationalistic and favoring Eritrean independence, was at the same time a loose coalition in which friction regarding ways and means created schisms in the organizational structure. It was during this period that the seeds of the present Eritrean organizational competition were sown. While today's unity issues superficially regard ideology as the major stumbling block, personality conflicts must be superimposed onto the picture to understand it in its entirety.

By the time Woldeab Woldemariam was beaming radio broadcasts against the Addis Ababa government into Eritrea, underground urban cells were being organized to challenge the impending Ethiopian incorporation of Eritrea. These cells were known as "Mahber Showate," Tigrinya for "Party of Seven," precisely because they proliferated in groups of seven. Mahber Showate identified with the ELM and went as far as carrying out occasional acts of terrorism against urban Ethiopian targets.

By 1961, one faction of the then strife-ridden ELM decided to establish a separate liberation organization with a military wing: thus, the birth of the Eritrean Liberation Front (ELF). The Supreme Council of the ELF included Idris Mohammed Adum as president, Tedla Bairu (former chief administrator of Eritrea) as a later vice-president, and Osman Saleh Sabbe as secretary-general. The Supreme Council was made up of middle- and upper-class men and led a group of politically unsophisticated cadres in a series of small armed clashes against Ethiopian installations. The Supreme Council has since come under severe criticism from a number of Eritreans who viewed their actions as lacking "revolutionary perspective." "They wanted to kick out the Ethiopian occupationists, only to replace them with Eritrean oppressors and exploiters."[2] The EPLF, in its National Democratic Programme, states that

> certain self-exiled traditional leaders and their collaborators established a small armed band under the name of Eritrean Liberation Front (ELF). This was done out of purely competitive considerations without consulting the forces that were already studying the means and preparing for armed struggle. . . . this front not only lacked a clear nationalist line with defined objectives, but it was also formed by and composed of an extremely backward clique.[3]

Between 1961 and 1965 there was a continuing struggle between the ELF, led by the Supreme Council, and the remnants of the ELM. The ELF claims that the ELM was slow in developing a military wing: not until 1965 did the ELM deploy guerrillas inside Eritrea. At that time, by the ELF's own admission, the Supreme Council decided to liquidate the ELM's military wing and proceeded with all deliberate speed.[4] With the disintegration of the ELM forces, a number of ELM cadres who wished to continue the armed struggle against Ethiopian occupation of Eritrea aligned themselves with the ELF.

Divisions within the ELF were just as serious as divisions between the ELF and ELM had been. Competition for power and control increased as the organization grew. The Supreme Council, many of whom were living abroad in the Middle East, attempted to curb the

competition for power by dividing Eritrea into five military zones.
The Supreme Council then divided the ELF into five divisions

> on the basis of religion and nationality and each division
> was made to operate in one of the zones. This zonal di-
> vision was detrimental to the unity of the Eritrean peo-
> ple.[5]

The five zones effectively became fiefdoms, largely reflecting the
mentality of their creators. The zonal divisions only increased the
competition for power and petty political jealousies. While the Eritreans bickered among themselves, the struggle against the Ethiopians
made little progress. The Ethiopian army exploited the zonal-ethnic
differences to the fullest, attacking one zone at a time and meeting
with very ineffectual resistance.

As the situation continued to deteriorate throughout 1967/68, a
kind of grass-roots "democratic movement" began to agitate against
the continued utilization of the devisive zonal structure. This movement, made up of both guerrillas and civilians, began an organizing
effort to convene a conference to resolve the issues of leadership and
unity of the zones. Although a number of the members of this movement met with repressive measures and even death for their efforts,
the movement finally succeeded in bringing about the Anseba Conference in September 1968. The Anseba Conference, in spite of the resistance of the Supreme Council, established the unity of three of the
divisions of the front. The remaining two zones, over which the ELF
leadership and zonal commanders had more influence, remained outside the unity agreement.

Although the Supreme Council constantly attempted to weaken
the new united zones, they met with little success. By August 1969,
the ELF leadership and the two autonomous zones agreed to meet the
united zones at Adobha. The Adobha Conference united the two remaining divisions with the three that were already united. However,
the ELF leadership attempted to fight back. With a little understood
series of behind-the-scenes power plays, bargains, and secret alliances, the Supreme Council, who controlled most of the purse strings,
was able to establish a new provisional military leadership called the
General Command. The General Command had 38 members: 18
from the three united zones and 10 each from the two zones joining
the other three. The Supreme Council continued to serve in its primarily political capacity from abroad.

The unity that emerged as a result of the Adobha Conference
was ill-fated and short-lived. The question arises as to why the three
previously united divisions would even agree to the new "packed"
General Command structure at all. The explanation is complex at

best, confusing at worst. In essence, the democratic forces were making one last-ditch effort to salvage a deteriorating political situation. The Supreme Council, primarily Osman Saleh Sabbe and Idris Mohammed Adum, insisted upon the new provisional structure as a precondition to any sort of meaningful discussions at Adobha. The three united zones could take it or leave it, thus ending communication between the groups and raising the specter of civil war on a large scale. They opted for "unity on any basis," which, in retrospect, was a rather poor choice, indeed.

Within a few months of the Adobha Conference, the General Command put six of its own members in jail and set out to purge a number of guerrillas that had previously opposed the majority policies while zonal divisions existed. In a relatively short period of time, 300 guerrillas were executed.[6] By early 1970 it was clear to a number of those who had attempted to attain "unity at any cost" that the agreement was fatal. Consequently, in order to guarantee their own survival as well as to establish a more progressive organization, in July 1970, a number of guerrillas from various divisions split from the ELF and proclaimed themselves the Eritrean Peoples Liberation Forces (later Front). Initially, the EPLF was dominated by Tigrinya-speaking Christian highlanders, leaving a predominance of Muslim lowlanders in powerful positions in the ELF. By as early as 1972 this was no longer the case: both fronts had attained more of an ethnic and regional balance.

Tom Farer, in discussing the factionalism of the Eritrean movement, has pointed out that

> divisive tensions wrack every liberation movement. They
> spring from many sources: abrasions between fighting
> units and the political directorate ensconced in some
> friendly foreign capital far from the zone of danger and
> unsure of its control; the temptations offered by competing,
> often mutually antagonistic, foreign patrons; disputes over
> the terms of settlement and the anticipated allocation of
> victory's benefits; difficulties of communication and supply;
> and the inevitable defectors and informants who intensify the
> paranoia native to an underground struggle. The ELF dem-
> onstrated all of these generic tensions plus others which
> vary with time and place.[7]

THE ERITREAN CIVIL WAR:
POLITICAL ASPECTS

At the same time that the Eritrean Peoples Liberation Front was being formed in 1970, the long-standing power struggle within the

Supreme Council intensified and resulted in yet another split in the Eritrean movement. One faction, headed by Idris Mohammed Adum, retained the name General Command while the opposing faction, led by Osman Saleh Sabbe, renamed itself the General Secretariat. By disassociating itself from the actions of the General Command and through its extensive contacts with Arab supporters, Sabbe's group hoped to gain a foothold and wield decisive influence in the newly formed EPLF. [8]

Throughout 1971, both a war of words and bullets continued to escalate among the three liberation organizations. During this period, and for the following three years, actions taken against the Ethiopians occupying Eritrea were minimal. Internal political alliances and infighting were the order of the day. In October 1971, the ELF-General Command held its first National Congress in western Eritrea. This Congress, attended by 561 delegates drew up a political program, with unity as its stated goal. But the schisms in the movement were too deep at this particular point in time for even the most preliminary unity discussions to take place.

In February 1972, two important events occurred. The first saw Sabbe's General Secretariat form a tactical alliance with the struggling EPLF. This event could only be described as a "marriage of convenience":

> The progressive fighters who formed the EPLF were clear on the opportunist nature of the General Secretariat. However, as the EPLF was in a transitional stage, i.e., in the process of consolidating its internal unity and defending itself from the savage attacks of the Ethiopian regime and the liquidationist attempts of the General Command, it established a tactical alliance with the General Secretariat. In February 1972, the General Secretariat changed its name to the Foreign Mission and agreed to work as the representative of the EPLF abroad. [9]

The second event was predicated upon the first: the outbreak of full-scale civil war between the ELF and the EPLF. In late February, the ELF passed resolutions calling for purges within the group itself as well as for the use of force against the EPLF. The Eritrean civil war had begun. One very quick political realignment occurred as a result of the outbreak of civil war: the group being purged within the ELF, the Obel group (Muslim fanatics from the Barka region), formed a tactical alliance with Sabbe and the EPLF in October 1972.

The EPLF maintains that it took a defensive posture during the civil war; considering the immense challenge of political consolidation facing this group at this time, this claim would seem to be fairly accurate. The EPLF, as a relatively young organization, spent a great deal of time in the political education of its own cadres and guerrillas as well as addressing itself to the previously ignored job of attempting to develop a revolutionary consciousness among the Eritrean people.

The toughest political challenge for the EPLF during the civil war years (1972-74) was from its own Foreign Mission, headed by Osman Saleh Sabbe. While the EPLF fighters inside Eritrea were developing an increasingly revolutionary political ideology, the Sabbe group remained opposed to any form of socialist direction. The Sabbe group:

> strove to create a basis for its line among the fighters by exploiting secondary contradictions. It opposed the extensive politicization of the masses and the dissemination of revolutionary theory. It suppressed the revolutionary journals published in the field . . . and distorted the consistently anti-imperialist line of the EPLF.[10]

The EPLF also accused Sabbe of abuse and misuse of money and goods he received from Arab states, particularly Iraq and Saudi Arabia. He would withhold goods from those inside Eritrea in an attempt to impose his own political preferences on the EPLF. Consequently, the EPLF (excluding the Foreign Mission) came to develop a strong concept of self-reliance in all matters relating to their needs: political, military, and economic.

The civil war, to be discussed more fully in the next chapter, came to a halt in October 1974, in large part due to the altered political situation in Ethiopia. The downfall of Haile Selassie and the advent of the Provisional Military Administrative Council (PMAC), or Dergue, in Addis Ababa presented the Eritreans with a new set of political questions to be addressed. Although unity was nowhere in sight, a tentative form of military cooperation between the ELF and EPLF against the Ethiopians emerged during the latter part of 1974.

A few words regarding the nature of the new Ethiopian regime are in order here. The coup d'etat by which the Dergue established itself on September 12, 1974, followed eight months of widespread, popular agitation against the Haile Selassie government. When the Dergue achieved power, they had very little ideological orientation, according to Donald Levine, the well-known Ethiopianist:

> They were mainly soldiers; they had general enthusiasms and patriotism and populism, but very little specific ideological orientation. That was injected into them by a few intellectuals around the University and by the student

movement, which was intensively Marxist oriented. . . .
How deeply committed they are ideologically to Marxist-
Leninism is something I am not sure about. [11]

The Dergue, like so many other essentially nationalist movements in
Africa and elsewhere, let the intellectual vacuum in Ethiopia be filled
by militant Marxist slogans. I would submit that the Dergue, in fact,
came to invoke their own brand of pseudo-Marxist rhetoric as justification for virtually any and all actions they might take. Rather than
base their concrete political and economic programs in Marxist theory,
the Dergue simply supplemented their military-proposed programs
with convenient socialist doctrine. [12]

To what extent the Dergue is a Marxist-Leninist or even a socialist entity is debatable and will not be discussed here at great
length. The Dergue has nationalized a good deal of agriculture and
industry in Ethiopia, putting previously privately owned holdings in
the hands of the State. However, the concept of nationalizing seg-
ments of the private sector is not particularly revolutionary, much
less a measure of socialism. Nationalization under the rule of a military council is hardly synonymous with socialism. In conducting their
"revolution from above" the new Ethiopian rulers have, I believe,
found justification for their attempts to transform Ethiopia into a
modern African state.

Throughout the course of the Eritrean struggle, a tension has
existed between the fighters inside Eritrea and their representatives
abroad. With the cessation of civil strife and with primary attention
once again directed at the Ethiopians, the contradictions between the
EPLF and Sabbe's Foreign Mission intensified to the breaking point.
The only surprising element is that the process actually took as long
as it did.

Once the Dergue had come to power the Foreign Mission expressed a readiness to negotiate what the Addis Ababa regime called
a "peaceful solution" to the Eritrean question. Sabbe declared that
he would not be opposed to granting Ethiopia "a corridor to the sea." [13]
Inside Eritrea, the EPLF took strong exception to Sabbe's proposals,
stating that

> the force that is waging a determined armed struggle in-
> side Eritrea is the sole representative of the Eritrean peo-
> ple on any issue, whether it is of minor or major signifi-
> cance. [14]

In September 1975, Sabbe's Foreign Mission finally went too
far for the EPLF. Four months earlier, in May, the ELF held its
Second National Congress. At the Congress a new, less rigid and en-

trenched set of political leaders was installed, though there was not as clean a sweep as some had wanted.[15] Idris Mohammed Adum and Tedla Bairu were removed from the executive and were replaced by younger men such as Ibrahim Toteel and Abdullah Idris. The new leadership of the ELF then met with Sabbe in Baghdad to discuss unity of the groups under the umbrella of ELF's revised political program. They met again shortly thereafter in Beirut, and finally on September 9, the Foreign Mission and the ELF Revolutionary Council (formerly General Command) signed a merger that came to be known as the Khartoum Agreement.

The problem with the Khartoum Agreement was that Sabbe had not bothered to consult his constituents inside Eritrea on the stipulations of the merger. The main provisions of the agreement were predicated upon the immediate merger of the ELF and the EPLF, even though it was clear from the outset that this was unacceptable to the EPLF since immediate merger was contrary to its proposal for a united front.[16] By a united front the EPLF meant a cooperative umbrella structure under which each organization would maintain its own committees, institutions, and so forth, yet be able to agree on goals and cooperate on joint military operations. The EPLF remembered all too well its experiences with "unity at any cost" in 1969 and wanted time to work out difficulties between the organizations prior to a formal merger.

Sabbe put tremendous pressure on the EPLF to accept the Khartoum Agreement: he stopped sending arms and other supplies to the guerrillas. On March 23, 1976, the Foreign Mission and an EPLF delegation met in Khartoum and, unable to resolve their differences, severed their relationship. The Foreign Mission tendered its resignation; however, it refused to divide any of the arms, money, or other goods it had collected in the name of the EPLF. This split left the EPLF politically isolated: on the one hand from the ELF and Sabbe, and on the other from virtually any source of foreign material. The principle of self-reliance would take on new, vastly increased meaning from this time onward.

The ELF and Sabbe, however, continued to receive foreign support. (No available sources can verify exact amounts, or even estimates.) Sabbe, through his network of conservative Arab contacts probably received more assistance than did the ELF. The ELF has for years received its largest amounts of assistance from Iraq and Syria, whose Ba'thist parties have tended to compete for ELF favor. Sabbe received most of his assistance from Libya (until 1977) and much smaller amounts from the more conservative Persian Gulf states, such as Abu Dhabi and Kuwait.

While up to this point the political aspects of the Eritrean revolution have been examined in chronological fashion, it is now necessary to take an in-depth look at the contemporary political ideologies of both the ELF and the EPLF, with special emphasis on their respective differences.

POLITICAL IDEOLOGIES: EPLF AND ELF

The split in the Eritrean liberation movement that occurred in 1970 is often described in facile generalities, notes Richard Lobban, a close follower of Eritrean affairs.[17] Yet the split was, as illustrated above, quite complicated. Lobban goes on to discuss some of

MAP 5

Guerrilla Operations

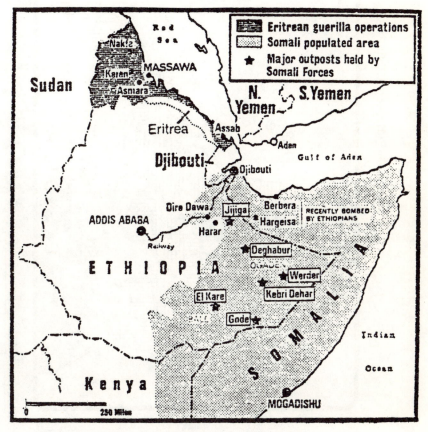

Source: Financial Times, January 19, 1978.

MAP 6

Areas of Influence within Eritrea

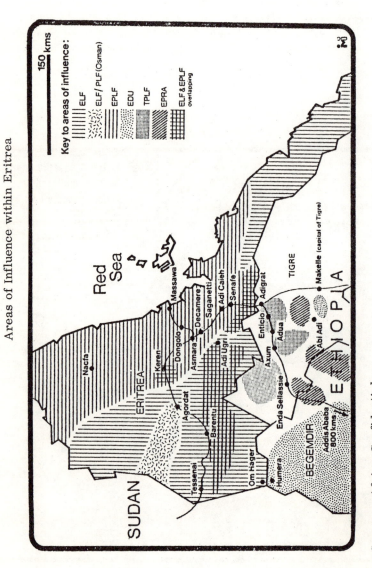

Source: Africa Confidential.

the generalities often used to explain the differences between the ELF and the EPLF: religious, ethnic, Sino-Soviet alignment, and ideological. These categories have been offered as the operational differences between the two fronts, yet Eritrean religious and ethnic lines have, in large part, been transcended by the fronts in recent years. I would agree with Lobban that these differences are not of a substantive nature, up until the last point, that of ideology. There are ideological differences between the two fronts, but these involve a number of qualifications.

Before the March 1976 break between the EPLF inside Eritrea and Sabbe's Foreign Mission, the position regarding the lack of ideological differences might have appeared more tenable. The political-ideological debate today tends to be over which front is more Marxist, or progressive, or more correct in their political line. Gerard Chaliand views the EPLF as "Marxist-oriented";[18] by most accounts the ELF is far less so. And yet, as David Hamilton has noted, the ELF has during the years 1975-77 developed a far more radical political stance, and many of its field commanders regard themselves as Marxists.[19] Where then, can the distinctions be made? I would submit that the substantive difference between the two organizations is one of political innovation versus response. While on paper their respective political programs share numerous similarities, the EPLF is the sociopolitical innovator, while the ELF often follows the EPLF's lead in a revised form sometime thereafter.

In addition to the innovation-versus-response distinction, there are political questions on which the two fronts differ. Four of these categories are examined in a 1978 Eritrean student political tract, In Defense of the Eritrean Revolution.[20] The ideological differences discussed in this book center around the concepts of class leadership, self-reliance, mass mobilization, and the socialist road to development. It might be noted that while a discussion of ideological factors can be quite useful in analyzing a revolutionary movement, the actions of the movement may or may not correspond to their theoretical tenets. The aforementioned categories are discussed below in the context of each organization's political ideology.

As noted above, Gerard Chaliand referred to the EPLF as "the most impressive revolutionary movement produced in Africa in the last two decades." When Chaliand calls the EPLF Marxist-oriented, he is referring to the EPLF political program of a national democratic revolution. For the EPLF to call itself a Marxist-Leninist party at this stage of its development would be premature, according to EPLF literature.[21] The national democratic revolution

> calls for the establishment of a solid worker-peasant alliance and the formation of a broad National United Front

under the firm leadership of a proletarian party that can
successfully rally all patriotic elements against the common enemy of colonial aggression. [22]

Although Marxist-Leninist oriented, the EPLF has no particular
ideological or tactical allegiance to "Moscow, Peking, or any other
Communist government."[23] Marx and Lenin are standard EPLF
reading as is Mao Tse-tung. However, the EPLF attempts to avoid
dogmatic application of Marxist principles to the Eritrean situation.

The objective of the EPLF, as stated in its National Democratic
Programme, is to establish a people's democratic state. (See Appendix B.) The front is firmly opposed to any continuing Ethiopian
administrative presence in Eritrea. In working toward this goal it
has, in both a military and political sense, operated in a remarkably
self-reliant manner. In the military struggle, to be discussed at
length in the next chapter, the EPLF has utilized the Maoist principle
of protracted warfare. While conducting a protracted struggle, the
organization strives to instill both revolutionary discipline and political consciousness in its cadres, fighters, and the larger Eritrean
population.

Today the EPLF views itself as a liberation front, rather than
any sort of formal political party. However, EPLF is acutely aware
of the need for a vanguard party "if the national democratic revolution
is to be consummated."[24] The revolutionary vanguard is the proletariat, who will not only consolidate its leadership in the future party
but who also have a vanguard role to play in the national democratic
revolution itself.

Although many Eritreans describe their country as "colonial
and semifeudal," the concept of a proletarian vanguard has sound
historical basis in the experience of the past 80 years. As noted in
the preceding chapter, the Italians, especially during their military
mobilization of the 1930s, created a number of wage-laborers in Eritrea. By the time of British Military Administration (1941-52), no
less than 20 percent of all Eritreans lived in cities and towns. In recent years this percentage has probably increased, although no accurate figures are available to verify this trend. As for the worker-
peasant alliance in the revolution, there would seem to be less reason
for tension between the two, when compared with other African countries. It may be noted that because of the relatively recent advent of
an Eritrean working class, many workers actually have their roots in
peasant society, thus forming a solid basis for the functioning alliance.
In addition, privileges for workers under colonial rule were few and
far between. Tensions that arise, according to the EPLF, tend to occur on the basis of class rather than along worker-peasant lines.

Marxist-Leninist political theory has been applied in other facets
of the EPLF program as well. Democratic centralism is the operative

principle of the organization at all levels, from Central Committee and the Political Bureau to the mass organizations.[25] The EPLF invokes the classical Leninist theory of imperialism in its analysis of international political economy. In its organizing efforts, the EPLF puts great emphasis on the participation of the masses to facilitate the revolutionary process:

> The EPLF maintains that the active and conscious participation of the masses of the people in the revolution is an absolute necessity for the success of the revolution and exerts great effort in organizing, politicizing and arming them.[26]

Finally, the EPLF maintains that the only acceptable road to development is along a socialist path, as befits a new democratic revolution.

The political ideology of the ELF is not as consistent as that of the EPLF. It appears to be, from firsthand observation, a very mixed ideological stance. The lack of a truly systematic approach to ideological commitments in the ELF is best illustrated in the homage paid to Pan-Arabism and Ba'thist "socialism" regularly in ELF publications. Over the years Iraq and Syria have given substnatial aid to the ELF; most of this assistance has been given as a result of the competition between the Ba'thist parties of these countries in attempting to gain political influence in the Middle East region. Yet, in the pamphlet, ELF: The National Revolutionary Vanguard of the Eritrean People, we find the following:

> Our relation with the Arab nation is not an emotional or superficial, but militant, organic, historical and cultural one based on bonds of the joint destiny, mutual and common interests, and solidarity in face of menace and aggression.[27]

> The liberation of the Eritrean people is interrelated to the security of the Arab nation.[28]

The basic contradictions in ELF political ideology, I would maintain, are those that exist between the leadership, some of whom possess Ba'thist sympathies, and the rank and file, who have little or nothing to do with any form of Pan-Arabism. Time after time in interviews, I was told that numerous rank-and-file ELF guerrillas were more "progressive" than the ELF Revolutionary Council and that tensions regularly arose from this dichotomy. Although the Second National Congress of the ELF took steps to make the leadership more reflective of ELF membership in May 1975, the Revolutionary Council still reflects a more rightist, Pan-Arab stance than does the organization as a whole.

The ELF is described by most observers as a movement with more nationalist tendencies than Marxist ones. Like the EPLF, it applies the principle of democratic centralism in organizational operations. There is no formal discussion of Marxist-Leninist classics in ELF training centers, although these books are readily available to interested individuals in Tigrinya and Arabic. The ELF sponsors mass organizations along the same lines as the EPLF, although, as noted above, these have generally been instituted in response to the EPLF initiative.

There are at least three areas where ELF ideology appears substantially at odds with that of EPLF. The first is class leadership: the ELF assigns the leadership of the revolution to the petty bourgeoisie, that is, people with better-than-average status in regard to property and education. In the rural areas middle and upper peasants maintain a disproportionate role in the decision-making process. The ELF, rejecting the notion of a working-class vanguard, maintains that the leadership is eventually dominated by the left wing of the petty bourgeoisie, which is seasoned in the armed struggle and which is committed to carry the revolution through to the end.[29]

The second area of divergence deals with the concept of self-reliance. Self-reliance is one of the EPLF's cardinal rules, whereas the ELF has always relied, to one degree or another, on external material support. The ELF has been quoted as saying that colonial and semicolonial countries "cannot solve their internal and external problems on their own by following the principle of 'self-reliance.'"[30]

The last area of divergence deals with the economic orientation of the revolution. While the EPLF is committed to a socialist path, the ELF has advocated a "non-capitalist road to development." The ELF believes that Eritrean society, being part of the Third World in general and of the African world in particular, has to follow the non-capitalist road of development.[31]

It seems clear, then, that the two liberation fronts do diverge in terms of political ideology. The EPLF is more consistently Marxist-oriented whereas the ELF appears to combine various ideologies, with a distinct nationalist bent. It is also worth repeating that where the political programs of the two fronts converge, the EPLF has usually initiated a given political practice that has been followed by the ELF. The best example of this practice is in the formation of mass organizations. These are examined in the following section on organizational structure.

STRUCTURE OF THE EPLF AND THE ELF

The organizational structures of the ELF and the EPLF are vaguely similar. Both hold their respective congresses to be the ul-

FIGURE 1

ELF Organizational Structure

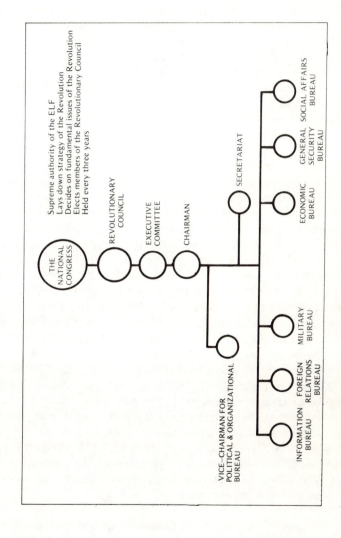

Source: Eritrean Liberation Front, The Eritrean Revolution (Beirut: ELF Foreign Information Center, 1977/78).

timate authority in their organizations, yet on a daily operating level the political power and decisions rest with other organs in the structure(s).

The ELF's organizational structure is illustrated in Figure 1. The National Congress is held every three years; the Second National Congress was held in May 1975, after the initial Congress was held in 1971. Members of the 41-member Revolutionary Council and 9-member Executive Committee hold the real power in the ELF. The ELF chairman, Ahmed Nasser, has very little organizational clout and is more a spokesman of the ELF than anything else. The two most powerful men in the ELF are Ibrahim Toteel and Abdullah Idris. Ibrahim Toteel is ELF vice-chairman and heads the crucial Political and Organizational Bureau. Abdullah Idris heads the Military Bureau.

The EPLF's Congress meets every two years and held its First Organizational Congress in January 1977. The EPLF's organizational structure is illustrated in Figure 2. In January 1977, the Congress elected a 43-member Central Committee (37 permanent and 6 alternate members) and vested in it all authority until January 1979. [32] The Political Bureau, the secretary-general and the assistant secretary-general of the organization were chosen from the Central Committee. As with the ELF chairman, the EPLF secretary-general, Ramadan Mohammed Nur, is largely without real political power. The single most powerful individual in the organization is Issayas Afeworki, the assistant secretary-general. Issayas joined the Eritrean movement in the mid-to-late 1960s, having previously been a student; little more is known about him. He has been the consistently most influential man in the EPLF since its inception in 1970.

The ELF's Political Bureau and the EPLF's Political Committee are particularly important in that they are the organizational conduits with the greatest number of Eritrean people: the mass organizations of both organizations come under their control. Both fronts have developed five mass organizations composed of workers, peasants, women, students, and youth.

Since the First Congress of the EPLF in January 1977, the development of formalized mass organizations has proceeded at a rapid pace. The EPLF believes that the Eritrean masses have a crucial role to play in the revolutionary process:

> A piece of iron has to be tempered in fire before it can
> be used for a plow. The masses are like iron. Once
> they are steeled in the crucible of struggle and their
> consciousness is raised, no obstruction can prevent their
> inevitable victory. [33]

The EPLF mass organizations began as clandestine groups in Ethiopian-occupied areas, but as EPLF scored one victory after another

FIGURE 2

Organizational Structure of the EPLF

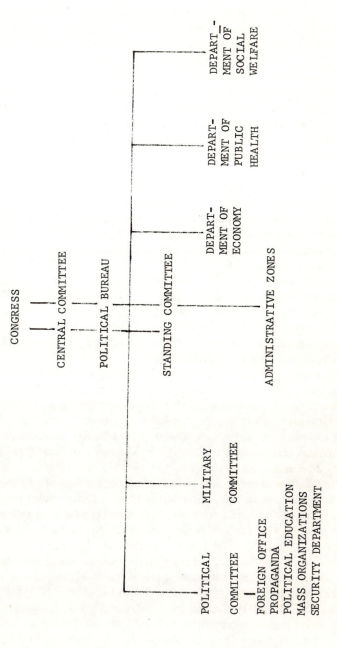

Source: Eritrean Peoples Liberation Front, Vanguard 2 (February–March 1977): 22.

throughout 1977, the respective mass organizations began to function openly in the liberated areas. The mass organizations function as a department within the Political Committee and are five in number: workers, peasants, women, students, and youth organizations.

The Eritrean Workers Organization is of particular importance for the EPLF "for the consolidation of the leading role of the proletariat in the liberation struggle."[34] The Workers Organization establishes cells in factories and plantations to conduct political discussion and raise the workers' national and class consciousness. The organization has been playing a crucial role in EPLF urban operations. In conjunction with the EPLF armed units, the workers have planned and carried out numerous operations involving the seizure and transport of medicine, machinery, arms, and clothing to EPLF-liberated areas.

The Organization of Eritrean Peasants attempts to mobilize the peasant population for active participation in the liberation struggle. The organization encourages the peasants to attend literacy classes, to build air raid shelters, and even to assist in combat situations. A number of the peasants recruited by the organization are in turn encouraged to become EPLF guerrillas. Very significantly, the peasant organization also pushes for land reform by agitating among the peasants for the necessity of redistributing land equally among those who till it. The organization is particularly concerned with uniting the poor and middle peasants, who comprise some 90 percent of Eritrean peasantry, in order to overcome the resistance on the part of large landholders and upper peasants.

The Organization of Eritrean Women gives high priority to raising the political consciousness of the women throughout the country. Since more than 95 percent of Eritrean women are illiterate, the organization gives special attention to literacy courses.[35] From among the most conscious members, recruits are sought for service in the EPLA and peoples militia. The women's organization is also working to sway opinion against dowry-based marriages.

Much less information is available regarding the students and youth mass organizations. Particularly at the university level, the role of Eritrean students may be more crucial outside Eritrea than at home. The Association of Eritrean Students in North America (AESNA) is heavily involved in publicizing the Eritrean struggle on college campuses, to community groups, and to religious organizations.

While information regarding the EPLF's formal mass organization for youth is scarce, the role of youth in the EPLF fighting force is well publicized. The young men and women who receive special political and military training are known as the Fitewerari, or Vanguard. Youths, aged 14 to 16 years old, are trained in special units that are particularly geared to their needs. Literacy, political education, and basic military training are all introduced at a level appropriate for this age group. The Fitewerari section is also used as a correctional measure for youths who have previously collaborated with the Ethiopians.

The major question surrounding the mass organizations of the ELF is just how operative these organizations are on a daily basis. Their formation, or in other cases activation from a virtually dormant state, has been in large part due to the immense push by the EPLF in forming their mass organizations. Nevertheless, five ELF mass organizations do exist: the General Union of Eritrean Workers (GUEW); the Eritrean Women's General Union (EWGU); the General Union of Eritrean Students (GUES); the General Union of Eritrean Peasants (GUEP); and the Eritrean Democratic Youth Union (EDYU).

The General Union of Eritrean Workers (GUEW) was founded in September 1973, but did not hold its first congress until December 1976.[36] Not offering as much opportunity for large-scale participation as some of the other organizations, the GUEW is seemingly more active abroad than in Eritrea itself. It is presently attempting to gain membership in the World Federation of Trade Unions (WFTU).

The Eritrean Women's General Union (EWGU) was founded in June 1974 but did not hold its first congress until May 1977. The union runs handicraft training centers and an elementary school with 500 students and has established a sweater factory in an ELF-liberated area.

The General Union of Eritrean Students (GUES) has been torn by internal strife the last few years. The ELF described the problem by admitting that "reactionary and subversive elements in the leadership weakened the union."[37] Translated, this probably means that some students in the ELF organization attempted to produce ideological or other changes and, having failed in their attempts, switched over to the EPLF.

Very little peasant mobilization has taken place in ELF-controlled areas. The ELF states that the formation of the General Union of Eritrean Peasants (GUEP) "was delayed due to unfinished mobilizational tasks in the field."[38] In fact, the ELF waited until its Second National Congress in May 1975 to resolve to form the peasants' organization at all. The GUEP, according to the ELF, is organizing peasants into cooperative unions for self-sufficient food production for themselves and the ELF units in their areas.

The Eritrean Democratic Youth Union (EDYU) was formed in September 1976, its formation also having been resolved at the ELF's Second National Congress. It is

making strenuous efforts to create a revolutionary generation capable of carrying out the programmes and consummating the gains of the Eritrean Revolution.[39]

THE TRAINING OF CADRES

While during the 1960s much of the guerrilla training that Eritreans underwent took place abroad (primarily in Syria and Iraq), by the mid-1970s the two fronts were able to conduct all of their training programs inside Eritrea itself. This was mainly due to the liberation movement's control of between 90 and 95 percent of the country. Little is available regarding the nature of the ELF fighter or cadre training programs. Each new ELF fighter trains for six months, undergoing intensive military and political training. Guerrilla warfare is stressed, I was told by a former ELF fighter, while the political education section of the program is not well organized. Many of the military trainers had received their own skills while in Iraq. Literacy in one's native language (Tigrinya or Tigre) is a requirement to advance to combatant status; the literacy program for prospective guerrillas is quite intense for the duration of their basic training period.

Training under the auspices of the EPLF is of a more systematic nature. The First Congress, held in January 1977, resolved to give increased importance "to raising the political consciousness of EPLF combatants."[40] New recruits are given a six-month training program with stress on political education as well as military training. Achieving literacy, as in the ELF, is a fundamental requirement for advancement to combatant status. The medium of instruction is one's native language, usually Tigrinya or Tigre, rarely Arabic, which is not indigenous to Eritrea.

The most conscious of the new combatants are often selected for the EPLF cadre school. The school's six-month program provides advanced political and ideological education for some fighters. The principal aim of this program is to transform the People's Army and train a mature vanguard. To integrate theory with practice, the cadres carry out many productive activities: they participate in the building of houses, construction of roads, and agricultural work.[41] In 1976 alone, approximately 1,000 cadres underwent advanced training under EPLF tutelage.[42]

PROPAGANDA

Both the ELF and the EPLF disseminate massive doses of propaganda inside Eritrea as well as for international consumption. Most of their propaganda is spread either by word of mouth, via print media, or by radio broadcasts.

For literate Eritreans, the ELF offers a wealth of information sources. The publications for internal consumption are issued by the

Information Bureau as an essential part of the ELF's political education program. Periodicals issued in the liberated areas appear in both Tigrinya and Arabic. The Eritrean People's Struggle is the official organ of the ELF. Awet (Victory) and Hisbawi Elama (The People's Goal) contain political education in simplified form, including Eritrean history and present ELF objectives. Zena Sewra (News of the Revolution) is a weekly news bulletin available in the field. The Military Bureau publishes a monthly called September One, which concentrates on military operations and strategies. All of the mass organizations have their own newsletters as well.

The Foreign Information Center of the ELF in Beirut publishes Eritrean Revolution bimonthly and The Eritrean Newsletter biweekly in both English and Arabic. The Rome office publishes the Notiziario Dell Eritrea; the Eritreagruppen in Stockholm publishes a periodical called Eritrea in Swedish.

For those who are not literate, the ELF conducts village meetings led by cadres who attempt to explain the historical and contemporary aspects of the revolution, as seen by the organization. The ELF also beams radio broadcasts into Eritrea from Khartoum four times a week for one hour via their organ, "Voice of the Eritrean Revolution."

The EPLF propaganda network is similar in format, if not greater in area covered, to that of ELF. The EPLF broadcasts their own radio program from Khartoum on the three evenings a week that ELF does not. Eritrean support groups in Europe and North America have raised money to fund a radio station known as "Radio Liberation Eritrea," which now operates from within Eritrea itself.

The literacy campaign conducted by the EPLF is also an important method for spreading propaganda. Materials used in the adult literacy campaign, as well as those used in primary education, are heavily laden with basic political material. The official monthly publication of the EPLF is Vanguard. Other EPLF publications include Mahta (Spark), the monthly theoretical organ; Aquai (The Peasant); Combatant, the internal organ of the EPLA (army); and Dimtsi Hizbi (Voice of the Masses) a bimonthly journal. These publications are generally available only in Tigrinya and Arabic, although Vanguard has been reprinted in English on occasion.

English language propaganda supporting the EPLF is available from the Association of Eritrean Students in North America. Eritreans for Liberation in North America, a group not formally associated with the EPLF, publishes the monthly newsletter Eritrea in Struggle and the occasional journal Liberation.

THE ELUSIVE ISSUE OF UNITY

When all of the political principles, differences, and structures of the EPLF and the ELF have been explored and debated, the Eritrean movement is left with one glaring issue: that of the disunity of the Eritrean liberation movement. The central political questions in the Eritrean struggle for independence are whether the Eritreans can defeat the Ethiopians and whether the Eritreans will defeat themselves. Between 1976 and the present, with precious few exceptions, there has been a paucity of cooperation between the two fronts. To complicate matters, or maybe to epitomize them, Osman Saleh Sabbe has regularly attempted to introduce a so-called third force, his splinter Eritrean Liberation Front-Popular Liberation Forces (ELF-PLF).

In addition to the hostilities between the EPLF and the ELF and the constant thorn of Sabbe's group, the two fronts have undergone internal turmoil, which has altered each group's complexion, particularly in the case of the ELF. These internal difficulties in addition to the massive Soviet-Cuban buildup have finally encouraged the new attempts at unity between the ELF and the EPLF.

The greatest point of contention between the ELF and the EPLF has been on which basis to cooperate with the other organization. The EPLF has held firm for a "united front" organization; that is a minimum basis for unity with the only essential point being the united front's objective: ridding Eritrea of Ethiopian occupation. During the same period, the ELF has been insisting on a merger of the two organizations, at all levels. The once numerically stronger ELF saw a merger as giving the Revolutionary Council the upper hand in the proposed union. By March 1978, ELF forces were estimated to have decreased to 7,000 men while EPLF forces had grown to between 25,000 and 30,000 fighters.[43] The previously weaker EPLF, all too cognizant of past attempts at mergers, had continually rejected "hasty reunification" of the fronts and regards a physical merger as

> necessarily of secondary importance in terms of building
> the foundation for a genuine unity. . . . The united front
> is the transitional stage which guarantees the attainment
> of the genuine unity of the two fronts.[44]

Against the background of united front versus complete merger enter Osman Saleh Sabbe. In control of a splinter group known as ELF-PLF, the head of the ex-Foreign Mission (of EPLF) has continually "spoken for himself while assuming the role of spokesman for the whole [Eritrean] movement."[45] Sabbe can well "afford" to do so. The EPLF refers to him as a "petty-bourgeoisie reactionary" and opportunist. He is, in any case, a representative of the semifeudal, predominantly Islamic segment of Eritrean society. He is well funded by Saudi Arabia, Kuwait, and Abu Dhabi[46] and is consequently thought of by many Eritreans as a representative of Pan-Arab interests.

Sabbe's ELF-PLF is estimated to be about 5,000 men strong.[47] It controls a small portion (between 5 and 10 percent) of Eritrea from the Sudanese border to Agordat. Sabbe tends to recruit new members among Eritrean refugees and deserters from the two major fronts.[48] He is reputed to pay his fighters, an idea completely alien to the EPLF and the ELF. Both the EPLF and the ELF have regularly denounced Sabbe's group over the past two years as complicating the unity struggle. However, in July 1977 the ELF forged a temporary agreement with Sabbe, which became a major stumbling block to any negotiations with the EPLF. Worse yet for the ELF, the short-lived agreement with Sabbe caused a new schism in the organization that ended with a number of defections from the once dominant organization.

The ELF underwent a massive upheaval process in the second half of 1977. It was estimated that the ELF may have actually lost as much as one-third of its strength, much of it to the EPLF.[49] The largest ELF faction remains the pro-Iraqi Ba'thist group led by Abdullah Idris and Ibrahim Toteel. There are, however, still a number of young ELF fighters who are not in agreement with the ELF leadership but have remained in the organization to attempt structural and ideological change from within.

It has been estimated that no less than 1,500 ELF members defected to the EPLF in the second half of 1977.[50] These defectors believe that the ELF leaders, primarily the Revolutionary Council, failed to implement a series of earlier military agreements made with the EPLF. On at least one occasion in September 1977 ELF forces refused to accept EPLF help and as a result lost a major base near Adi Caieh.[51]

An even larger group of defectors is referred to as fallol ("anarchist") by the ELF leadership. They broke away from the ELF in July 1977 after the ill-fated agreement with Sabbe. Hundreds of these young fighters who rejected the Revolutionary Council-Sabbe power axis were executed by the ELF. Still others escaped to Khartoum, where, approximately 1,000 strong, they refer to themselves as the Eritrean Democratic Forces, or Eritrean Democratic Movement. They criticize the ELF leadership for maintaining too close a relationship with Iraq; for a lack of internal democracy; for the ELF's alleged failures to cooperate fully with the Eritrean peasantry; and for associating with Sabbe.[52]

A number of these ex-ELF fighters are said to be rallying around former ELF leader Hirui Tedla. Hirui, the son of former chief administrator of Eritrea, Tedla Bairu, was demoted from ELF leadership for opposing earlier moves toward the Sabbe group. It has been speculated that Hirui's Eritrean Democratic Movement may join the EPLF in the future.[53] However, when interviewed in Khartoum in December 1977, Hirui assured me that he had no such intentions, as he viewed the EPLF as too sectarian an organization for his support. At the same time, he was not entirely clear as to the direction of his so-called Democratic Movement, but did emphasize the necessity for more democratic political forms in Eritrea and less need for ideological polarization.

The EPLF has been the beneficiary of some of the ELF's recent political losses. Yet, while the EPLF has no truly serious internal divisions, it is not completely united either. Africa Confidential notes that EPLF's 1977 military and promotional successes have helped to heal the divisions that did previously exist.[54] A few years ago a very small group known as Menkaa ("Bat") surfaced in the organization. In 1976 perhaps as many as 200 young EPLF intellectuals were arrested. Many were executed for "radicalism"—for following an alleged Maoist line.[55] The Menkaa group, believing itself more leftist than the EPLF leadership, challenged a number of EPLF structures and operations as early as 1973 and, as noted above, was liquidated for what amounted to an attack on the democratic centralism of the EPLF.

The ELF and the EPLF, in large part responding to the increased pressures exerted by Cuban and Soviet presence in Ethiopia and Eritrea, finally did sign an accord forming a joint political command:

> The ending of the Ogaden war, the airlifts of troops and military supplies into Asmara and the series of Ethiopian thrusts south and south-east of the provincial capital have brought a unity which had previously never resulted from any amount of Sudanese pressure or Eritrean bilateral discussions.[56]

In October 1977, the two fronts agreed on a series of general principles at a unity meeting in Khartoum, which became known as the October 20th Agreement. The two groups met again in Khartoum from March 6 to 15, 1978, and signed another document on March 15 outlining the specific principles and procedures for implementing the October 20th Agreement. Finally, from April 22 to 24, 1978, the ELF and the EPLF met inside Eritrea to implement formally the previously signed accords.

In essence, this unity agreement looked toward the forming of a single national democratic front in Eritrea. The essential features of the agreement were: (1) the formation of a joint political leadership; (2) the formation of joint committees for military, information, economics, social affairs, and foreign relations; (3) an agreement that the joint political leadership will be responsible for the preparation of a unification congress sometime in the future; and (4) a call upon the rank and file of Sabbe's organization to join either the ELF or the EPLF.

Practically speaking, the new agreement created a united front rather than a complete merger of the two organizations. Each front was to maintain its organizational and political independence with the major aim of the joint committees being to establish minimum joint programs. The information offices of both the ELF and the EPLF began joint broadcasts from Khartoum in late March. [57] The long-standing political differences, to say nothing of the personal rivalries, will take much longer to overcome.

If the Soviet-Cuban threat was the primary factor in facilitating the October 20th Agreement, then the ELF's internal problems were an important secondary one. It has been estimated that ELF membership fell to as few as 7,000 armed fighters by March 1978. The same source estimated EPLF strength in the 25,000-to-30,000 fighter range. [58] The ELF, having lost fighters to the EPLF, Sabbe, and to the Eritrean Democratic Movement, undoubtedly felt that they needed to come to terms with the EPLF while they were still in a position to do so.

One factor inhibiting the implementation of the unity agreement was the existence of Osman Saleh Sabbe's forces. The March 15th declaration along with the October 20th Agreement clearly dealt Sabbe's group out of any, even minor, role in the Eritrean revolution. Yet, Sabbe has as many as 5,000 men under arms and might attempt to challenge the two fronts' demands that his organization disband. Africa Confidential has speculated that

> there is a strong likelihood of a joint ELF and EPLF military action against Sabbe's forces following the announcement of an alliance between the two organizations. [59]

However, real unity between the two competing organizations did not take place as a result of the October 20th Agreement. The Ethiopian offensive, rather than having a unifying effect upon the movement, only exacerbated the already plentiful internal problems. Specifically, no serious military cooperation took place and this hurt the Eritreans badly in their respective attempts to repulse the onslaught of Soviet and Cuban military might:

> Joint operations around Barentu in June [1978] under the auspices of the military committee suffered, say fighters in both fronts, because cooperation was weak. [60]

While the rank and file of both organizations seem to want unity, unconfirmed reports said that fighters from the EPLF were skirmishing with those from the ELF in isolated incidents in early 1979.

On January 21, 1979, the two fronts reactivated the joint leadership command, pledging themselves to a streamlined version of the October 20th Agreement. This was, however, the fourth accord of its kind to be signed in Khartoum in the past four years. The six-man joint supreme political leadership would, in theory, operate out of one central headquarters, command a single unified army, and draw up a master plan for all military and political activities.[61]

The January meetings were held under the auspices of the Sudanese government and attended by Ahmed Nassar, Ibrahim Toteel, and Abdulla Suleman of the ELF, and Issayas Afeworki, Ramadan Nur, and Ibrahim Aafa of the EPLF.[62] This new arrangement would seem to be fragile at best. The threats of the joint leadership are as great, if not greater, from the inside as they are from Ethiopian and Cuban forces.

THE THEORY AND REALITY
OF ERITREAN POLITICS

The October 20th Agreement opened up a number of possibilities, not the least of which was that many Eritreans who in the past had hesitated formally joining one of the fronts for fear of becoming involved in the feuding may now see fit to openly support the united front. Virtually the entire Eritrean population supports the independence movement,[63] and the liberation fighters will need all the help they can garner in the face of the continuing Ethiopian counteroffensive.

Yet, the potential stumbling blocks facing the Eritreans, both substantive and secondary, continue to pose the most serious questions in analyzing the revolution.

Real ideological and tactical differences have separated the EPLF and the ELF. The ELF emphasizes the theory of noncapitalist development for a future independent Eritrea. They acknowledge the necessity of winning a military victory over the Ethiopians before proceeding with extensive socioeconomic changes. Consequently, they emphasize the establishment of a strong central administrative structure that would guide postindependence, state-supported economic and social development while playing down the concept of the "class struggle."[64] On the other hand, the EPLF looks toward the Maoist theory of "national democratic revolution,"

in which intensive political organization of the workers and the peasants lays the basis for sweeping social and political reforms at every level carried out simultaneously with the war for independence.[65]

Superimposed upon the ideological differences are the persistent personality conflicts. The feelings of hostility run deep between the various leaderships: the EPLF dislikes and distrusts Sabbe; Sabbe has use for the other two groups only when he can exploit contradictions between them for his personal benefit; the ELF (Revolutionary Council) leadership has felt increasingly threatened by the other two groups as the ELF's membership has declined; and all of the respective leaders have been very protective of the areas under their control.

There are a number of other problems that merit mention as well. These are the hazardous remains of successive colonial legacies in Eritrea. Colonial policies of divide and rule tended to exacerbate such differences as geography, religion, and ethnicity. The more conscious Eritreans, whether Christian Tigrinya-speaking highlander or Muslim Tigre-speaking lowlander, recognize that these differences were easily exploited, especially by the Italians, in keeping Eritreans artificially divided. Today, the liberation movements are doing everything in their power to de-emphasize such differences.

At one time the ELF was more Muslim lowlander dominated, at least in the positions of leadership. At its inception, and for some years following, the EPLF was dominated by Christian highlanders. By 1978, however, the generalization that the ELF was predominantly Muslim and the EPLF more Christian in background was no longer valid.[66] The EPLF now gives first priority in their recruitment program to Muslim lowlanders. The ELF is, by all accounts, divided nearly evenly between Christians and Muslims, with a slight Muslim majority. Highlanders of both religions made up about 75 percent of the EPLF's forces a year ago; that balance is undergoing a gradual shift. The 37-member EPLF central committee is almost evenly divided between Christian and Muslim members. The EPLF has been clear to emphasize that the highlander domination of that organization has been a reflection of social rather than religious composition. The better-educated, more politically conscious highland population has, in the past, been in a far better position to serve as the vanguard of the revolution.

One interesting point regarding religious background and leadership roles in Eritrea is the large number of Eritrean Protestants found in the revolution's hierarchy. The Evangelical Church of Eritrea has no more than 10,000 members, yet many of these individuals were favored by the British during their military administration and thus advanced to positions of some authority. Woldeab Woldemariam, the elder statesman of the EPLF, is a Protestant, as is Assistant Secretary-General Issayas Afeworki. Hirui Tedla, formerly of the

ELF and now attempting the formation of the Eritrean Democratic Movement, is a Protestant as well. This disproportionate number of Protestants in leadership positions would seem to illustrate the point that the most politically conscious elements in Eritrean society have tended to be most prominent in the revolution.

Religion and ethnicity need not, from all indications, be substantially divisive factors on the road to independence. Both fronts, with occasional exception, have worked hard to ensure that these easily exploitable differences will not be exacerbated. Hirui Tedla has stated that he views the EPLF as enhancing social contradictions between Christians and Muslims. It should be emphasized, however, that the factor of social class underlies most of the social differences between Christians and Muslims at this time in Eritrea. By the process of protracted warfare, the movement can go a long way in redressing such grievances. The person most capable of fanning religious and ethnic differences is Osman Saleh Sabbe. Sabbe, an extremely articulate man, is capable of combining Arab money and a traditionalist following to undermine any sociopolitical progress being made in Eritrea. The manner in which any new united front might deal with Sabbe may well determine the extent of the potential divisiveness in a new Eritrea. The manner in which the ELF and the EPLF deal with each other for the duration of the armed struggle may well determine the future of Eritrea itself.

NOTES

1. Gerard Chaliand, "The Horn of Africa's Dilemma," Foreign Policy 30 (Spring 1978): 126.

2. Eritreans for Liberation in North America, Reactionary Clique Forced Out of EPLF (n.p., 1976), p. 2.

3. Eritrean Peoples Liberation Front, National Democratic Programme of the Eritrean People's Liberation Front (n.p., 1977), p. 8.

4. Eritrean Liberation Front, Eritrean Revolution 1 (August-September 1976): 12.

5. Eritrean Peoples Liberation Front, op. cit., p. 10.

6. Eritreans for Liberation in North America, op. cit., p. 3.

7. Tom J. Farer, War Clouds on the Horn of Africa (Washington, D.C.: Carnegie Endowment, 1976), pp. 33-34.

8. Eritreans for Liberation in North America, op. cit., p. 4.

9. Ibid.

10. Ibid.

11. U.S., Congress, Senate, Subcommittee on African Affairs of the Committee on Foreign Relations, Ethiopia and the Horn of Africa, Hearings, 94th Cong., 2d sess., August 4, 5, and 6, 1976, p. 52.

12. John Markakis and Nega Ayele, in their book Class and Revolution in Ethiopia (Nottingham: Spokesman, 1978), provide an in-depth analysis of this theme.

13. Eritreans for Liberation in North America, Eritrea in Struggle 1 (May 1977): 3.

14. Eritreans for Liberation in North America, Reactionary Clique, p. 5.

15. Africa Confidential 16 (October 24, 1975): 5.

16. Eritrean Peoples Liberation Front, op. cit., p. 16.

17. Richard Lobban, "The Eritrean War: Issues and Implications," Canadian Journal of African Studies 10 (1976): 341. In a letter to me dated July 2, 1979, Lobban modifies his previous comments. Part of his letter states:

> When my article was first drafted, serious and sincere
> efforts were being made to establish unity between the two
> main segments of the Eritrean independence movement.
> Since the later group had, in fact, split from the former
> and since unity was being discussed it appeared that the
> major differences were less than ideological and were, in
> good measure, personal. The period between final draft
> and today, almost five years, has seen unity as elusive as
> ever and ideological cleavages growing rather than nar-
> rowing. The EPLF has moved considerably further to the
> left of the ELF. One perspective would insist that the
> EPLF has become more "revolutionary", while my own
> perspective is that it has, in fact, become "ultra-left".
> Some characteristics of this "ultra-leftism" are: 1) a
> pre-occupation with leftist and radical terminology,
> 2) emphasis on "self-reliance" rather than international-
> ism at a period when they have few foreign allies, 3) in-
> ternal splitting tendencies, viz., Osman Saleh Sabbe, and
> 4) emphasis on military, rather than political, dimensions
> of the struggle, and 5) isolation or separation from their
> foreign based student, youth, and women's organizations.
> These judgments are made in the context of the Eritrean
> political spectrum, which itself must be placed into the
> spectra of Ethiopia and the Horn in general. Admittedly,
> the revolutionary process in Ethiopia is not complete, but
> its politico-military consolidation of the conflict in the Oga-
> den and over its domestic opponents such as EPRP, has
> drastically altered the situation which existed recently and
> saw the Eritreans in near achievement of their goal of ter-
> ritorial separation.

18. Chaliand, op. cit., p. 127.

19. David Hamilton, "Ethiopia's Embattled Revolutionaries," Conflict Studies 82 (April 1977): 17.

20. Association of Eritrean Students in North America and Association of Eritrean Women in North America, In Defense of the Eritrean Revolution (New York, February 1978), pp. 161-63.

21. Ibid., p. 100.

22. Eritreans for Liberation in North America, Liberation 2 (April-May 1973): 1.

23. Chaliand, op. cit.

24. Association of Eritrean Students in North America and Association of Eritrean Women in North America, op. cit., p. 94.

25. For a complete discussion of this point see ibid., pp. 161-63.

26. Ibid., p. 162.

27. Eritrean Liberation Front, ELF: The National Revolutionary Vanguard of the Eritrean People (n.p., 1978), p. 20.

28. Ibid., p. 21.

29. Eritrean Liberation Front, Gedli Hizbi Eritrea, November 1976, pp. 17-18, quoted in Association of Eritrean Students in North America and Association of Eritrean Women in North America, op. cit., p. 161.

30. Ibid., p. 162.

31. Ibid., p. 163.

32. Eritrean Peoples Liberation Front, Vanguard 2 (February-March 1977): 24.

33. Eritreans for Liberation in North America, Liberation 6 (November-December 1976): 5.

34. Ibid., 6 (July-August 1977): 28.

35. Ibid., 6 (March-June 1977): 20.

36. Eritrean Liberation Front, The Eritrean Newsletter, September 1, 1977, p. 14.

37. Ibid., p. 15.

38. Ibid.

39. Ibid.

40. Eritreans for Liberation in North America, Eritrea in Struggle, March 1977, p. 6.

41. Eritrean Peoples Liberation Front, Vanguard 2 (February-March 1977): 6.

42. Ibid.

43. Africa Confidential 19: 2.

44. Association of Eritrean Students in North America and Association of Eritrean Women in North America, op. cit., p. 147.

45. Fulvio Grimaldi, "The Eritrean Road to Unity?" Middle East, no. 38 (December 1977), p. 58.

46. Africa Confidential 18 (November 18, 1977): 1.
47. Ibid., 19 (May 26, 1978): 3.
48. Ibid., 19 (March 3, 1978): 2.
49. Ibid., 18 (November 18, 1977): 2.
50. Ibid.
51. Ibid.
52. Ibid.
53. Ibid.
54. Ibid., p. 3.
55. Ibid.
56. Ibid., 19 (March 31, 1978): 5-6.
57. Sudanow 3 (April 1978): 22.
58. Africa Confidential 19 (March 3, 1978): 2.
59. Ibid.
60. Sudanow 3 (November 1978): 27.
61. Ibid., 4 (February 1979): 16.
62. Ibid.
63. Chaliand, op. cit.
64. Africa Confidential 19: 1.
65. Ibid.
66. Ibid.

3
ARMED STRUGGLE IN ERITREA

By early 1978, the only Eritrean towns and cities under Ethiopian control were the capital, Asmara, the seaports of Massawa and Assab, and the provincial centers of Barentu and Adi Caieh. Eritrean forces of the Eritrean Peoples Liberation Front (EPLF) and the Eritrean Liberation Front (ELF) controlled all other towns as well as the Eritrean countryside, including the extensive network of roads.

Since mid-1978, however, the struggle for control of Eritrea's cities and towns has tilted decidedly in favor of the Ethiopian forces. Forces of Ethiopian regular army and irregular militiamen, backed by massive Soviet and Cuban ground, sea, and air support, have virtually pushed the Eritrean guerrillas back into the countryside.

Eritrea's terrain is well suited for guerrilla warfare. For effective guerrilla operations, based on clandestine presumptions, rugged terrain is almost a prerequisite. Much of the land is deeply folded, as well, which mades guerrilla activity virtually impossible to halt by conventional military means. [1] (See Map 5.)

By 1961, believing that all avenues of peaceful resolution were finally closed, a number of Eritreans felt the use of armed force the only option left to them. The ensuing armed struggle in Eritrea can be understood by systematically exploring the various phases the revolution itself has undergone. There are four distinct periods that demand analysis. These periods are hinged upon particular sets of events in the development of the revolutionary process in Eritrea. The first is the initial period of armed struggle from 1961 to 1963. The second could be viewed as a general broadening of the military effort, from 1964 to 1970. The third phase deals with the split of the liberation forces in 1970 and the civil war in Eritrea itself, with rival liberation groups directing much of their energies against one another, rather than against the Ethiopians. The most recent phase has been the war against Ethiopia's Provisional Military Administrative Council (PMAC), better known as the "Dergue."

THE INITIAL PERIOD

In spite of the serious political constraints and schisms discussed in the previous chapter, the ELF launched its first armed unit on September 1, 1961, under the leadership of Hamid Idris Awate. The first ELF engagement of an Ethiopian police unit was at the Battle of Mount Adal, in western Eritrea. As one observer has noted, "Scrounging together ₤ 6500 [pounds sterling], the ELF purchased a consignment of superannuated Italian rifles and in late 1961 opened the conflict with a scattering of hit-and-run engagements."[2]

In 1962, the ELF's forces were divided into two separate (but not equal) categories: a small urban guerrilla section and the more numerous six-man moving squads. The urban unit remained relatively inactive during these early years. The rural ELF squads, made up of western Eritrean peasants and nomads, began a campaign of harassment against the Ethiopian government. This consisted of hit-and-run attacks on isolated police stations and other rural government installations. By focusing attacks on police stations, the ELF replenished its arms supply with captured Ethiopian hardware.

By the end of 1963, the now 250 Eritreans under arms had made their presence felt in the rural areas of western Eritrea. The Ethiopian government responded by organizing counterinsurgency forces. These commando forces, consisting primarily of Eritreans, failed to halt the activities of the ELF. At the same time, the Ethiopians launched a two-pronged propaganda campaign at the Eritrean population. On the one hand, they dismissed ELF movement in the west as shifta ("bandit") activities. The endemic banditry in this part of Eritrea was a well-known fact. The Ethiopian authorities also began to exploit regional and religious differences in an attempt to "divide and rule" the Eritrean population. They implemented a policy "of currying support primarily among Christian Eritreans with doses of development funds and imperial patronage."[3]

THE BROADENING WAR

During the initial period 1961-63, the ELF leadership living abroad was so preoccupied with petty jealousies that little could be agreed upon, politically or militarily. However, by late 1963 a Supreme Council emerged with Idris Mohammed Adum as president, Woldeab Woldemariam as director of the Cairo office, and Osman Saleh Sabbe as secretary-general and ambassador-at-large.

The ELF was supported during this early period mainly by the Sudan, where most of the early Eritrean political refugees had taken shelter. However,

> Sudanese aid was limited and inconsistent as it depended on internal political developments and was influenced by the fact that the Ethiopians could retaliate by supporting the Southern Sudan rebels. Nevertheless, the Sudan provided the ELF with essential facilities such as staging bases, supply depots for smuggled arms, and shelter from the Ethiopian army.[4]

By 1964 the ELF began to receive direct material assistance from the Syrian Ba'thist regime.[5] Syria championed the ELF, which, it claimed, was an Arab liberation movement fighting a reactionary pro-Israeli regime.[6] In spite of the fact that the ELF could not, by definition, be an "Arab liberation movement," the military and financial support received from Syria helped the front immensely. "ELF forces grew from a few hundred men armed with antiquated weapons to about 2,000 men with relatively modern weapons."[7] During this period the ELF employed Kalashnikov automatic rifles, Czech Stens, World War II British Enfields, some Soviet AK-47s, an assortment of captured U.S. M-1s, Chinese rockets and mortars, and Chinese-made explosives.

The ELF continued to grow and gradually gained control of most of rural western and northern Eritrea. It also claimed to have moved beyond purely military endeavors to the actual administration of liberated areas. As the ELF grew larger in men and arms, the discord between various factions grew worse. To minimize competition in the field, the ELF leadership abroad divided Eritrea into five military zones in 1964/65. They also divided the ELF into five divisions on the basis of religion and nationality, and each division was made to operate in one of the zones. These zonal divisions would last until 1970; the colonial concept of divide and rule was functioning well in Eritrea. The period of the military zones was a time when the zones were rivals, competing and contending against each other and squabbling over territorial boundaries. The leaders of the zones, far from helping each other, were rejoicing at the defeat of one another. Not only were they collecting money from the local population through taxes, fines, and donations but also were accumulating property for the future by looting cattle and other property from the people they ruled.[8]

Despite the internal divisions within the ELF, the Ethiopian authorities perceived the front as an increasingly threatening force. It has been noted that in response to ELF activity the Ethiopians relied heavily on two stratagems—not to overreact and to isolate the front:

The policy of isolation as manipulated from Addis Ababa revealed the Emperor at his most effective, formed as it was by a combination of diplomatic initiatives, proxy revolution, veiled threats, the exploitation of his own image, others' fears, and shifts in the international climate. Ethiopia repeatedly closed off the ELF, not only in the forums of the United Nations and the Organization of African Unity, but also along the wild borders of the Sudan and across the Red Sea. Simultaneously, whenever possible, Ethiopia simply denied the existence of the ELF insurgency and rarely indicated publicly that allied help, i.e., American or Israeli, would be welcome.[9]

Increasingly, what the Ethiopians could not accomplish with finesse they attempted to accomplish with military might. And their military capacity did, indeed, depend significantly upon the United States. From 1953 to 1970 the United States provided $147 million in military assistance to Haile Selassie's government. This amounted to almost one-half of the total U.S. military assistance to all African countries during that time span. In 1970 military assistance to Ethiopia was $12 million and equaled almost two-thirds of the total for all of Africa. Of the 6,733 African students trained under the military assistance program between 1963 and 1970, 2,813 were Ethiopians.[10] Between 1953 and 1975, a total of 3,552 Ethiopian students was trained in U.S. military institutions at a total cost of $21.8 million.[11] (For a more complete accounting of the specific hardware supplied to Ethiopia by the United States see Appendixes C and D.)

The United States was not the only source of material support for the Ethiopian armed forces during this period. The Israelis, who along with the Ethiopians perceived themselves to be "islands in a Muslim sea," contributed directly to Haile Selassie's counterinsurgency efforts. Israel has repeatedly stated that an independent Eritrea might made the Red Sea completely inaccessible to Israeli shipping, to say nothing of the oil that Eritrea received before 1979 from Iran, which passed through the straits of Bab el Mandeb. Consequently, Israeli advisers took responsibility not only for training Haile Selassie's Imperial Bodyguard in Addis Ababa but also for providing counterinsurgency training to Ethiopian commandos at their camp in Dacamare, south of Asmara. An Israeli also served as military attaché to the then governor-general of Eritrea, Asrate Kassa. The Israeli military contingent serving in Ethiopia and Eritrea regularly numbered between 20 and 200 men.

The year 1967 was a critical juncture in the Ethio-Eritrean conflict. A series of events occurred both within Eritrea and externally that would influence the future course of the revolution.

The Ethiopians had been carrying on discussions with the Sudanese government for some time regarding both the Eritrean guerrillas and the southern Sudanese rebels, the Anyanya. In early 1967, these discussions finally paid off: in return for reduced Sudanese support of the ELF, Ethiopia curtailed assistance that Israel was funneling through Ethiopia to the Anyanya. [12] This was only the first of three severe blows the ELF would suffer in rapid succession.

While the ELF was faced with reduced support from Khartoum, regular troops of the Ethiopian army were used for the first time against the front. These regular army troops had little difficulty in exploiting the weaknesses of the divided (five zones) ELF forces. The Ethiopians launched their unprecedented campaign by attacking one zone at a time:

> There was no zone that put up sufficient resistance in its respective region let alone cooperated with the others during the whole time Ethiopia was burning hundreds of villages, massacring, bayoneting and burning thousands of children, women and old people, butchering innumerable livestock, forcing thousands of people to take refuge in the Sudan, and displacing thousands more from their homes. [13]

Air and ground forces swept through suspected ELF areas, most of which were predominantly Muslim, routing both the ELF and civilians alike. It has been estimated that over 300 villages were burned. [14] It is believed that during 1967 more than 28,000 Eritreans were driven across the border to the Sudan. [15]

The third development to threaten the ELF in 1967 was the Six-Day War between Israel and its Arab neighbors. Tom Farer believes that by its overwhelming victory, "Israel trivialized Arab interest in events on the periphery of the Middle East." [16] In fact, the Arab states supporting the ELF, particularly Syria, were too much preoccupied with their own affairs following the Six-Day War. Funds and arms previously available to the ELF dwindled to a trickle, reinforcing the already drastically reduced activities of the front. By the end of 1967, the Ethiopian army had regained control over much of western Eritrea. This was, indeed, a low ebb for the ELF.

It was a full year before the Eritreans could reassert themselves in the field. The impetus for this resurgence was a dramatic increase in external aid during the years 1968/69. During 1968 various Arab countries stepped up their aid to the ELF. In their propaganda and public relations efforts, some ELF leaders found it prudent to identify openly with certain Middle Eastern movements, particularly the Palestinian struggle.

Syrian aid began to flow to the Eritrean guerrillas once again. ELF fighters were known to have received training in Syria side by side with Palestinian fedayeen.[17] Iraq initiated a small assistance program to the front: the program was limited and mostly aimed at undermining growing Syrian influence in the ELF. More conservative regimes, such as Saudi Arabia and Kuwait, sent a trickle of financial assistance. Southern Yemen (later the People's Democratic Republic of Yemen [PDRY]), reborn with the triumph of its own revolution, also became an ardent supporter of the ELF. With the PDRY commitment to world revolution and its hostility toward both Israel and Ethiopia, Aden considered the ELF worthy of support.[18]

In 1969 three new regimes in or adjacent to the Horn area also engaged in moral and material support of the Eritrean cause. The new Libyan regime, under Muammar al-Qaddafi, soon adopted the Eritrean movement. Arms were transported to the PDRY and from there moved across narrow straits of the Red Sea to points along the Eritrean coast.[19] A coup d'etat in the Sudan produced a government, led by General Numeiri, less willing to cooperate along the lines of the 1967 Ethio-Sudanese agreement of noninterference in the other country's armed struggles. Later in 1969, another coup d'etat by the military brought Siad Barre to power in Somalia. Both the Sudan and Somalia soon began a program of stepped-up aid to the ELF.

In early 1969, the still badly divided ELF instituted a three-pronged strategy in attempting to deal with the Ethiopian presence in Eritrea. In the countryside, the ELF tried to avoid direct confrontations with the Ethiopian army and resorted to hit-and-run guerrilla tactics. In the cities, terrorism and sabotage were the forms of harassment deemed most practical. And in the international arena, the ELF initiated a series of bombings and hijackings aimed at Ethiopian Airlines (EAL).

After a bitter defeat at Hal-Hal in northwest Eritrea in September 1968, in which the ELF lost 60 guerrillas, a strategy of avoiding direct confrontations with the Ethiopian military was practiced. Ambushes of Ethiopian forces on patrol became much more common. In August 1969, in two separate ambushes, the ELF killed 113 soldiers in the Massawa area. Buses moving along the Eritrean section of the Asmara-Addis Ababa road could only do so under armed escort. Bridges were blown up on the road between Asmara and Keren in October 1970. In the same month, the ELF began stopping trains on the Asmara-Keren-Agordat route and, after forcing the passengers to disembark, destroyed the trains and their cargo. In September 1969, an ELF unit detained the U.S. consul-general in Asmara, Murray Jackson, for seven hours. Jackson, who had been traveling outside of Asmara, was indoctrinated by the guerrillas and was forced to sign a statement acknowledging he had seen them. A similar incident took place in March 1970, when a guerrilla unit kidnapped and briefed a team from the National Geographic Society.

During this period, more attention was paid to urban guerrilla tactics than in previous years. In the early stages of urban warfare, the ELF had three objectives: the first was to obtain needed goods/supplies from the cities and towns; the second was the kidnapping of certain wealthy residents in return for which a substantial ransom was demanded; and the third was to assassinate those considered to be "enemies of the Eritrean revolution." In mid-1970 two high court judges who had sentenced ELF sympathizers to death were themselves machine-gunned to death while sitting in a bar on Asmara's Haile Selassie I Avenue.

In conjunction with the war being waged in Eritrea, the ELF felt the need to dramatically publicize its struggle against the Ethiopians in an international setting. As previously noted, the Haile Selassie government effectively prevented the Eritreans from being heard in such forums as the United Nations and the Organization of African Unity. Consequently, the ELF began a series of attacks on EAL planes in March 1969 that would persist intermittently into 1972. On March 11, 1969, the ELF bombed and badly damaged an EAL jet at Frankfurt (Germany) airport. On June 18 of the same year, the ELF struck again at the Karachi (Pakistan) airport, badly damaging a second EAL jet. On September 13, three ELF members hijacked an EAL plane to Aden, interrupting an Addis Ababa-Djibouti flight. On December 12, two ELF guerrillas attempted to hijack an EAL jet bound for Athens from Madrid, but were shot to death by Ethiopian security men aboard the plane. In 1972 the anti-EAL campaign culminated in a bloody shoot-out several thousand feet over Addis Ababa. All seven ELF guerrillas aboard the plane were shot to death by government agents within moments after the hijacking was announced.

THE EARLY 1970s: CIVIL WAR IN ERITREA

The best way to understand the Eritrean revolution in the early 1970s is in the context of the tremendous internal upheaval that took place within the liberation movement itself. With the Eritrean preoccupation concerning the 1970 split and its surrounding politicomilitary ramifications, it comes as no surprise that the Ethiopian army took the offensive once again. This is not to suggest, however, that the Eritrean movements were idle militarily during the years 1970-71. By the beginning of 1970, ELF forces reportedly numbered 10,000 men, of which 2,000 to 3,000 were regulars and the rest militia.[20] It has also been estimated that there were about 250 Eritreans training in Syrian and Lebanese camps, about 150 in Algeria, and another

400 in the Sudan.[21] Soviet weapons supplied to the Sudan, Somalia, the PDRY, and Syria continued to reach the Eritrean guerrillas.

Sporadic urban guerrilla warfare continued. But the emphasis, or what little there was, centered on attempts to make inroads into different areas of the Eritrean countryside. It has been noted that the ELF's greatest success during this period was the opening of a third front, in addition to the western and northern ones, by conducting joint ventures with a group of Danakil.[22] Some of these Danakil, or Afar, emerged a few years later as the nucleus of what came to be known as the Afar Liberation Front. The Afar helped the ELF smuggle arms and personnel into Eritrea from the PDRY, across the Red Sea. Operating near the Bay of Zula, the ELF used this area of Dankalia as a staging ground for operations against Ethiopian installations along the coast and the important Assab-Addis Ababa road.

In the last half of 1970, the ELF intensified their ambushes in the highlands. A district governor was killed in Serai in August. Then, on November 21, the commander of the Ethiopian Second Division, Teshome Erghetu, was ambushed and killed outside Asmara on the Keren road. This particular incident precipitated a series of important changes in Ethiopian strategy for "pacifying" Eritrea. Ras Asrate Kassa was replaced as governor-general of Eritrea by Lt.-Gen. Debbebe Hailemariam. At the same time, feeling that sterner measures were overdue, a state of emergency was declared in much of Eritrea on December 16, 1970. Much of the lowland countryside was placed under martial law. Asmara, Massawa, Assab, and the two highland provinces of Hamasien and Akkele Guzai were not affected. The state of emergency empowered the Ministry of National Defense to "evacuate the inhabitants and keep their movements under surveillance in the prohibited areas." It was also empowered to set up military courts to try criminals, criminals being those as so defined by the military administrator, Lt.-Gen. Kebede Gabre.

The Ethiopian Second Division, with substantial help from the air force, opened a massive military operation against ELF-held areas during December 1970. The Second Division consisted of about 8,000 soldiers armed with American M-1 rifles; 3,000 anti-ELF commandos were unleashed as well. Part of an armored division was brought to Eritrea for the offensive. The Ethiopian Air Force was, in 1970, considered to be the best and strongest in sub-Saharan Africa (excluding South Africa). It consisted of a squadron of six Canberra B-2 bombers (purchased from Britain), a squadron of eight SAAB-17 ground support planes (purchased from Sweden), a squadron of eight supersonic F-5A fighter-interceptors (U.S. aid), a reconnaissance squadron of six T-28 and three T-33 trainers, a transport squadron of DC-3s, and several small helicopters.[23] Several of these squadrons were deployed in Eritrea for the Ethiopian offensive.

The Ethiopian Air Force began systematically bombing villages along the coast and in northern and western Eritrea. The army moved into ELF-held areas, burned villages, and executed or detained these suspected of collaborating with the ELF. Waves of new refugees poured into the Sudan.

From the beginning of 1971, Ethiopian army engineers began opening new roads into the fertile lowlands of western Eritrea, the lowlands along the Sudanese border, and the coast area, which had previously been inaccessible to motor vehicles. Once the roads were finished, the army moved in and gained a large degree of control in those areas.

After some semblance of order had been established over much of rural Eritrea, the Ethiopians "exploited the heterogeneous character of the population and resorted to tactics similar to those used by the Americans in Vietnam."[24] As with the "strategic hamlet" program in Vietnam, the Ethiopians moved the inhabitants of numerous villages to larger, fortified villages and organized many of the people into anti-ELF militia units. In a number of areas, particularly the Gash and Baria-Kunama regions, the Ethiopians successfully utilized a divide-and-rule strategy to encourage volunteers for anti-guerrilla auxiliary units.

Furthermore, a portion of the coastal strip of Eritrea, with its large Afar population, was summarily detached from Eritrea and divided among adjacent provinces of the Ethiopian plateau.[25] Most notably, the Eritrean port of Assab was annexed to Wollo Province. Thereafter, the governors of the various Ethiopian provinces were responsible for administering, developing, and policing the part of the coast attached to their respective areas.

The immediate effect of the Ethiopian offensive was a sharp reduction in Eritrean guerrilla operations. However, in the process of "pacifying" the countryside, the army was increasingly alienating the rural population. The Ethiopian soldiers often dealt with the Eritrean villagers harshly. The average Ethiopian, who had no medium to communicate with the rural Eritrean, was contemptuous of the people he was pacifying and regarded the Muslims, especially, with suspicion and hatred.

The Ethiopian campaign was by no means limited to the battlefield. Haile Selassie was once again on the attack in the diplomatic arena. He conducted diplomatic offensives on three fronts. The first dealt with Sudanese President Numeiri's decision to grant a degree of autonomy to the Anyanya in the south. When the Ethiopian emperor volunteered to mediate between Numeiri and the Anyanya, Numeiri responded by withdrawing semiofficial support from the Eritrean liberation movement.

The second coup for Haile Selassie was the establishment of full diplomatic ties with the Peoples Republic of China. Whatever trickle of assistance the Eritreans had been receiving from the Chinese was terminated shortly thereafter.[26]

The third initiative was aimed at the government of the PDRY. The Aden government

> was reminded that the large Yemeni population in Ethiopia and its valuable remittances to relatives in the PDRY existed at the Emperor's sufferance. While this warning did not eliminate Aden as a transshipment point for Libyan and other arms, it allegedly produced a lower level of open cooperation in the arms traffic.[27]

THE ERITREAN CIVIL WAR: MILITARY ASPECTS

With the schism in the liberation movement created by the 1970 split, and the short-term effectiveness of the 1970/71 Ethiopian offensive, civil war became more and more imminent. The ELF and more recently formed Eritrean Peoples Liberation Forces, later Front (EPLF) differed on various points, virtually all of which could be divided into two categories: clashes of personality and ideology. Most, though not all, of the military activity in Eritrea between February 1972 and October 1974 took place between the warring Eritrean movements, with much less time and energy being directed toward the Ethiopian presence in Eritrea.

Unfortunately, accurate details about military aspects of the civil war are scarce. Much of the hostilities were conducted on the political level rather than on the battlefield. For a civil war, casualties were relatively low; by the best estimates, no more than 400 guerrillas from both organizations were killed during the sporadic battles during this two-and-one-half-year period.[28]

What does seem clear is that declaring the EPLF "counter-revolutionary," the ELF passed a series of resolutions on February 29, 1972, aimed at liquidating its rivals.[29] The militarily weaker EPLF was forced to maintain a defensive position for the duration of the civil war. In 1972, the EPLF set up its first permanent base in Eritrea's northern Sahel Province. Throughout the period of civil strife, the EPLF worked on consolidating military and political training for its members. During the course of the civil war, the EPLF generally inherited some of the ELF's strength, as the ELF tended to grow weaker and lose some of its military superiority.

Although the number of dead resulting from the civil war was not particularly high, the war did serve as a terribly divisive experience for the nationalist movement. In addition to the loss of human

life, the destruction to property was enormous, and the fighting between Eritrean groups provided the Ethiopians a chance to further
consolidate any military and political gains they had been able to effect. Moreover, the civil war served to create low morale among
the Eritrean populace. Especially in the countryside, the people were
being pacified by the Ethiopians, on the one hand, and were being
asked to choose sides by the warring Eritrean factions, on the other.

Adversity within the Eritrean liberation movement was often
overcome in spite of the various leaders. So it was with the cessation
of hostilities between the ELF and EPLF in October 1974. The events
that occurred in Ethiopia throughout 1974 seemed to point toward a
more favorable atmosphere for ending the civil war. For 1974 was
the year that Haile Selassie, King of Kings, Lion of Judah, Elect of
God, and 225th direct descendant of Solomon and Sheba was deposed
as emperor of Ethiopia after ruling for more than 50 years.

Some of the more democratic, progressive elements in both
the ELF and EPLF had been lobbying for an end to the civil war,
which they viewed as a result of "secondary contradictions," and to
proceed with the main task of the revolution: ridding Eritrea of Ethiopian occupation. A good portion of the Eritrean population shared in
these sentiments.

In early October 1974, two mass meetings were held 15 miles
outside of Asmara, which led to the end of warfare between the ELF
and the EPLF. It is estimated that between 20,000 and 30,000 people
attended the meetings to reunite the guerrilla factions.[30] The Eritrean people, who "came by car, bus, bicycle, and even airplane
from Addis Ababa," demanded an end to the civil strife that was so
clearly counterproductive to anything the liberation movement represented. These rallies culminated in only the most tentative reconciliation of the rival fronts. Needless to say, these mass meetings
could only, and did, take place in the midst of an extremely fragile
(and short-lived) cease-fire between the Ethiopian army and the
fronts. For their part, the Ethiopians would come to very much re-
gret the end of the civil war in Eritrea.

Throughout the civil war, the Eritrean guerrillas had continued
to militarily harass the Ethiopian army and other governmental installations. Hit-and-run attacks and ambushes remained the major
Eritrean strategy for the countryside. Urban guerrilla units began
operating in a more organized and systematic manner. More sophisticated techniques were used to win support from the urban population, especially in Asmara. The EPLF reorganized its urban units
into three categories. The first was economic: these were the tax
collectors and donation seekers. The second was more novel: these
were the cells of mass organizers that conducted political education
programs among the populace. The third group of urban cadres car-

ried out assassinations of selected Ethiopians as well as Eritreans who actively opposed the liberation movement. In addition, these units were also responsible for urban sabotage and an occasional bank robbery, which netted the EPLF much needed currency to conduct other facets of its program.

By the summer of 1974, with the end of Eritrean civil strife in sight, incidents of guerrilla activity had so multiplied as to encourage "a perceptible migration of Italian capital and drive a Japanese firm to suspect copper-mining activities."[31] The British journalist Colin Legum, having just returned to London from the Horn, wrote that

> there can no longer be any serious hope of defeating the
> rebels by military force. The only practical question now
> is what kind of political settlement is possible.[32]

THE WAR AGAINST THE DERGUE

The Provisional Military Administrative Council, or Dergue, that deposed Haile Selassie in 1974 would have done well to take Legum's advice more seriously. Upon coming to power, the Dergue found itself with a large arsenal of largely U.S.-supplied weapons (see Appendix E). By 1976 the United States had provided Ethiopia $278.6 million in military assistance, not to mention the $350 million in economic aid. The strength of the army stood at 41,000 men; the navy, 1,500 men; and the air force, 2,300 men. The question facing the 120-man Dergue vis-à-vis Eritrea was whether to seriously attempt to negotiate with the Eritrean liberation movements or to attempt to crush the revolution militarily. It came as little surprise that they opted for the latter course:

> The Dergue refused to recognize the anti-colonial essence
> of the Eritrean war of national liberation. It pretended,
> instead, to conceive [of] the Eritrean struggle as that of
> a people having legitimate grievances against the corruption
> and maladministration of a handful of officials of the for-
> mer regime.[33]

The Dergue had failed to recognize and/or understand the same central tenet that continually escaped the former emperor: that the Eritrean struggle was not one of "secession," or "separatism," or even "rebellion," but had increasingly become a very popular movement for national liberation.[34] By the time the Dergue had eliminated the imperial leaders of the ancien régime in late 1974, Eritrean independence was considered a nonnegotiable demand by a vast majority of Eritreans.

The first, titular, chairman of the Dergue, Gen. Aman Andom, was believed by some observers to be capable of negotiating with the liberation fronts as he was, himself, an Eritrean. However, the two fronts saw no substantive difference between General Aman and the rest of the Dergue. It is believed that in the face of an escalating war in Eritrea, Aman might have become increasingly angry and, actually, could have been a worse enemy to the Eritrean movement than even the present Dergue leadership has been. General Aman, due to upheaval within the Dergue itself, never had a chance to establish a clear direction vis-à-vis the Eritrean struggle.*

The Dergue initially utilized a two-pronged strategy in attempting to neutralize the Eritrean forces. The first tactic was political and allegedly aimed at achieving a peaceful solution in ending the hostilities. Accordingly, the Dergue called upon the Eritrean fighters to lay down their arms in favor of a peaceful solution. It set up a 38-man committee of prominent Eritreans in an effort to create a body with whom to negotiate the peaceful solution. At the same time, the Dergue dispatched a peace delegation on a tour of African and Arab states to try to isolate the Eritrean movement from friends and supporters.

While continuing to press for a negotiated settlement, the Dergue mounted a series of brutal campaigns against not only the guerrillas but the civilian population as well. In the town of Om Hager, 250 unarmed civilians were executed in July 1974. More than 50 youths in Asmara were mysteriously strangled with piano wire in December of that same year. Numerous Eritreans were detained and jailed, in most cases without formal charges filed against them. Ultimately, the Dergue cemented Eritrean opinion firmly and actively against it by the systematic brutality and repression leveled at the civilian population.

With the Eritrean civil war at an end, the EPLF and ELF began to direct their respective energies against the Ethiopian occupation of Eritrea. The EPLF, especially, invoked the strategy of a "people's war." In Eritrea, they believed, this would of necessity be a protracted war:

The overall strategy was to build strong base areas, use these to liberate the countryside step by step, proceed to

_____

*On November 23, 1974, Aman died at his home in a gunfight with soldiers who had been sent to arrest him. That same night, 59 imprisoned members of the ancien régime, including two former prime ministers, were executed by the Dergue without benefit of any sort of hearing or trial.

liberate the large villages and towns and finally encircle and liberate the main cities. [35]

In putting this plan into practice, the EPLF was forced to invoke the aforementioned concept of self-reliance. In matters military, self-reliance is expressed by the slogan: "Destroy the enemy with his own guns and bullets."[36]

During the final months of 1974, the EPLF began to implement its plan to extend its forces "to broader strategic areas in order to mobilize and organize the masses against the Ethiopian forces.[37] However, before implementing its systematic plans to drive the Ethiopians from Eritrea, the EPLF, in conjunction with the ELF, decided to mount an operation against the Ethiopian Army in and around Asmara, as a show of their combined strength. The Battle of Asmara, which began on the evening of January 31, 1975, was more than just a symbolic attack on the Eritrean capital—it was the only major offensive in which the EPLF and ELF cooperated as of mid-1979.

The Eritrean offensive clearly took the Ethiopian forces by surprise. The Dergue had just finished reinforcing garrisons throughout Eritrea in anticipation of a major offensive of its own, when, on the night of the thirty-first, several hundred guerrillas infiltrated into Asmara and launched attacks on Ethiopian military posts as well as the major barracks within the city. Asmara underwent heavy fighting for the next ten days, and scattered skirmishes continued for another month. Most of the major battles, however, took place on the main roads leading in and out of Asmara: from Massawa, Keren, and Decamare. Guerrillas proved able to delay convoys of heavily armed troops for several days on all of these roads, while convoys more lightly armed were either wiped out or forced to turn back.[38] The combined Eritrean forces were estimated to have between 15,000 and 25,000 men under arms throughout Eritrea at this point in time.

As a result of the Battle of Asmara, the morale of the Eritrean guerrillas as well as the larger civilian population received an enormous boost. The propaganda effects of the Eritreans' successes were emphasized not only among various Arab supporters but in the world press as well. And, finally, the Ethiopians had been dealt a severe blow: if the series of military losses were not enough, the Eritreans also captured numerous Ethiopian weapons—including rifles, ammunition, hand grenades, and the like. The Battle of Asmara had the effect of announcing to the Dergue that the revitalized liberation movement was a formidable force to be dealt with in the future.

Throughout 1975 the violence in Eritrea continued to escalate. The Ethiopian military instituted a policy of massive retaliation against Eritrea's civilian population. The razing and burning of villages that were suspected of having given aid or shelter to the guerrillas became commonplace. The air force bombed villages and food crops in indiscriminate reprisals. A number of My Lai-type situations occurred throughout Eritrea.[39]

The EPLF, "guided by the strategy of 'liberating the countryside piece by piece,' which is based on the theory of people's war,"[40] continued to extend its control into broader areas of rural Eritrea. Constant battles were waged against Ethiopian military encampments in the countryside. By their own estimate, in 1975 the EPLF engaged the Ethiopians in no less than 110 battles, 15 of these in conjunction with the ELF.[41]

By the spring of 1976, the Dergue had devised a new, two-pronged plan to deal with the Eritrean movement. On the one hand, the Dergue, now nominally headed by Gen. Tefari Banti, proposed a nine-point peace plan appealing to the "broad masses and progressive forces of Eritrea to give their fullest support and cooperation to the effort the Government is making to solve the region's problem."[42] The nine-point plan proposed "immediate autonomy to the people of the Eritrean Administrative Region" (see Appendix F). Both the EPLF and the ELF rejected the plan, which they claimed was nothing more than a disguise for the Dergue's real plans.

The other part of the Dergue's program to deal with Eritrea was much more in keeping with its previous actions. Never having put much credence in the nine-point plan, the Dergue had been preparing for a major offensive against the Eritrean liberation forces. The Dergue had begun mobilizing thousands of Ethiopian peasants for its ill-fated peasants' march on Eritrea earlier in the year. In organizing this ragtag band, the Dergue had appealed to the peasants on two bases.[43] First, the government appealed for "a kind of Christian holy war against the Eritreans," who they made out to be foreign-backed Arab puppets. The second inducement was that many of the peasants had been promised land grants in Eritrea itself.

The peasant march became a disaster for the Dergue. The government had attempted to raise a 160,000-man peasant force, but by June 1976 only 25,000 or so were amassed at the Ethio-Eritrean border.[44] The peasants were an ill-trained and -armed militia; many of them were provided with surplus World War II equipment, and others with no arms at all. Apparently, the Dergue had planned to deploy "human wave" formations of peasants against the well-disciplined, if not smaller, Eritrean forces. None of the peasants ever crossed into Eritrea: "two sizable groups suffered bloody defeats and heavy casualties before the Dergue recalled them."[45] Eritrean guerrillas, mostly from the ELF, crossed into Ethiopia's Tigre Province and dealt the hapless peasants a demoralizing defeat.

The peasant march into Eritrea was postponed in mid-June, reportedly as a result of logistical problems and the successful Eritrean initiative against the peasant force. News reports also credited diplomatic pressure by both the Sudanese and U.S. governments with helping to abort the campaign.[46] Wherever the emphasis is placed, the withdrawal of the peasant militia gave the Eritrean forces another morale boost: one that helped propel them to any number of military victories over the next year and a half.

The defeat of the peasant militia is only peripherally related to a topic little mentioned thus far; that is, the relationship between the Eritrean liberation movements and the various groups within Ethiopia that have taken up arms against the Dergue. Generally speaking, joint military ventures in the area have been rare. The ELF gave tactical support to the ancien régime-oriented Ethiopian Democratic Union (EDU) in the EDU's February 1977 attack and consequent occupation of Humera. Humera has strategic importance for the Eritreans as it is located in Begemder on the Ethio-Eritrean border just across from Om Hager. Neither Eritrean organization has fostered a particularly cooperative relationship with the rightist EDU, which, since being chased from Humera, has declined steadily both politically and militarily.

The Western Somali Liberation Front (WSLF), which began the war for control of the Ogaden region of Ethiopia with the help of Somalia itself, has also experienced very little interaction with the Eritreans. Aside from possible mutual assistance in arms movements, there would appear to be no evidence of a militarily cooperative relationship between the WSLF and the Eritreans.

The Ethiopian group having the greatest contact with the Eritrean forces is the Tigre People's Liberation Front (TPLF). Tigre Province, Ethiopia, lies immediately south of Eritrea and they share a long, common border. The people of Tigre, like those of highland Eritrea, are predominantly Christian, speak Tigrinya, and feel they have suffered systematic Amhara domination over many centuries. The TPLF initiated guerrilla training and resorted to armed struggle against the Dergue in 1975. On occasion, the Eritreans have found it expedient to conduct joint military efforts with them. The TPLF cooperated with the ELF against the peasant militia, which was stationed in Tigre waiting to invade Eritrea, in mid-1976. There were said to be other joint efforts, as well, although these cannot be accurately verified.[47]

A number of significant military accomplishments by Eritrean forces were registered throughout 1977. At the same time, crucial political events were taking place throughout the entire Horn area. The First Congress of the EPLF was held in January. Eritrean forces amassed victory after victory in the military arena, liberating most of Eritrea's towns. The United States cut off military aid to Ethiopia, after 25 years of close cooperation. In May Somalia launched a tremendous offensive in its "irredentist" attempts to regain the Ogaden desert region. Finally, foreign involvement in Ethiopia, and consequently Eritrea, underwent a drastic change with the introduction of large-scale Soviet and Cuban presence in the area. New, or redefined, roles by the governments of the Sudan, PDRY, and Libya also contributed to the changing picture in Eritrea.

The overt actions of Sudan's President Numeiri aided the Eritrean cause considerably throughout 1977. Ethiopian-Sudanese relations have been an on-again, off-again proposition for years. Throughout 1976 Numeiri persisted in his efforts to start negotiations for a "peaceful solution" between the Ethiopian government and the Eritreans. More than likely, for Numeiri, this meant some form of Eritrean autonomy within a greater Ethiopia, similar to the solution that is operational in the southern Sudan. However, by January 1977, relations between Ethiopia and the Sudan had greatly deteriorated, leading to the mutual recalling of ambassadors. On January 30 Numeiri announced that the Sudan now supported the Eritrean people in their fight for independence.[48] This relative freedom of movement for Eritreans operating from the Sudan became a significant factor in both military and political terms.

At the same time, the end of January, the EPLF held its First Congress, out of which came its National Democratic Programme. The military implications of this program were clearly spelled out a month later in Vanguard, the official monthly organ of the EPLF. The liberation of Eritrea and its people would be done step by step through a strategy of people's war. This war would be carried out in three phases:

1. Positional warfare to defend the liberated areas from enemy encroachments and destroy its bases to expand the liberated areas step by step;
2. Mobile warfare in the semiliberated areas to liquidate enemy agents, destroy its bases, block its mobility, inflict great loss on its forces, and liberate the semiliberated areas; and
3. Guerrilla warfare in the enemy-controlled areas to wipe out its ammunition, fuel and supply storages, demolish its military and economic installations, and create favorable conditions for the general strategic war.[49]

The EPLF began to put this program into action. After a siege that began in September 1976, the Eritrean Peoples Liberation Army finally took control of Nacfa, the capital of Sahel Province, on March 22, 1977. This was the first major town to come under Eritrean control; for it to be the capital of a large province made the victory doubly important. The liberation of Nacfa was the first in a series of successful EPLF attempts to take control of Eritrea's provincial centers.

Less than two weeks later, on April 2, the EPLF liberated Afabet, the last remaining town under Ethiopian occupation in Sahel Province. One week later, on April 9, the Ethiopian garrison at Elabered was forced to retreat to Keren, both of which are in Senhit Province. By abandoning Elabered, 18 miles southeast of Keren, the Ethiopians had left Eritrea's largest plantations in the EPLF's hands. These Italian-owned and -operated plantations were producers of dairy products, fruits, and vegetables, much of which was exported to the Middle East and Europe. Thus, by gaining control of the Elabered plantations, the EPLF not only deprived the Ethiopians of valuable export revenues but greatly aided the EPLF's drive for self-sufficiency in food production.

At about this time, on May 5, the Eritrean Liberation Army (ELA), the military wing of the ELF, defeated the Ethiopian garrison in the town of Tessenei, 25 kilometers from the Sudanese border. It took the ELA little more than a month of fighting to rid Tessenei of Ethiopian forces. A spokesman for the ELF said that the loss of Tessenei would cost Ethiopia about $16 million worth of crops produced in that area each year.[50] During the first week in June, the ELA launched a surprise invasion into the historic Ethiopian town of Adowa, some 60 kilometers south of the Eritrean border. They overran the Ethiopian garrison there and seized a fair number of weapons before retreating back into Eritrea.[51]

At this point in time, a series of international realignments took place with potentially serious implications for the continuing Eritrean revolution. In particular, the huge buildup of Soviet weapons combined with the thousands of Cuban troops presented a vastly improved arsenal confronting the Eritreans. With President Carter's new foreign policy directives tying military assistance and arms sales to human rights programs in selected countries, the Ethiopian government began to anticipate the cutoff of U.S. military aid. On April 23, the Dergue closed down four U.S. organizations: Kagnew Station in Asmara, the U.S. Military Assistance Advisory Group, the U.S. Naval Medical Research Group, and the U.S. Information Service. Although the U.S. State Department protested this action as "unwarranted,"[52] the military tilt in Ethiopia had already been determined. The United States had turned down an Ethiopian request for $65 million worth of ammunition within the preceding two months.[53]

Shortly thereafter, in May, the U.S. Congress confirmed a set of prohibitions against military assistance and sales credits to Ethiopia. It recommended these prohibitions for Ethiopia because its government:

1) by all available sources of information is consistently engaging in gross violations of human rights, including summary executions; 2) it has recently concluded a $100 mil-

lion plus arms transaction with the Soviet Union; and 3) recently closed down the U.S. military mission as well as other U.S. facilities.[54]

In fact, the USSR had agreed the previous December (1976) to supply Ethiopia, and a long-term military aid deal worth more than $100 million was completed.[55] By July 1977, it was reported that, in a secret pact signed in May, the Soviets had agreed to supply Ethiopia with $500 million worth of arms, including MiG-21 jets and surface-to-air SA-7 missiles.[56]

A great deal of the men and matériel that found its way to Ethiopia from the Soviets and Cubans was more directly related, in its initial stages, to the war that began in the Ogaden desert region of Ethiopia in mid-1977 (see the concluding chapter for further discussion of the Ogaden war). Weapons and personnel came to Ethiopia from five sources: the Soviet Union and Warsaw Pact countries, Cuba, Libya, the PDRY, and Israel.

The main Soviet contribution to the Ethiopians' new arsenal is sophisticated military hardware in tremendous amounts. It has reportedly reached the $1 billion level; Time reports that by the end of January 1978, $850 million worth of Soviet arms had been airlifted to Ethiopia.[57] The array of weapons is astounding: BM 21 Katyusha rocket launchers; BTR 60 and 152 armored personnel carriers; T54, T55, and T62 tanks; 122-, 155-, and 185-mm. long-range artillery; MiG-21 fighters; and even MiG-23 ground attack fighters.[58] Soviet advisers in Ethiopia have been estimated at about 1,000, and the German Democratic Republic has a number of troops there.[59] There has also been a steady buildup of Cuban fighting men in Ethiopia. Before the massive January 1978 airlift, their number was believed to approximate 1,000; by November 1978, the U.S. government estimated that 18,000 Cubans were in Ethiopia.[60] By mid-April of the same year, 3,000 Cubans had reportedly flown to Eritrea to reinforce the Ethiopian garrison there.[61]

Libya has heavily subsidized the Ethiopian government as well. It is estimated that Colonel Qaddafi had committed $100 million in military aid to Ethiopians by mid-1977.[62] Much of this weaponry went for equipping the reorganized people's militia, formerly conceived of as the peasant militia. In addition, Libya promised to provide substantial development assistance to the Dergue.[63]

The People's Democratic Republic of Yemen (PDRY), has played an increasing combat role in the Dergue's fight against the Eritreans. The South Yemenis "are piloting Soviet supplied MiG fighters, operating tanks and artillery and flying reconnaissance helicopters" in Eritrea.[64] The South Yemenis were believed to be the only people flying the MiGs on combat missions in Eritrea; a South Yemeni pilot had reportedly been captured by the ELF after his MiG-21 was shot down near Agordat in mid-February. [65] It is also believed that 100 to 120 South Yemeni troops are in Asmara operating Soviet tanks and heavy artillery. [66]

Finally, Israel, though it has maintained no formal diplomatic relations with Ethiopia since the 1973 Yom Kippur War, lent military assistance to Ethiopia until February 1978. Israeli pilots not only maintained but also flew combat missions in U.S.-made F-5 jet fighters. They also served as suppliers of ammunition and spare parts for the U.S.-manufactured arms that were still in use by Ethiopia's regular army. [67] Some Eritreans believed that Israel also supplied Ethiopia with napalm, cluster bombs, and aircraft-fired missiles, but no real confirmation for this exists. Israel's Ethiopian role apparently came to a rather abrupt end when Foreign Minister Moshe Dayan made public disclosures about Israel's military cooperation with Ethiopia, in February 1978. [68]

While the Ethiopians were reaping this tremendous amount of foreign assistance, the Eritrean movement was getting very little outside help. The EPLF, in particular, received virtually no foreign support and depended heavily on a program of self-reliance, using captured Ethiopian weapons and other supplies. The ELF has been receiving a limited degree of financial help from Iraq, with aid from Syria much reduced. Both fronts have benefited immensely from the virtually unlimited use of the Sudan as an adjacent (foreign) center of activity. Most of the foreign assistance funneled to the Eritrean struggle goes to Osman Saleh Sabbe's ELF-PLF (Popular Liberation Forces). Sabbe's Pan-Islamic appeal to the more conservative Arab states has kept his 5,000-man force well funded.

In spite of the Ethiopian buildup during the latter half of 1977, the Eritreans continued to score significant victories and to bring an increasing amount of territory under their control. A large majority of the foreign military personnel in Ethiopia were, from the time of their arrival until March 1978, involved more directly in the Ogaden war than in the Dergue's battle against the Eritreans.

One of Cuba's roles in Ethiopia was the responsibility for training the people's militia, or peasant army. By June 1977, the militia, which had been organized into five divisions, was paraded through Addis Ababa at a strength of 70,000 men. [69] This initial peasant force "wearing North Korean uniforms and carrying Russian AK-47 automatic rifles," were to be "only the vanguard of an intended force of 300,000 men." [70] Fifty thousand peasant militiamen had been sent to Eritrea by mid-year and were apparently involved in breaking the ELF siege of Barentu. [71]

Early in July the EPLF scored its greatest military gains by capturing Keren and Decamare in rapid succession. Decamare, the largest city in Akkele Guzai Province, was taken on July 7, after a five-hour heavy assault on the 2,500 Ethiopian troops there. A day later, on July 8, the EPLF took Keren, Eritrea's second largest city and the capital of Senhit Province. It took the EPLF five days of heavy fighting, including hand-to-hand combat, to defeat the 4,000-man Ethiopian force stationed at Keren. A week later, on July 15, the EPLF staged a spectacular operation in freeing more than 800 Eritrean political prisoners from the Sembel maximum security prison in Asmara. The towns of Sageneiti and Digsa were taken in early August, and Agordat, the capital of Barka Province, was liberated on August 30. On October 13, the EPLF destroyed a large Ethiopian convoy trying to reach Asmara from Massawa. By capturing the town of Dogali at the same time, the EPLF had cut a strategic supply route to Asmara.

On December 13 the EPLF launched an offensive against the port of Massawa, Eritrea's third largest city. The Eritrean offensive almost succeeded. Only by rushing reinforcements to the city by sea did Ethiopia manage to stave off the fall of Massawa, a victory that would have certainly led to the capture of Asmara itself.[72] Many of the city's 50,000 residents fled the city while the EPLF gained control of three-quarters of Massawa, and the Ethiopians continued to hold the port area itself. Casualties were reportedly heavy on both sides. The virtual standoff, which lasted for almost a year, was initially due to the heavy air and sea support the Ethiopians received. MiG-21 fighters constantly strafed EPLF positions; offshore, ships fired in close support. It has been speculated that some of the ships may well have been from the Soviet Navy, but there was no hard evidence to confirm this.

The failure of the EPLF to occupy Massawa successfully proved costly for the Eritrean movement as a whole. By the time of the EPLF assault on Massawa, in December 1977, Eritrean forces had spread themselves very thin in occupying virtually all major Eritrean towns. The advances of the movement throughout 1977 were so rapid as to hardly allow for military consolidation of fortified positions, particularly with the threat of increased Soviet and Cuban military participation.

The EPLF attack on Massawa was a tactical error of immense magnitude. The Eritreans may have believed that the successful occupation of that port city would significantly decrease the possibility of a large-scale, Soviet-backed Ethiopian counteroffensive in the near future. Yet, their failure to capture Massawa lent momentum to the anticipated Ethiopian assault.

Once the Ethiopians and their Soviet and Cuban backers defeated the Somalian forces in the Ogaden in March 1978, they immediately turned their attention toward Eritrea. By May the Dergue had announced a major offensive against the Eritrean guerrillas.

The Soviet Union had almost completed a key part of its air and naval base in the Dahlak Islands by June 1978.[73] Other Soviet personnel were busy building an airbase at Makele, Tigre, south of the Eritrean border:

> Some 50 Soviet MiG-21 and MiG-23 fighters were trans-
> ferred there, together with Russian and Cuban pilots, most
> of the Soviet helicopter fleet in Ethiopia and 50 T-55 and
> T-62 tanks with South Yemen crews.[74]

With this sort of firepower and foreign personnel assisting the Ethiopian forces it is easy to understand how even the well-disciplined Eritrean guerrilla forces could be forced to retreat from the towns they had been occupying.

By November most of the major towns were again under Ethiopian control. The EPLF siege of Massawa was finally broken late in the month. Keren fell to the Ethiopians on November 27. In many cases, such as Keren and Decamare, much of the civilian population left the towns along with the Eritrean forces.

The 1978 Ethiopian assault was, for the most part, engineered by the Soviets and carried out by Ethiopian, Cuban, and South Yemeni forces:

> Soviet and East German engineers are believed to have
> built flanking roads for the Ethiopian tanks to come up be-
> hind Eritrean lines. The Eritreans were caught in a pincer
> thrust by tank forces crewed by Ethiopians and Cubans, sup-
> ported by artillery and rocket units operated by East Ger-
> mans and South Yemenis.[75]

CONCLUSION

By the summer of 1979, the Ethiopian forces were attempting to push the EPLF out of the Nacfa area, the last stronghold of the guerrilla group. (The ELF had previously been expelled from all of the towns it had controlled.) As many as 50,000 Ethiopian regulars and militia were involved in the offensive.[76] The best the Eritreans can hope for here is a military stalemate, which could easily be construed as a defeat for the significantly stronger Ethiopian forces.

The most likely prospect for the future is that both the ELF and the EPLF, together or separately, will regroup in smaller armed units to revert back to more conventional, hit-and-run guerrilla warfare. This will necessarily be protracted warfare, not only because of the Ethiopian reoccupation of the towns but also because of the continued infighting between the movements themselves.

For how long and to what degree the Dergue will continue to receive Soviet and Cuban support in Eritrea remains to be seen. If the Eritreans can eventually unify against the Ethiopian forces, the time factor may well work in their favor. Yet, the movement has never been tested as it was in 1978/79 and may well be into the early 1980s.

Basil Davidson, in his classic work on the Guinean revolution, believes that

> liberated zones are a proof of a nationalist fighting movement's efficacy, a demonstration of what is to come after victory, but also a vital means of achieving that victory.[77]

As the liberated zones of Eritrea have, at times, illustrated the movement's military capability, they also offer a look at putting the Eritreans' ideology into practice. The Eritrean struggle has produced some remarkable forms of social organization in the areas under guerrilla control, as a closer examination of this emerging social order will indicate.

NOTES

1. Africa Confidential 16 (October 24, 1975): 8.
2. Tom J. Farer, War Clouds on the Horn of Africa (Washington, D.C.: Carnegie Endowment for International Peace, 1976), p. 29.
3. Ibid., p. 30.
4. Ibid.
5. Africa Research Bulletin, January 15, 1971, p. 1957.
6. Mordechai Abir, Oil, Power and Politics (London: Frank Cass, 1974).
7. Ibid., p. 170.
8. Eritrean Peoples Liberation Front, National Democratic Programme of the Eritrean People's Liberation Front (n.p., 1977), Introduction, p. 10.
9. J. Bowyer Bell, "Endemic Insurgency and International Order: The Eritrean Experience," Orbis 18 (Summer 1974): 427-50.
10. U.S., Congress, Senate, Subcommittee on United States Security Agreements and Commitments Abroad of the Committee on Foreign Relations, United States Security Agreements and Commitments Abroad: Ethiopia, Hearings, 91st Cong., 2d sess., June 1, 1970, p. 1888.
11. U.S., Congress, House, United States Arms Policies in the Persian Gulf and Red Sea Areas: Past, Present and Future, Report of a Staff Survey Mission to Ethiopia, Iran, and the Arabian Peninsula, Pursuant to H.R. 313, 95th Cong., 1st sess., 1977, p. 175.

12. Farer, op. cit., p. 31.

13. Eritrean Peoples Liberation Front, op. cit., p. 10.

14. Farer, op. cit.

15. Robert L. Hess, Ethiopia: The Modernization of Autocracy (Ithaca, N.Y.: Cornell University Press, 1970), p. 216.

16. Farer, op. cit.

17. John Franklin Campbell, "Background to the Eritrean Conflict," Africa Report, May 1971, p. 20.

18. Abir, op. cit., p. 173.

19. Farer, op. cit.

20. Abir, op. cit., p. 175.

21. Africa Confidential 11 (March 13, 1970): 2.

22. Abir, op. cit.

23. Mordechai Abir, "The Contentious Horn of Africa," Conflict Studies 24 (June 1972): 13.

24. Abir, Oil, Power and Politics, p. 186.

25. Ibid.

26. Farer, op. cit., p. 33.

27. Ibid.

28. Interview with a former ELF guerrilla in Khartoum, Sudan, December 1977.

29. Eritrean Liberation Front, The Eritrean Revolution: Sixteen Years of Armed Struggle (Beirut: ELF Foreign Information Center, 1977), p. 45.

30. David Ottaway, "Eritrean Rebel Front Gains Support," Washington Post, October 18, 1974.

31. Farer, op. cit., p. 35.

32. Ibid.

33. Eritreans for Liberation in North America, Revolution in Eritrea (New York: EFLNA, 1975).

34. Ibid.

35. Eritreans for Liberation in North America, Liberation 5 (July–August 1976): 6.

36. Ibid., p. 7.

37. Eritrean Peoples Liberation Front, Vanguard 13 (January 1976): 12.

38. Ibid.

39. Africa Research Bulletin, September 15, 1976, p. 3731.

40. Vanguard, op. cit., p. 14.

41. Ibid.

42. Africa Research Bulletin, June 15, 1976, p. 4024.

43. David Binder, "Ethiopia Said to Prepare Attack on Eritrean Rebels," New York Times, May 12, 1976, p. 1.

44. David Hamilton, "Ethiopia's Embattled Revolutionaries," Conflict Studies 82 (April 1977): 17.

45. Ibid.

46. Tamene Asmara, "Ethiopia Pulls Back, Cites Signs of Peace," Washington Post, June 21, 1976.

47. Interview with the TPLF Representative in Khartoum, Sudan, December 1977.

48. Africa Research Bulletin, February 15, 1977, p. 4282.

49. Eritrean Peoples Liberation Front, Vanguard 2 (February–March 1977): 15–16.

50. Africa Research Bulletin, May 15, 1977, p. 4393.

51. Eritrean Liberation Front, Eritrean Revolution 2 (May–July 1977): 24.

52. Africa Research Bulletin, May 15, 1977, p. 4396.

53. Ibid.

54. U.S., Congress, Senate, The International Security Assistance and Arms Export Control Act of 1977: Report No. 95–195 to Accompany S. 1160, 95th Cong., 1st sess., May 1977, p. 30.

55. Africa Research Bulletin, February 15, 1978, p. 4705.

56. Newsweek, July 25, 1977, p. 14.

57. Time, February 6, 1978, p. 42.

58. Mesfin Gabriel, "Ethiopia Promises 'the Year of the Offensive,'" New African 126 (February 1978): 23.

59. Newsweek, January 23, 1978, p. 35.

60. Los Angeles Times, November 29, 1978, p. 14.

61. Daniel S. Papp, "The Soviet Union and Cuba in Ethiopia," Current History 76 (March 1979): 113.

62. Time, July 25, 1977, p. 36.

63. Africa Confidential 18 (August 5, 1977): 6.

64. Weekly Review (Nairobi) 156 (February 13, 1978): 11.

65. Agence France-Presse, Africa 2457 (February 21, 1978): 23.

66. Weekly Review, op. cit.

67. Africa Confidential 18 (August 5, 1977): 6.

68. Agence France-Presse, op. cit., p. 2457.

69. Africa Research Bulletin, July 15, 1977, p. 4464.

70. Ibid.

71. Ibid., August 15, 1977, p. 4507.

72. Ibid., January 15, 1978, p. 4675.

73. Foreign Report 1547 (August 16, 1978): 2.

74. Ibid.

75. Ibid.

76. New York Times, July 19, 1979, p. 6.

77. Basil Davidson, The Liberation of Guine (Baltimore: Penguin, 1969), pp. 117–18.

4

THE ERITREAN ALTERNATIVE:
SOCIAL PROGRAMMING

IDEOLOGY AND SOCIAL PROGRAMMING

The Eritrean movement has made significant gains in the field of social programming. The programs introduced by the Eritreans are unique for the Horn of Africa, if not for much of the continent itself. The programs are special in both degree and content and are, for the most part, outgrowths of the respective fronts' political ideologies.

Both the Eritrean Liberation Front (ELF) and the Eritrean Peoples Liberation Front (EPLF) have, to different degrees, invoked a set of categories in their quest for change in Eritrea: equality, democracy, political participation, mass organizations, and self-reliance. The essential concern, particularly for the EPLF, is to alter the semifeudal consciousness of the Eritrean people, which is seen as a necessary step in the physical liberation of Eritrea itself. This new consciousness is elucidated by a 13-year-old member of the EPLF's "Vanguard" youth organization, and is worth citing at length:

> Before we left our homes to join the revolution we used to live it in our games. Kids of the village would gather daily outside their home and then divide into two groups: one pretending to be the revolutionary forces and the other the Ethiopian army. . . . In the end we would be happy in the outcome—the defeat of the Ethiopian soldiers, an outcome we knew in advance. We used to relish this game even though we did not see an actual fight between the guerrillas and the Ethiopian army. But it was not long before we began to see Ethiopian soldiers entering villages, spreading death. . . . But we also saw the revolutionary forces avenging and protecting the people. It was then that we knew that

our place was in the midst of the struggle and not at home.
That is how we came to join. [1]

Not as much can be said for the ELF's social programs as for
those of the EPLF. The feeling among many Eritreans is that the
ELF feels forced by the competitive conditions to institute programs
it otherwise would not choose. One former ELF guerrilla believes
that the ELF is much more comfortable simply administering liberated
areas rather than initiating new programs. [2] The ELF does, however,
have a growing network of social programs under its Social Affairs
Bureau (SAB) of the Executive Committee. This bureau is divided
into six sections: education and literacy, health and popular services,
care of refugees, care of the families of martyrs and militants, care
of the near-handicapped, and social guidance. While not as mass-
participation oriented as the EPLF, the ELF does attempt to involve
some of the people it administers in self-help schemes, particularly
in the previously mentioned mass organizations: students, workers,
peasants, women, and youth. The SAB, in its attempts to mobilize
parts of the Eritrean population, has titled its program "From the
People, To the People."

The EPLF, as noted previously, is organizationally superior to
the ELF in several ways. The EPLF's political ideology, analysis of
conditions in Eritrea, and general application of its program make
for a stronger, better-organized, more coherent set of social programs in the areas under its control. The EPLF is acutely aware of
the operational relationship between culture and consciousness. (See
Appendix B, section 3A.) It asserts:

> Culture affects and exerts a great influence on the economy
> and politics. The concrete material conditions of social
> existence are the bases of human consciousness while con-
> sciousness, in turn, plays a big and important role in the
> transformation of the natural and social conditions of exis-
> tence. . . . Culture, in general, expresses the relations
> between man and nature, the relations among various so-
> cial classes, the material and spiritual life of society, and
> the identity of a people. [3]

The EPLF, through its social programming, is attempting to
build a new Eritrea with the creation of a new culture. In its attempted
transformation of society, the EPLF believes it has attained great
success in building the foundations for large-scale change. The EPLF
is addressing itself to the problems of health care, education, economic restructuring of society, and mass participation in these programs. The EPLF sees the social progress being made in Eritrea

manifesting itself in different ways. These social programs have indicated that the dislike for and prejudice against work and workers is gradually disappearing. The EPLF also believes that social and political relationships based on domination and favoritism are slowly being eroded, in turn giving way to religions based more substantially on democracy and equality.[4]

Before analyzing the nature of the specific programs of the liberation fronts, it is necessary to take a closer look at some of the people who are either actively participating in or being served by various social programs. These people are the Eritrean refugees.

THE REFUGEE PROBLEM

Accurate information regarding the refugee situation inside Eritrea itself is extremely difficult to obtain. The number of displaced people certainly exceeds 500,000, though it is probably less than 1 million. Since the total Eritrean population is between 2.5 and 3 million, possibly one-third of the population of Eritrea could be classified as refugees. It has been estimated that between February 1975 and August 1976 alone, 350,000 Eritreans became displaced persons.[5]

The Ethiopian government has prevented all relief and humanitarian organizations from providing any sort of relief supplies to these displaced people. Both liberation fronts have created relief-oriented humanitarian organizations to help alleviate some of the refugees' most pressing problems. The EPLF manages the Eritrean Relief Association (ERA), and the ELF operates the Eritrean Red Cross-Red Crescent Society (ERCCS). Unfortunately, the two organizations have rarely found grounds for cooperation with one another.

Much better information exists regarding the number and plight of the refugees who have fled Eritrea for the safety of neighboring Sudan. The United Nations High Commission for Refugees (UNHCR), admitting a lack of adequate statistics, estimated that by the end of 1976, 100,000 Eritrean refugees had arrived in the Sudan.[6] The Sudanese Ministry of Interior's Office of the Commissioner for Refugees believes that by December 1977, 200,000 Eritreans were in the Sudan as displaced persons.[7] The refugees generally can be divided into two groups: the first consists of rural people and those with large families who remain in the eastern Sudan; the second consists of those former urban and town dwellers who gravitate toward Khartoum and other Sudanese towns and cities.

A large number of this latter group have gravitated toward Khartoum. The number of Eritreans actually registered in Khartoum by the end of 1977 was 16,140; there may be as many as 25,000 in the greater Khartoum area.[8] At the end of 1977, the stream of new refugees was leaving Eritrea via a northern route. Heading for Port Sudan, they reflected the intense fighting in the areas from Asmara to Massawa. In 85 percent of the cases, refugees with urban backgrounds either look for work or a place to study or they attempt to go abroad.[9] These people are usually in better financial positions than their rural counterparts and often receive money from relatives already working abroad.

The refugees coming from rural Eritrea can be divided into two additional groups. The first, which the UNHCR representative estimated approaches 50 percent, settled spontaneously in the eastern Sudan.[10] For many, especially the Beni Amer and other lowland groups, the conditions of this region of the Sudan closely approximated their life in Eritrea. Many of these people have integrated into life in the region, either settling with relatives or on a broad social basis.

The remainder of the rural Eritreans are resettled in temporary refugee camps or semipermanent agricultural resettlement areas. The largest of the temporary camps is Wad el Hillayu, where 30,000 refugees live. It is generally agreed that in the smaller, semipermanent agricultural resettlement developments, such as Qala en Nahl, living conditions for the refugees are decent. The people are given land, seed, tools, and an occasional tractor. As for the large camp at Wad el Hillayu, Berhane Woldegabriel states that "medical facilities are good, with more than five clinics operating, but food supply is often irregular."[11]

Most of the aid offered to Eritrean refugees is either from international organizations or from the Sudanese government. Eritrean agencies such as the ERA and the ERCCS each maintains a clinic at Wad el Hillayu but concentrate most of their efforts within the liberated areas of Eritrea itself. Agencies assisting Eritreans in the Sudan are the UNHCR, the World Food Program, the semiautonomous Refugee Counseling Services, the Sudan Council of Churches, and the Office of the Commissioner for Refugees in the Sudanese Ministry of the Interior.

Two other groups of refugees warrant mention here: those who are working in Persian Gulf states and those living in Europe and North America. Thousands of Eritreans have made their way from Khartoum, Sudan, to the oil-rich Gulf states where they are able to find menial employment at very good salaries. This particular group of refugees is generally educated and has the financial means to purchase visas and roundtrip airline tickets in order to obtain the necessary UN Conventional Travel Document for passage to the Gulf.

Thousands of other Eritrean refugees and expatriates now reside in Europe and North America. Those living in North America support the Eritrean revolution under two umbrella organizations:

Eritreans for Liberation in North America (EFLNA) and the Association of Eritrean Women in North America (AEWNA), both of which have supported EPLF in the past but at present are reevaluating their support of that organization. EFLNA and AEWNA are heavily involved in publicizing the Eritrean struggle in the United States through a series of cultural and political programs, documentary slide and film showings, and other fund-raising activities. Both groups have reprinted a number of EPLF publications, such as the monthly, Vanguard, in addition to their own publications: Liberation and Eritrea in Struggle.

SOCIAL PROGRAMMING IN THE LIBERATED ZONES

Both the EPLF and the ELF conduct a number of specific socially oriented programs that at once serve and involve a large proportion of the Eritrean population in the liberated areas. The emphasis in this section will be placed on those programs conducted by EPLF, as their social network is broader in scope and more systematic than that of the ELF. As was noted in a previous chapter, the ELF tends to focus on the military aspects of liberation before addressing itself to more socioeconomic issues. The programs explored below are health care, education, and the changing role of women in Eritrean society.

During the Italian colonial period (1806-1941), the few hospitals and clinics in Eritrea were located in Asmara and the larger towns and were for the exclusive use of the colonists. A few Eritreans were trained as dressers, but for the most part the indigenous population was forced to rely solely on traditional medicine. This situation changed little during the British occupation, and then only in a cosmetic sense during federation with Ethiopia. For the overwhelming majority of Eritreans, the annual 40-cent, per capita health expenditure of the Ethiopian government had no visible effect.[12]

Before the end of the Eritrean civil war in 1974, the two fronts provided medical services that could only be described as deficient in both quality and quantity. Since the end of 1974, the ELF has begun to initiate medical services in the areas it controls. The ELF founded the ERCCS in late 1975, in addition to establishing more than 50 clinics and dispensaries.[13]

For the EPLF, public health is an essential social concern, as described in its National Democratic Programme (Appendix B, section 3C). The EPLF adheres to the tenet that necessary medical services be rendered to all Eritreans free of charge. Interestingly, it also proposes to attempt to scientifically develop traditional medicine. Since 1975 medical services provided by the EPLF have expanded substantially. The number of outpatients that received one or another medical service provided by the EPLF in 1975 was almost half a million, or five times greater than the 1974 figure. The number of outpatients for the first half of 1976 was nearly equal to that of all of 1975.[14] The scope and effects of the EPLF's health services can best be understood by a brief discussion of their medical personnel and training, hospitals, clinics, mobile teams, preventive medicine, and medical supplies.

By late 1976, EPLF medical personnel included 12 doctors (6 of whom are surgeons, 2 of whom are pediatricians), 67 nurses, 80 practical nurses, 6 nurse anesthetists, 8 laboratory technicians, 4 X-ray technicians, and 15 pharmacists.[15]

Two levels of medical training programs are given in each of the EPLF's four hospitals to increase the number of badly needed medical personnel. The elementary program trains the squad doctors, who might be considered similar to China's barefoot doctors. This program consists of a three-month intensive course focusing on common diseases, dressing techniques, first aid, and basic nursing procedures. Most of these squad doctors are then assigned to clinics or mobile teams.

Those who complete the elementary program and serve for at least two years in the field are eligible to take an intermediate level program. This six-month training program, while stressing common diseases, is more comprehensive, covering medicine, surgery, pediatrics, and gynecology and obstetrics. Essentials of disease and minor operative techniques are presented. Emphasis is made on history taking and physical examination, so that the student can later work independently. Those who finish the intermediate course are assigned to head clinics or mobile teams.[16]

The EPLF's four major hospitals have become multifaceted medical networks with a combined capacity, as of February 1977, of 1,392 beds.[17] The hospitals, all of which function in the liberated areas, boast modest laboratories, X-ray machines, and different wards for general medicine, surgery, pediatrics, and obstetrics. The 500-bed central hospital has a 60-bed tuberculosis unit, a 60-bed orthopedic and physiotherapy unit, and a 15-bed fistula unit.[18] In the first half of 1976, these hospitals performed close to 2,000 operations, of which 382 were considered to be major.[19]

One major benefit that has accrued to the EPLF from the operation of its hospitals is that virtually all battle injuries can be treated inside Eritrea. In 1974, 31 percent of those with battle injuries were sent outside of Eritrea to be treated; by 1975 it was necessary to send less than 1 percent of those injured abroad for treatment.[20]

In addition to the four hospitals, EPLF operates 20 stationary clinics in the liberated and semiliberated areas. These clinics are attached to army battalions, and, in addition to outpatient services, they have an average of 20 beds each for inpatient treatment of basic medical cases and deliveries. Each clinic has a health officer and between five to seven squad doctors. During the first six months of 1976, nearly 300,000 patients were treated in these clinics, more than a third of which were malaria or anemia cases.[21]

The last institutional feature of the EPLF health services program is the mobile team. In late 1976 there were 11 of these mobile teams, each consisting of one medical assistant and two-to-five squad doctors, accompanied by armed members of the team. The mobile teams visit remote areas of the EPLF-controlled liberated zones, visiting people who often have never received any kind of modern medical treatment in their lives. The mobile teams usually visit one village a day and travel between two and six hours a day. In addition to treating patients, the teams are increasingly involved in disease prevention. They now teach selected people from the villages visited the "elementary principles of hygiene" and train them in the giving of injections and dressing of wounds.

The EPLF not only emphasizes curative medicine but focuses its efforts on preventive medicine as well:

> BCG and smallpox vaccination campaigns have been conducted in some areas. In early 1975 over 20,000 people were vaccinated against smallpox in the lowlands, and at present [1976] a campaign is underway to vaccinate 100,000 people against BCG. . . . The serious limitation has been the lack of vaccines, which have been hard to get despite repeated efforts.[22]

The most pervasive handicap encountered by the EPLF in its health services program has been "the inconsistent and inadequate supply of drugs and medical equipment." The pharmacies attached to the hospitals store and distribute medical supplies but usually run short of essential drugs. Due to the lack of any substantial foreign aid, EPLF is forced to spend its own money to purchase drugs and medical equipment from abroad. In addition to these purchases, the EPLF has repeatedly seized drugs and equipment from the Ethiopians. In the largest single raid of this sort, on September 10, 1976, EPLF units captured approximately $100,000 worth of drugs and medical equipment from the Ethiopian central medical warehouse in Asmara. Finally, in keeping with the policy of self-reliance, the EPLF pharmacies have been able to prepare certain basic drugs—such as cough syrup, ointments, and antiseptics—from indigenous raw materials; however, these efforts have fallen far short of the needed supplies.

Education, both general and political, has been an important part of the liberation struggle's social programming. The Eritrean movements believe that by educating the broad masses of people in the country, political, social, and economic change will be facilitated both during and after the military struggle. As in the case of their respective health services offerings, the EPLF's mass education programs are broader in scope and better organized than those of their rival organization. However, a few words are in order regarding the ELF's program before proceeding to a discussion of the EPLF's.

During the 1976/77 academic year, more than 12,000 students attended 157 ELF-run schools. Most of these students attended first and second grades; for the 1977/78 school year, 25,000 students were enrolled in grades one through three.[23] Textbooks, in both Tigrinya and Arabic, are prepared by the Education and Literacy Department of the ELF's Social Affairs Bureau. Other materials have been solicited from abroad, but the major problem remains a shortage of qualified teaching personnel. The ELF also is planning to open a junior secondary school in Kassala, Sudan, with the assistance of the United Nations.[24] An adult literacy program is in effect in ELF-controlled areas of Eritrea, with night classes being offered at all elementary schools.

The EPLF's National Democratic Programme outlines the organization's educational objectives (see Appendix B, section 3B). Education, for the EPLF, is clearly part of a larger political consciousness: it is to be integrated with production and "put in the service of the masses." It is also to be divorced completely from religious considerations. In line with these theoretical dictums, EPLF's Department of Education established the first Revolution School in January 1976, to educate the children of deceased fighters and refugees; 36 more schools were opened during 1976. Emphasis is on educating students in grades one through four, although some older students are involved as well.

The Revolution School is meant to be a holistic experience for these Eritrean youngsters:

> The children are raised in a healthy atmosphere where they
> are taught to love labor and are educated in the spirit of
> self-reliance. The students, along with the teachers, farm
> small plots of land and have already become self-sufficient
> in vegetables. Sports and physical culture [sic] are given
> importance. Simple military training is also given to the
> students.[25]

The formal educational curriculum for second and third graders includes courses in Tigrinya, Arabic, English, geography, science, arithmetic, and general politics. An important by-product of this entire educational process is the integration of Eritrea's different cultures. As one member of the EPLF describes it:

The pupils in the "Revolution School" who come from all
of Eritrea's nine nationalities show great enthusiasm to
learn from and integrate with each other. Free from narrow nationalist or chauvinist thinking, they are forging deep
unity among the nationalities. During cultural programs
the pupils participate vigorously in songs and dances of all
nationalities.[26]

Throughout the EPLF-controlled areas, a mass literacy campaign is conducted among the largely illiterate rural population. Especially important has been the literacy program conducted for new
recruits of the Eritrean Peoples Liberation Army (EPLA), a large
number of whom could not read or write. Each new recruit is now
required to learn to read and write before he finishes his six-month
training period.

Political education, along the lines of the EPLF's National Democratic Programme, is another aspect of the education program propa-
gated in EPLF-liberated zones. For example, in the city of Keren,
captured by the EPLF in July 1977 but retaken by Ethiopian forces the
following year, political education teams actively conducted sessions.
In a weekly period, more than 50 political education meetings were
held in the six zones of the city. Not only the general populace under-
goes such political training; most of the lower- and middle-level government employees are in the process of being "rehabilitated" through
a rigorous political education process.[27]

THE NEW ERITREAN WOMAN

It is important to note the radically altered role of women in
Eritrean society in the past five years, particularly those women associated with the EPLF. Women's rights are spelled out in the EPLF's
National Democratic Programme (Appendix B, section 4B). Full equality with men, not just in theory but in practice, is the organization's
goal.

Traditionally, the Eritrean woman suffered the most extreme
forms of oppression. She was excluded from any direct ownership of
land. In patriarchal Eritrean society, women had little or no role in
even the most obscure social or political decision making. Marriage,
basically an economic transaction, was decided upon between the male
heads of the concerned families. Among Tigrinya-speaking, predominantly Christian Eritreans, the bride's parents must pay a dowry to
the parents of the groom. Among the other eight cultural groupings,
the groom's parents must pay the dowry.[28] Polygamy is common in
Eritrea, particularly among the lowland Muslims. Divorce is the
prerogative of the man, "who can throw his wife out at any moment."

Under EPLF ideological tutelage, much of this is changing for some Eritrean women. The Association of Eritrean Women has been organized as an expression of women's consciousness within the EPLF. The association

> fights to mobilize Eritrean women so that they can realize their role and participate in the political and armed struggle "against colonial aggression and for social transformation." It gives high priority to raising the political consciousness of Eritrean women so they can grasp the source of their oppression and the road to emancipation.[29]

The EPLF is critical of the ELF, whom they view as postponing fundamental changes, such as women's status in the revolution, until independence has been achieved.

Women members of the EPLA oftentimes fight right alongside of their male counterparts. Women fighters are also engaged in agricultural and small-factory production. Women are sharing duties with men in medical, educational, and cultural departments of the organization. Women are encouraged, though not always successfully, to participate in village assemblies; girls attend EPLF schools in nearly equal numbers and on an equal basis with boys.[30] By June 1977, women fighters made up 13 percent of the EPLA; six months earlier, 11 percent of the delegates to the EPLF's First Congress were women.[31]

These social programs and changes serve as guidelines for prospective programs in an independent Eritrea. What a truly independent Eritrean state might resemble is, of course, open to conjecture. However, the socioeconomic direction of the revolution is on a course radically different from the previously accepted structure of Eritrean society. These social programs, which continue throughout the Eritrean-controlled countryside, along with the potential for economic development (to be explored in the following chapter), indicate the genuine possibility of a unique transformation of the Horn of Africa.

NOTES

1. Eritreans for Liberation in North America, Liberation 6 (November-December 1976): 9.

2. Interview with a former ELF member, Khartoum, Sudan, December 1977.

3. Association of Eritrean Students in North America, Selected Articles from "Vanguard", October 1977, pp. 3-4.

4. Eritreans for Liberation in North America, Liberation 6 (January-February 1977): 30.

5. Eritreans for Liberation in North America, Eritrea in Struggle, August 15, 1976, p. 6.

6. Interview with A. J. Kozlowski, UNHCR representative in the Sudan, Khartoum, Sudan, December 1977.

7. Interview with Omar Muhammed Ismail, commissioner for refugees, Ministry of the Interior (Sudan), Khartoum, Sudan, December 1977.

8. Ibid.

9. Berhane Woldegabriel, "The Refugee Problem," Sudanow 2 (July 1977): 9.

10. Interview with A. J. Kozloswki, op. cit.

11. Berhane Woldegabriel, op. cit.

12. Eritrean Peoples Liberation Front, EPLF: Serving the Masses on the Medical Front (New York, October 1976), p. 6.

13. Eritrean Liberation Front, Eritrean Newsletter 13 (September 1, 1977): 13.

14. Eritrean Peoples Liberation Front, op. cit., p. 7.

15. Ibid., p. 14.

16. Ibid.

17. Eritreans for Liberation in North America, Liberation 6 (January-February 1977): 18.

18. Eritrean Peoples Liberation Front, op. cit., p. 8.

19. Eritreans for Liberation in North America, Liberation 6 (January-February): 19.

20. Eritrean Peoples Liberation Front, op. cit., p. 10.

21. Eritreans for Liberation in North America, Liberation 6 (January-February 1977): 19.

22. Eritrean Peoples Liberation Front, op. cit., p. 13.

23. Eritrean Liberation Front, Eritrean Newsletter 15 (October 16, 1977): 4.

24. Ibid., p. 5.

25. Eritreans for Liberation in North America, Eritrea in Struggle 1 (June-July 1977): 5.

26. Ibid.

27. Eritreans for Liberation in North America, Eritrea in Struggle 2 (February 1978): 4.

28. Eritreans for Liberation in North America, Liberation 6 (March-June 1977): 16.

29. Ibid., p. 20.

30. Jean Louis Peninou, Eritrea: The Guerrillas of the Red Sea (n.p., 1975).

31. Ibid., p. 22.

5
PROSPECTS FOR
AN INDEPENDENT ERITREA

The prospects for an independent Eritrean state are heavily dependent on a series of interrelated factors. The internal political issue of Eritrean unity is at a crucial stage and will undergo severe tests in the next few years. The military situation in Eritrea is also at a critical juncture: On what basis and by which tactics will the Eritreans attempt to continue the armed struggle against the Ethiopians and their Soviet and Cuban patrons?

This chapter will concern itself with examining the proposed solutions to the conflict and then proceed to evaluate the Eritrean economic outlook. Should independence become a reality? One also needs to question what type of state Eritrea might be: In the achievement of an egalitarian, socialist-oriented Eritrea a feasible reality? Before examining the viability of an independent Eritrea, let us first turn to a discussion of the proposed solutions to the present conflict.

PROPOSED SOLUTIONS TO THE
ETHIO-ERITREAN CONFLICT

The Ethiopian government, since May 1976, has stood on its nine-point program as a means of achieving a peaceful accommodation with the Eritrean movement (Appendix F). The Ethiopian head of state, Mengistu Haile Mariam, has reaffirmed this program, which would give Eritrea regional autonomy "in collaboration with progressives in the rest of Ethiopia and on the basis of the programme of the Ethiopian National Democratic Revolution."[1]

In early 1978 there was a suggestion being discussed in Addis Ababa that would involve the creation of 12 or more socialist republics within the framework of a greater Ethiopia.[2] Two of these republics would, of course, be Eritrea and the Ogaden. The East Germans managed to get the Eritrean Peoples Liberation Front (EPLF) and the Ethiopians together in Berlin on February 1 and March 22, 1978.[3] The Dergue met with the EPLF in Berlin again in June 1978.[4] The meetings ended unsuccessfully, as each side found the other intransigent.

The details of any sort of regional autonomy for Eritrea would have to be worked out if and when the Ethiopians and Eritreans sat down to hammer out an agreement. If the Eritrean movement is "truly progressive," Ethiopian Foreign Minister Feleke Gedle Giorgis stated, then "they must join with socialist Ethiopia. Those who refuse are reactionaries."[5] This approach would seem to leave the Eritreans with very little leverage in any future negotiations with Ethiopia.

James Buxton, writing in the Financial Times, believes that the Dergue's approach effectively rules out compromise with the Eritreans.[6] The only solutions acceptable to the Dergue are within the context of present Ethiopian borders, absolutely precluding the possibility of an independent Eritrean entity:

> The overriding impression one gets in Addis is that though many lives will be lost, both in battle and by starvation resulting from the disruption of supplies, this Government at least, with its considerable talent for survival, is determined not to compromise either its revolutionary principles or the inherited frontiers of imperial Ethiopia.[7]

If the Ethiopian position and resulting proposals seem intractable, then the Eritrean position is no less so. The Eritreans have repeatedly stated that they see no alternative to full independence. They see the Dergue's nine-point program as a hoax, since shortly after it was proposed the Dergue unleashed its "peasant militia" against Eritrea.

Both the Eritrean Liberation Front (ELF) and the EPLF have expressed the desire to conduct some form of negotiations with the Ethiopian government. The EPLF once spelled out three preconditions for negotiating a peaceful solution with Ethiopia. They are:

1) Ethiopian recognition of the right of the Eritrean people to self-determination and independence;
2) Ethiopian recognition of the two fronts, the EPLF and ELF, as the only legitimate representatives of the Eritrean people; and
3) Agreement that the dialogue be conducted on the international forum of the United Nations.[8]

By December 1978, the EPLF had declared its willingness to hold talks with the Dergue without preconditions anywhere except in Addis Ababa.[9]

Other parties have offered political solutions in addition to those presented by the Eritreans and Ethiopians. Most of those solutions, however, have envisioned various degrees of autonomy for Eritrea within a larger Ethiopian framework. Both the Soviets and the Cubans are said to favor a political, rather than a military, solution. According to one report, the Soviets contacted the Eritrean movement early in 1978 and proposed a settlement granting Eritrea autonomy on all but foreign affairs if Ethiopia were assured of the use of the port facilities at Assab.[10]

Tom Farer, in War Clouds on the Horn of Africa, states that the Eritreans and Ethiopians must "transcend the conventional architecture of sovereignty or resign themselves to endless and mutually ruinous conflict."[11] This transcendence can only be achieved through external involvement. The same international guarantors (the United Nations?) of Eritrean autonomy in a federal arrangement with Ethiopia could also ensure Ethiopian access to the Red Sea ports. The question of sovereignty could be waffled, according to Farer. While the relationship between the two units might be federal, Eritrea could be admitted to the United Nations, following the precedent of the Ukraine and Byelorussia.

The problem with both the Soviet and Farer solutions is that neither the Ethiopians nor the Eritreans are really willing to compromise at this point in time. Other dimensions must be introduced into the present situation for any kind of negotiations to occur. The nature of the Dergue itself might be one of these variables; the recent Eritrean military reversals could also be a factor in the negotiating process. Should Mengistu be replaced with a less militant leader, some sort of negotiating process might seem more feasible. (However, this possibility appears more remote the longer Mengistu remains chairman of the Provisional Military Administrative Council and consolidates his power.) If the Ethiopians continue to inflict serious blows to the guerrillas on a number of fronts, the fronts might be forced to reevaluate their own reticence to negotiate.

The Eritreans are adamant about struggling for complete independence. The Ethiopians, armed with Soviet and Cuban assistance, are in no mood to negotiate a settlement. The two once-powerful members of the Dergue who seriously debated a negotiated settlement, Aman Andom and Atnafu Abate, were executed. Not even a quick military victory for either side can be predicted. As long as the large Soviet-Cuban presence in Eritrea continues, victory can be denied to the guerrilla forces. On the other hand, even with massive foreign assistance, the Ethiopians cannot seriously hope to militarily defeat the Eritrean forces in an unconventional, protracted guerrilla war. At present, then, there appears to be no feasible solution to the conflict. A stalemate has occurred and, with some possible alternations, will continue until new political or military elements are introduced.

AN ECONOMICALLY VIABLE ERITREA

Should Eritrea become independent, how viable would its economy be? There have been surprisingly few answers offered. The effects of the war on Eritrea have obfuscated the possibilities for economic development in the country. Yet, based on data from the past and from the economic programs introduced by the liberation movement, one can envision an economy capable of meeting its people's basic needs.

Eritrea became vitally important to Ethiopia not only for its Red Sea ports of Massawa and Assab but for its industrial, agricultural, and human resources as well. In 1970 more than 35 percent of Ethiopia's industrial activity occurred in Eritrea.[12] Ethiopia's only oil refinery, owned and operated by the government, is located in Assab. A large proportion of Ethiopia's imports (75 percent) and exports (77 percent)[13] passed through the ports of Assab and Massawa before the 1977 shift in the war. By 1978 the entire Ethiopian economy had been weakened to the point where the rate of inflation was 30 percent a year.[14]

An independent Eritrea would be a blow to Ethiopian economic development, but by no means a fatal one. The two countries would necessarily remain linked economically, as the ports of Massawa and Assab are useless unless they service the highlands, both Eritrean and Ethiopian. Production of Ethiopia's major exports, coffee and hides and skins, would be virtually unaffected by the loss of Eritrea. However, Ethiopia would revert to being a landlocked country with no guaranteed access to the sea.

How capable of development would the economy of an independent Eritrea be? In the survey of Eritrea's economic potential that follows, an examination is made in the areas of agriculture, livestock, light industry, extractive industry, marine wealth, and commerce.

Many analysts believe that in Eritrea the possibilities for large-scale agricultural development are limited. Two of the reasons usually given for this pessimism would have little relevance should Eritrea realize independence. Often cited as reasons for the low level of agricultural production are the traditional land tenure systems and the unscientific farming methods in use in the country. Should Eritrea become independent, neither of these practices will necessarily continue. This will be discussed further in the section on the liberation movements' economic programming.

A more substantive argument is that rainfall in Eritrea can be irregular, and even fail altogether, in one part of the country or another in a given year. G. K. N. Trevaskis has noted that "rainfall is generally scarce, capricious, and torrential; and less than three percent of the territory's land surface is cultivated."[15] In addition, the best agricultural land is found in the Gash-Setit lowlands, where rainfall is often inadequate. In the wetter highland areas, the soil is not as fertile and the terrain is much more rugged. The principal crops grown in the lowlands are sorghum, corn, maize, cotton, and an indigenous millet known as teff. No accurate estimate of total production for these crops exists, but teff is grown far more widely than any of the other commodities.

The hypothesis that Eritrea cannot feed its population has been based on political and technological considerations rather than objective agricultural potential. Italian colonial policy was mainly concerned with producing cash crops for the Italian market:

> Nothing, however, was done to encourage the production of grain or vegetables, in which Eritrea was deficient and dependent on imports. . . . Because the war had made it difficult to import foodstuffs the British endeavored to make the territory self-sufficient in vegetables, fruit, and grain. . . . By 1950 they were not only meeting the local European demand for fruit and vegetables, but were exporting a small surplus. [16]

In the past, therefore, political decisions actually determined to what extent Eritrea could feed its people. Eritrea has continued the export of fruits and vegetables while under Ethiopian rule, as illustrated in Figure 3 and Table 1.

In addition to the administrative decision by the British to make Eritrea self-sufficient in certain foodstuffs, two other factors explain the tremendous jump in agricultural output in the 1940s. Ten thousand acres were given out in concession to Italian agriculturalists from which large successful plantations were created. At the same time, efforts were made to increase the productivity of the Eritrean cultivator "by propaganda, the establishment of demonstration plots, and, in some areas, the provision of tractors and motor ploughs."[17] By 1946, 640,000 acres were under cultivation versus 141,000 acres in 1939; the grain harvest was 118,000 tons, up from 28,500 tons.[18]

Annual crop production in Eritrea for the years 1962-72, inclusive, is illustrated in Table 2. In 1962, the year that Ethiopia formally abrogated the federal agreement with Eritrea, crop production stood at 226,456 tons. As Table 2 shows, agricultural output never approximated that figure again during the course of the next ten years.

The decrease in production may be attributable to a variety of factors: climate, drought, guerrilla activity, and so forth. Yet it is certain that the Ethiopians were not encouraging the growth of the Eritrean economy during this period and were most definitely concentrating their meager productive energies in other parts of Ethiopia.

FIGURE 3

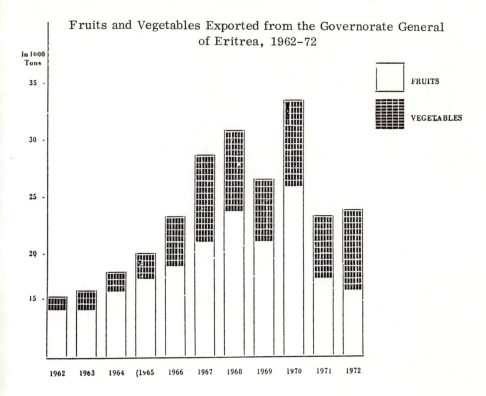

Fruits and Vegetables Exported from the Governorate General of Eritrea, 1962–72

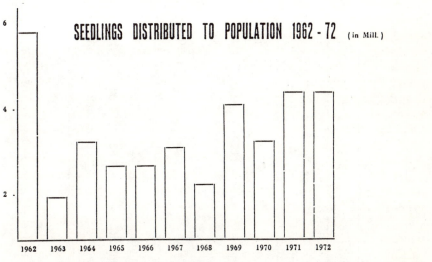

SEEDLINGS DISTRIBUTED TO POPULATION 1962 - 72 (in Mill.)

Source: Eritrea Chamber of Commerce, Trade and Development Bulletin, vol. 2 (March–April 1973).

113

TABLE 1

Fruits and Vegetables Exported from Eritrea, 1962–72
(in tons)

Type	1962	1963	1964	1965	1966	1967	1968	1969	1970	1971	1972
Fruit	13,380	13,377	14,946	16,077	17,391	19,257	22,279	20,000	24,930	16,150	14,934
Banana	12,377	12,317	14,456	14,719	16,082	18,141	20,551	18,704	21,728	15,295	14,159
Mango	25	31	16	60	52	35	115	34	102	85	—
Citrus	905	946	442	1,116	1,091	961	1,423	1,200	3,000	769	775
Other	73	83	32	182	166	120	190	62	100	1	—
Vegetable	896	1,402	1,507	2,612	4,283	7,550	7,508	5,335	7,950	5,349	7,500
Pepper	200	303	400	872	1,400	2,480	3,000	1,960	3,020	3,769	7,000
Tomato	306	686	550	746	1,200	2,430	1,900	1,400	2,030	631	—
Eggplant	82	92	107	144	183	190	208	215	200	45	—
Other	308	321	450	850	1,500	2,450	2,400	1,760	2,700	902	500

Source: Eritrea Chamber of Commerce, Trade and Development Bulletin, vol. 2 (March–April 1973).

An examination of concession agriculture in Eritrea gives an idea of the agricultural potential in the different regions of the country. Concession agriculture in Eritrea, as of 1964, was

> characterized by land leased from a central government, operated by a manager and laborers, geared toward producing for the market, and worked by means of modern facilities, e.g., motor-pumps, irrigation canals, wheel-barrows, etc.[19]

Most of the large concessions were concentrated in the western lowlands and the Red Sea coastal plains. Particularly fertile areas are those around Tessenei, Agordat, and Barentu, mainly along the banks of the Gash and Barka rivers. The physical diversity of Eritrea has encouraged the cultivation of a variety of crops (see Table 2).

In the highlands, small farms produce such items as pears, apples, peaches, bananas, lemons, oranges, onions, and tomatoes. In some of the river deltas of the Red Sea coast, papayas, mangos, and dates are grown. In the western lowlands the largest quantities of tropical and citrus fruits are cultivated.

Cotton is cultivated in three main areas: the Red Sea coastal region, the Barka-Anseba Valley, and the Gash Valley. The dum palm, which is found growing wild along the banks of the Gash and Barka rivers for great distances, is of great economic importance. Its leaves provide raw material for the extraction of fiber, and the fruits are used for the manufacturing of buttons, alcohol extraction, and fodder for cattle. The harvest of the dum palms' leaves had, at one time, led to an easily exportable agricultural product.

Both coffee and tobacco production have existed on a very limited scale in Eritrea. Yet both could easily be developed to meet the needs of the indigenous population. Coffee is cultivated on mountainside terraces around Merara, Faghena, and Sakur. The coffee plants are unshaded and need no irrigation, as these regions benefit from two rainy seasons per year.

Tobacco is cultivated in a variety of locations from Keren and Agordat in the western lowlands to the Dogali River near the Red Sea coast. Tobacco grows very well in these areas and enough could be harvested for export, after satisfying local needs. One drawback to the increased production of tobacco in the past was the (Ethiopian) Tobacco Monopoly. All tobacco production was licensed by this government agency, and the policy was to limit production to domestic requirements.[20]

At this point, it might be well to examine some specific agricultural projects and potential ventures in various areas of Eritrea. In 1973 the Eritrean Chamber of Commerce, in its Trade and Develop-

TABLE 2

Annual Crop Production in Eritrea, 1962–72
(in tons)

Crop	1962	1963	1964	1965	1966	1967	1968	1969	1970	1971	1972
Wheat	17,205	8,612	7,018	4,000	14,000	8,997	10,982	5,511	3,674	8,480	3,222
Barley	26,050	18,419	14,627	12,000	23,200	22,202	31,826	9,160	7,372	16,309	7,897
Durra	89,582	26,563	78,184	45,000	9,100	38,000	53,977	14,545	11,794	27,008	17,000
Maize	7,663	10,815	7,282	3,000	2,100	3,600	7,275	5,725	1,779	4,118	3,038
Millet	26,668	6,842	24,607	4,000	3,800	10,629	11,902	2,701	2,196	6,677	4,759
Dagusse	9,860	10,185	6,853	2,500	3,500	2,910	10,638	3,060	2,250	4,980	2,865
Teff	6,102	6,335	7,838	1,000	9,600	11,878	7,402	3,429	3,250	6,008	3,666
Pulse	3,500	3,024	3,607	1,500	1,665	6,912	7,436	2,609	2,656	4,767	1,800
Oilseed	4,642	10,047	7,353	10,999	4,292	11,339	13,061	5,622	3,866	5,078	3,800
Potato	4,438	4,428	1,774	3,200	2,560	5,175	3,580	4,745	3,821	5,802	8,943
Tomato	4,009	2,510	5,610	2,600	1,500	4,994	4,100	10,332	8,208	15,258	17,431
Pepper	642	700	810	1,000	3,434	3,930	6,554	8,482	9,614	11,408	12,497
Watermelon	110	265	57	100	139	385	616	208	280	1,031	928
Other vegetable	2,272	3,350	1,320	2,200	1,884	2,609	6,332	6,930	6,486	10,428	12,158
Banana	16,655	18,250	19,450	17,500	18,000	21,000	31,310	34,196	32,407	31,476	32,534
Citrus	2,071	2,130	2,120	1,960	1,566	1,598	3,705	4,782	3,511	6,001	9,235
Other fruit	731	1,305	179	750	871	741	776	683	576	978	278
Seed cotton	4,137	2,898	2,960	5,001	5,000	5,016	6,030	9,084	8,872	11,520	11,002
Coffee	72	65	103	65	141	98	41	30	52	10	—
Tobacco	47	32	36	61	—	7	42	27	39	16	8
Total	226,456	136,775	191,788	118,436	106,352	162,320	217,585	131,861	112,703	177,353	153,061

Source: Eritrea Chamber of Commerce, Trade and Development Bulletin, vol. 2 (March–April 1973).

116

ment Bulletin, outlined a series of development schemes aimed at improving water systems and, consequently, production in various areas of the country.[21] The various proposals that follow were in the discussion stage only as of 1973. They are hypothetical only in that the Ethiopian government has never seriously attempted to implement any of these schemes.

A number of areas in the highlands could be utilized in agricultural development projects provided that a constant water supply is guaranteed by drilling wells or building dams where needed. The rivers Sebene, Tsorona, and Mareb, dammed at strategic places, would supply a continuous flow of water to irrigate a large portion of the Hazamo Plain. Other highland areas where such schemes are applicable are Ubel, the Plain of Ala, Daro Paulos, Adi Mesguag, Shecketi, Embakittai, Adi Hadid, Akurur, and Mai Aini.

The eastern lowlands (between the plateau and the Red Sea) could be more effectively developed by the use of a water-spreading system. In such a system, intermittent rivers and streams that swell during a heavy rainfall are diverted to nearby fields. This system has two advantages: it would not only provide water for irrigation but also would reclaim more land by depositing rich soil on the fields adjacent to the river banks. The main sites for water-spreading schemes in the eastern lowlands would be Mersa Taklai in the north, along the Falkat riverbed; Mersa Gulbub, Mersa Kuba, Kufrilla, and Abararat, along the Sebka riverbed; Sheb and Wakiro, along the Laba riverbed; Emberemi, along the Desset riverbed; Zula, along the Hadas riverbed; and Bada, in Dankalia, along the Ragale riverbed.

The western lowlands could be extensively developed by means of irrigation. It was in the western lowlands that Italian concession agriculture was most widely practiced. The Hagaz and Barbaru valleys in the Anseba Basin could be irrigated from an artificial lake created by the damming of the Tsebab Straits.

There are a number of other plains and valleys that can be extensively developed by drilling wells for an underground water supply or by making full use of water from nearby rivers. These areas are fertile and expansive as well. The best areas are the Tessenei Gullui Plain, between the Gash and Setit rivers, comprising 120,000 hectares;* Om Hager-Gullui (100,000 hectares); Bashis, or Bashuka (45,000 hectares); the Gash Valley (36,000 hectares); and Mansura (25,000 hectares).

---

*The hectare is a metric unit equal to 10,000 square meters, or 2.47 acres.

LIVESTOCK

One of Eritrea's principal sources of natural wealth has always been its livestock. Large herds of sheep, goats, and camels have enjoyed sufficient grazing area throughout the country. Cattle rearing was a particularly important activity especially in the rural areas where the number of cattle owned was indicative of an individual's social status.

As with agriculture, little was done to exploit Eritrea's potential wealth in animal by-products under Italian colonialism. The Italians did, however, effectively combat common animal diseases, mainly rinderpest and trypanosomiasis. The British managed to develop milk, butter, and cheese processing to meet local European needs and actually had a surplus of cheese available for export. By 1946 there were 1.2 million cattle, 2.2 million goats and sheep, and 105,000 camels in Eritrea.[22] In 1973 the Eritrean Chamber of Commerce estimated that there was one head of cattle and two goats or sheep per each person living in Eritrea.[23] This translates into roughly 2.5 million cattle and 5 million goats and sheep. Pig rearing has also become an increasingly popular activity since the 1940s.

Of the three breeds of cattle found in Eritrea—the Arado, the Arabic, and the Barka—the latter is the most important. The Barka is a medium-sized breed with a large hump and is best for both meat and milk production. Found primarily in the western lowlands, it was crossbred with imported Frisian and Ayrshire cattle in the early 1960s "with very satisfactory results."[24] Before the 1975 escalation of the present conflict, the dairy farms in Eritrea had surpassed the local demand for milk and had even supplied markets in parts of Ethiopia.

Camel herding is essential to the Eritrean lowlands, as camels have provided a major source of food and clothing in addition to serving as transportation in desert areas. However, the camel population as well as the other livestock population has been reduced by the Ethiopian Army and Air Force in what the Eritreans describe as "wanton extermination campaigns."

INDUSTRIAL ACTIVITY

What was once a moderately productive light industrial economy has, in the 1970s, been almost totally dismantled by the Ethiopian government. As noted in the first chapter, Italian industrial concerns were war related; the British made a more serious attempt at developing light industry to produce goods for internal consumption. New industries spring up to manufacture soap, beer, wine, matches, leather goods, bottles, glassware, and paper.

It is instructive to examine Eritrean light industrial development previous to its recent destruction by the Ethiopian government and armed forces. Since 1974, the Ethiopians have systematically transported industrial equipment out of Asmara, transferring it to various destinations in Ethiopia itself. Whole factories, such as canning and slaughtering facilities, have been dismantled and the machinery shipped to Addis Ababa and elsewhere.

As stated earlier in this chapter, more than 35 percent of Ethiopia's industrial activity took place in Eritrea in 1970. This included the only oil refinery, located at Assab. In 1970 Eritrea had 165 industrial establishments employing more than 14,000 people.[25] Because of the difficulty in obtaining updated information on industry in Eritrea, much of the following industrial survey dates back to 1957.[26] (The most plausible explanation for so little industrial information being available is that since 1962 the Ethiopian government has de-emphasized industrial development in Eritrea, focusing instead on the development of the Addis Ababa industrial area.)

The three largest industrial plants in Eritrea were the Baratello Cotton Company, Melotti Brewery, and INCODE, a meat-packing company. Baratello was the second largest cotton company in Ethiopia. Melotti was the country's largest brewery, as well as being one of the largest in eastern Africa. INCODE was Ethiopia's leading meat-packer.

The S.A.V.A. Glass Factory utilized the abundance of sand and limestone in Eritrea suitable for glass production. In factories at Agordat and Keren, S.A. Industriale De Rossi manufactured a large variety of buttons from the dum nuts found along the Rivers Barka and Gash. Fabbrica Chiodi turned out nails, while plywood was produced in another factory located in Decamare, 40 kilometers southeast of Asmara.

The African Match and Paper Factory produced matches by utilizing the euphorbia, a softwood tree that grows in the Anseba Valley, 35 kilometers from Asmara. Cartiera Eritrea also manufactured a variety of paper goods, especially for use in binding and packaging. Finally, worth mention again, was the Elabered Estate, now under Eritrean control. This is the largest agro-industrial estate in Eritrea, possibly in Ethiopia as well.

No comprehensive systematic survey of mineral deposits has yet been taken in Eritrea. Indications are, however, that at least modest amounts of mineral wealth do exist and can be commercially exploited. Mineral deposits in Eritrea include gold, copper, saline deposits, mica, zinc, nickel, asbestos, kaolin, manganese, magnesium, titanium, marble, feldspar, potash, and, possibly, oil offshore from Massawa.[27]

The only commercially exploited mineral on a large scale up to the 1970s was gold. Fair quantities of gold have been found both in the highlands and the Gash-Setit lowlands. The gold content of the veins in the lowlands has been about nine grams per ton, while it was between four and five grams on the plateau.[28] Between 1937 and 1940,* the gold production of Eritrea totaled 1,072 kilograms.[29] As with agriculture and livestock, political considerations proved to be pivotal in the case of Eritrea's gold-mining industry:

> By 1940 gold production had risen to an annual rate of 17,000 ounces and the industry showed promise of development. Then most of the mechanical equipment in the mines was requisitioned, dismantled, and removed by the British and American military authorities. . . . Replacements were difficult and often impossible to obtain.[30]

One of the most recent developments regarding mineral exploitation in Eritrea has been the discovery of copper at Debarwa. The Debarwa site became operative in 1973, and production by April 1975 was expected to reach 17,000 tons of 35 percent copper concentrates.[31] However, the ELF disrupted production in late 1974, and the site has since been left standing idle. Estimates for total production from the Debarwa site range up to 160,000 tons, and there are at least three other exploitable sites in the same area. While the Debarwa site would be important to a budding Eritrean state, the estimates of copper that can be exploited are quite small when compared with those found in Zambia or Zaire.

A Japanese firm had major responsibility for the copper-mining project at Debarwa. The ELF has claimed that the Japanese firm, Nippon Koei Company, has been in contact with the ELF regarding operations in the country should Eritrea become independent.[32] Nippon Koei has, naturally, denied any such reports. The ELF also claims to have had feelers from Italy's Agip Oil Company, another claim that has been denied. Mobil has drilled offshore from Massawa but has only admitted to finding traces of oil.

Iron-ore deposits of varying quality and quantity are found in several different parts of Eritrea. Deposits of iron ore estimated at 17 million tons lie near Ghedem, in the foothills behind Massawa.[33] Reserves in locations throughout Hamasien and Serai provinces in the highlands have been estimated to be between 15 and 200 million tons.[34]

Kaolin is found in several parts of Hamasien, in amounts sufficiently large for commercial utilization. Five thousand metric tons

---

*Between 1937 and 1939, gold was valued at $34 per fine ounce, using the U.S. equivalent of the London price.

of manganese ore were extracted in Ghedem, near Massawa, before the British defeated the Italians in 1941.[35] Eritrea also contains substantial deposits of potash in the northern Danakil. Much of the potash in the region lies on the Ethiopian side of the border, but Eritrea apparently does possess a commercially profitable amount.

The Red Sea has long provided Eritrea with a tremendous variety of marine wealth. Of particular importance here are the fishing and salt industries. Eritrea's 1,000-kilometer coastline should have excellent potential for development.

As was the case with extractive industry, the fishing industry suffered greatly "as a consequence of the British requisitioning of mechanical equipment which later proved difficult to replace."[36] The Red Sea possesses a rich variety of fish—such as snapper, rock cod, mullets, sardines, and shrimp, to name but a few. Much of the catch is absorbed by fish-meal industries in Massawa, which process it and export it to Europe. Fishing statistics for the Massawa area are illustrated in Table 3. The growth of the fishing industry was limited in the past by the fairly low level of technology and equipment in use, the small scale of most of the operations, and inadequate refrigeration facilities at the various ports.

The principal source of salt for both Eritrean use and export has been from the evaporation of seawater, particularly at Massawa, Assab, and Wachiro. The commercial production of salt began in Massawa, dominated by Le Saline Di Massawa. As far back as 1957, this company produced 100,000 tons of salt annually, 75 percent of which was exported.[37]

Closely related to the marine wealth that exists in Eritrea is another important source of income. The major ports of Massawa and Assab would go a long way in helping to make Eritrea economically viable. The overwhelming majority of imports and exports entering and leaving Eritrea and Ethiopia go via Massawa, Assab, or Djibouti (see Tables 4 and 5). In the past, the port of Djibouti played the most dominant role of the three as far as Ethiopia was concerned. However, the importance of Assab has been growing in recent years, owing to its direct roadway link to Addis Ababa. By 1963 Massawa handled 41.5 percent of Ethiopian imports and 33.4 percent of the exports; Assab handled 25 percent of the imports and 43.9 percent of the exports; and Djibouti had fallen off to handling 25.6 percent of the imports and 23 percent of the exports.[38] During the Ogaden campaign, the Western Somali Liberation Front cut the railway linking Addis Ababa with Djibouti, increasing Ethiopian reliance on Assab, the only port available to them. More recently, the Ethiopian government concluded an agreement with the German Democratic Republic for East German help in large-scale expansion of the port facilities at Assab.

Assab is very close to the straits of Bab el Mandeb, which link the Red Sea with the Indian Ocean. It is an artificial port consisting

TABLE 3

Massawa: Fishing Statistics for the Period 1965–72

	1965	1966	1967	1968	1969	1970	1971	1972
Fishing crafts registered in Massawa and Thio	319	414	368	376	390	421	436	450
Type of fish caught for foodstuffs (in tons)								
Anchovy	579.5	580.1	263.4	258.8	532.0	486.0	600.5	430.5
Sardine	465.5	908.6	696.5	38.1	51.0	599.0	502.7	108.4
Small shrimp	96.5	113.5	172.5	125.0	88.0	256.0	100.0	100.2
Fresh fish for local consumption	319.0	374.4	369.5	544.5	686.6	434.7	464.4	436.6
Fresh fish for export	836.0	827.2	756.8	510.0	613.0	522.8	548.0	530.1
Shark	7.0	71.0	17.0	150.0	27.5	73.7	106.0	79.5
Shell and other marine products collected (in tons)								
Mother of pearl	5.0	7.3				5.2	5.4	7.9
Trochus	147.0	130.4	199.3	228.0	159.0	333.0	368.7	466.5
Ornamental shell	2.0	0.5	1.4	2.0	1.0	1.1	2.0	1.4
Other marine products	5.0	9.0	0.4	—	1.0	1.7	1.0	1.7
Marine products exported (in tons)								
Fish meal	730.0	980.0	1,430.0	530.0	385.0	720.0	480.4	258.0
Dry fish	341.0	298.0	176.8	38.4	225.2	338.0	535.1	550.5
Refrigerated fresh fish	631.0	827.2	756.8	510.4	595.6	557.7	545.6	528.0
Dried shark	16.0	—	—	—	—	—	—	—
Shell products	129.0	171.0	192.2	160.1	278.8	372.7	249.0	330.3
Number of persons engaged in fishing industries	124	142	121	95	76	111	148	193
Fishing licenses granted	14	15	16	15	16	14	13	11

Source: Department of Fisheries Office, Massawa.

TABLE 4

Exports, 1953–63
(percent of value)

Commodity	1953	1954	1955	1956	1957	1958	1959	1960	1961	1962	1963
Coffee	59.0	62.0	55.6	53.0	64.0	58.0	47.5	52.0	49.6	53.3	49.5
Hides and skins	10.9	10.1	10.1	10.7	7.9	10.7	15.6	10.5	13.4	12.5	10.5
Oilseeds and the like	9.9	7.6	11.8	12.4	9.8	8.6	7.7	9.8	9.2	12.0	14.3
Cereals and pulses	9.7	7.2	5.9	5.4	5.4	4.8	9.9	12.4	9.5	8.5	8.3
Chat	1.1	3.2	4.1	4.6	2.4	3.6	4.9	4.5	5.7	5.3	5.6
Total	90.6	90.1	87.5	86.1	89.5	85.7	85.4	89.2	86.4	90.8	88.2

Source: Ethiopian Geographical Journal 3 (1965): 40.

TABLE 5

Imports, 1953–63
(percent of value)

Commodity	1953	1954	1955	1956	1957	1958	1959	1960	1961	1962	1963
Textile	43.0	36.3	33.0	35.7	36.1	26.7	25.0	28.8	28.5	30.0	24.4
Machinery and transportation equipment	21.4	26.3	32.2	29.2	30.3	38.7	30.6	34.0	28.6	33.2	40.1
Foodstuff	11.3	9.2	6.9	8.2	6.2	8.2	8.0	10.1	11.5	5.9	6.7
Fuel	5.5	4.9	5.3	5.8	6.3	5.4	6.1	5.4	5.3	6.4	5.3
Chemical products	3.8	4.1	4.1	4.7	5.5	5.7	5.3	6.3	5.1	7.3	7.2
Total	85.0	80.8	81.5	83.1	84.4	84.7	84.0	84.6	79.0	82.8	83.7

Source: Ethiopian Geographical Journal 3 (1965): 40.

mainly of two jetties, on which major reconstruction was last completed in 1962. Massawa, on the other hand, is a natural port and possesses one of the best natural harbors on the whole Red Sea coast. Massawa's port facilities are somewhat older than those of Assab, with maximum development having taken place in the 1930s when Italy was making preparations to conquer Ethiopia.

A brief note is in order regarding Eritrea's inland transportation network. Eritrea's cities and various production regions are connected by a series of good roads, primarily constructed by the Italians. The country possesses 776 kilometers of all-weather highways, 2,240 kilometers of secondary roads, and 306 kilometers of railway tracks.[39] Particularly in regard to the extractive industrial areas, good all-weather roads are in existence, and, in most cases, the rains are not extremely heavy where many of the already-known mineral deposits lie.

Based on the above economic survey of Eritrea, one could make a reasonable case for the existence of a potentially viable Eritrean state. That is not to say that such an entity would be wholly self-contained and not interdependent. It is to say that the basis for a viable economy exists but has, for the most part, been lying in a semidormant state.

The potential for growth in the Eritrean economy has existed for some time. There are diverse areas in which a motivated population can economically develop far more than has been attempted in the past. As illustrated throughout this economic survey, economic potential was never the central problem in developing a healthy economy; the untapped potential generally took a backseat to other, more political, priorities. When the political priorities themselves are redefined, as they are being now by the Eritreans themselves, the economy of the country will have a better than fair chance to be developed as it never was before. If what is taking place in contemporary Eritrea is in fact a revolution, then the "new Eritrean" that the revolution is creating will be the key to not only political but economic development as well.

PROSPECTS FOR THE FUTURE

Both the ELF and EPLF plan on utilizing Eritrea's land and resources in a fundamentally more cooperative mode of production than existed in the country previously. Their respective ideas are voiced not only in their organizational programs but are being illustrated daily in the economic programming taking place throughout Eritrea. To what extent the economy will develop along these more socialist lines will depend on the resources themselves as well as solid organizational implementation of appropriate policies.

The ELF believes that because much of the industrial infrastructure of Eritrea has been destroyed or dismantled by the Ethiopians, an independent Eritrea would initially focus on industrializing agricultural production.[40] In believing that Eritrea cannot simply skip "the stage of non-capitalist development," the ELF, in its Political Programme, outlines a model where state ownership predominates and yet leaves room for smaller private enterprises as well.[41] In the same tract, the ELF states that all Eritreans will gain from a change in the relations of production. While any heavy, or major, industries would be nationalized, individual, small lighter industry would be encouraged. The government would also be in control of all mineral wealth and commerce, and would further democratize and organize landownership "for the realization of social justice and greater productivity." In giving land to landless peasants, the ELF envisions some form of collective landownership in the not-so-distant future.* The ELF is initially interested in building "a prosperous agricultural community" without the domination of foreign influence.[42]

The EPLF's focus is on building a self-reliant and planned national economy (Appendix B, section 2). As noted in previous chapters, the EPLF envisions an Eritrean state as playing a broader, more all-encompassing role than does the ELF. This applies to the economic sector no less than in other areas. The EPLF is aware of the necessity in maintaining a proper balance between agriculture and industry in the context of the planned economy. The organization's ideas for implementation of the socialist economy are enumerated clearly in its National Democratic Programme.[43]

Important elements of EPLF agricultural programming revolve around the creation of large nationalized farms utilizing modern agricultural techniques and equipment. Abolition of traditional land tenure systems and encouragement of cooperative farming is at the top of the EPLF's priorities. More will be said about land tenure, traditional and prospective, below.

The EPLF calls for the nationalization of all major industries in the country in addition to the ports, mines, transportation, and communication. It would permit Eritreans to own "small factories and workshops compatible with national development and the system of administration."[44] The EPLF also looks toward the development of heavy industry in promoting light industry, advancing agriculture, and combating industrial dependence.[45]

---

*There is still a large landless class in Eritrea, particularly in areas under ELF hegemony. Even in EPLF areas, the redistribution process can be a slow one, depending upon the receptiveness of the local populace to EPLF political education programs.

The EPLF envisions the state nationalizing finance, trade, and urban housing. Nationalization of banks and insurance companies, essential communications and transportation utilized in trade, and all urban land is clearly spelled out by the organization. It seems clear that when compared with the ELF's economic plans, the EPLF's program is broader in scope and that implementation of an overtly socialist system might become a reality in a relatively short period of time.

The economic programs introduced by the two organizations in their respective liberated areas would seem to indicate a real commitment to the programs outlined above. Many of the social programs discussed in the previous chapter have gone a long way in promoting the restructuring of Eritrean society. Of course, at this point in the revolutionary process the scope and effect of any such program are necessarily limited. Yet, there are indications that feasible aspects of the programs are being implemented.

In its zones, the ELF has attempted to facilitate numerous economic programs. Agricultural cadres are assigned to administrative units in the country to introduce better methods of cultivation and stock breeding. Cooperative unions are formed in villages and collective work is encouraged for higher production of foodstuffs. The Economic Bureau of the ELF runs several large plantations, orchards, and vast irrigated farms taken from the Ethiopians. One of the ELF's largest projects is the cultivation of 1,700 hectares of sorghum in Ali Gidder, on what used to be the largest cotton plantation (Italian-owned) in the Horn of Africa. Workers are being paid twice the wage they were receiving for work on the cotton plantation and producing a bumper crop, which will greatly aid the ELF drive for self-sufficiency in food production.[46]

Small-scale and cottage industries are also being put into operation in ELF-liberated areas. Plants established include iron and wood workshops, sweater and textile factories, edible oil, and flour mills. Cottage industries such as basketry, pottery, and other handicraft centers are also being encouraged. Finally, an infrastructure of roads and small bridges is being built by the ELF and the people, connecting often inaccessible parts of the country to regional centers.

In all ELF-occupied towns, the price of commodities is under strict control. Basic goods are supplied by the Trade and Commerce Department of the ELF and sold at cost.[47] Individual merchants are therefore forced to lower their prices to remain competitive with the ELF shops. In Tessenei, approximately 75 percent of the houses in town were previously owned by foreigners (mainly Italians) who have since left the country. All houses in the town were put under ELF control, while it occupied the town. The front, in conjunction with a committee of local residents, resettled refugees who arrived in Tessenei from other parts of the country in these houses.

For the EPLF, self-reliance is the overriding concern in the establishment of any economic program. The foundations of a new Eritrea can be evaluated by looking at the broad array of the EPLF's programming.

The EPLF focuses on changing the entire structure of Eritrean society. When it controlled a number of towns and small cities in the country, the EPLF was very concerned with the standard of living in cities. Not only did the EPLF raise workers' wages but also established a policy of price controls for goods circulating in the cities. In Keren, for instance, the EPLF set a minimal profit range (10 percent) for the city merchants and, at the same time, helped establish cooperative stores where the price of food is about 30 percent less than in private shops.[48] In most areas, the EPLF meets little objection from farmers (producers), as the EPLF political cadres have encouraged a spirit of cooperation through political education and propaganda. In the cities and towns, the EPLF also ran orphanages, maternity homes, and family and child care centers in addition to attempting to help resettle those refugees who wanted to return to their homes.

In the field of transportation, the EPLF has had notable success. Members of the army have, with very little in the way of materials, constructed a 1,500-kilometer network of roadway that has been named the "Liberation Road":

> Traversing a difficult terrain of steep mountain sides,
> deep valleys and extensive plains, the Liberation Road
> connects all the liberated areas, from the Sudanese border
> through the heart of the country to the Ethiopian border.
> It alleviates the problems of transportation, creates effi-
> cient communication among the administrative zones, and
> greatly accelerates the revolutionary work.[49]

The EPLF has also deployed a chain of buses and trucks captured from the Ethiopians to implement a kind of public transportation system throughout much of the area under its control.

The EPLF has been attempting to change the relations of production in the agricultural arena via the context of the Association of Eritrean Peasants. For the EPLF, the raising of political consciousness must accompany changes relating to production for the overall process to be truly meaningful. Land reform programs are carried out by the EPLF-sponsored peasant organization in conjunction with the local population:

> Village branches of the Peasant Association play decisive
> roles in crushing the resistance of the landlords and rich

peasants. To implement the land reform resolution a people's revolutionary committee is elected and again the Peasant Association struggles to ensure that the committee is dominated by landless and poor members of the Association. The people's revolutionary committee fulfills its task of making an equitable distribution of land.[50]

The EPLF then begins to help the peasants adopt scientific farming methods, set up cooperatives, and generally raise the level of production in the areas under EPLF control. In some of these areas, the peasants have even "begun pooling their land and implements for collective work."[51]

Toward the development of a planned national economy, the EPLF has addressed itself to a series of programs dealing with livestock and agriculture. During 1976 the organization vaccinated nearly 450,000 head of livestock against a variety of diseases.[52] In 1975 the EPLF was able to harvest 25 percent of its food requirements; in 1976 that figure jumped to 50 percent.[53] The remainder of the EPLF's food needs came from donations and purchases from local farmers. Like the ELF, the EPLF has taken over the operation of a number of large plantations previously owned by foreigners. The immense fruit and vegetable plantation at Elabered is now producing tremendous dividends for the EPLF, rather than for the Ethiopians.

Finally, the EPLF has set up a number of small-scale factories throughout Eritrea. These factories attempt to make the EPLF self-sufficient in various and sundry areas: manufacture of small arms and spare parts; electronic repairs; repairs such as radios, watches, and mechanical tools; iron welding; carpentry; manufacture of household utensils; and the tanning and tailoring of hides.[54]

The question arises, in light of the above description of economic resources and prospective and current programs, as to how dependent an Eritrean state would be on foreign aid. This is a matter of speculation, and it is very difficult to suggest an accurate answer here. The liberation movements themselves seem adamant that any future aid (as has been with past assistance) will not be accepted if conditions are attached. Ahmed Nasser, chairman of the ELF's Revolutionary Council, has stated that, "We have never accepted any aid that had conditions attached and that we never will accept such aid."[55] The questions of foreign aid and foreign investment will no doubt be better defined by the political realities of any new Eritrean state. As for foreign investment, an EPLF politburo member, Sebhat Efrem, believes that Eritreans will need to judge from experience whether the country would permit such investments, adding that,

We have the policy of self-reliance and may produce all
we need ourselves. But if we find we need something that
we cannot escape, we may have to do it.[56]

ALTERNATIVES FOR DEVELOPMENT

In a recent book that explores the prospects for Third World
development, Felix Greene states that for underdeveloped countries
to develop industries that might compete with those in the advanced
countries is often self-defeating. He, along with other dependencia
theorists, such as Carlos Fuentes and Pierre Jalee, believes that

the main task for an underdeveloped country wanting to develop an independent economy is not to compete with the
advanced capitalist countries but to supply the needs of
their home population through the development of their own
resources.[57]

This concept is especially relevant in the case of Eritrea. The liberation movement, particularly the EPLF, has addressed itself to precisely this kind of ideology through the implementation of self-reliance
in conducting the revolution.

Greene further believes that when a country has secured real
independence from foreign economic control and has been able to meet
the needs of its own people by establishing local industries to produce
goods for local use, "then, and then only, is the time ripe to develop
an export trade in manufactured goods."[58] The road to this sort of
economic independence is full of potential hazards, prompting the
elaboration of three necessary steps to avoid the worst pitfalls.
Greene believes that:

1) No underdeveloped country should under any circumstances permit foreign corporations to own and operate
   enterprises within its borders.
2) Where enterprises owned by foreign corporations already exist they should be nationalized.
3) The only acceptable assistance from abroad is in the
   form of technical help and loans (never investments)
   without strings and which vest ownership of new enterprises developed with these loans wholly in the hands
   of the receiving country.[59]

Nationalization and state ownership of major industries are
clearly on the Eritreans' economic agenda. Greene's third dictum,

that regarding conditions of loans and technical assistance, is probably wise advice in the long run, although it might make early economic programming and growth appear slack. Yet in terms of the self-reliance so regularly preached by the EPLF, the care taken in accepting various forms of aid should pay dividends for the Eritrean people, as they are the ones who will be developing some sort of stake in whatever is accomplished.

The Eritrean movements have already made a good start on the road to self-reliance. Self-reliance as an ideology pervades EPLF literature and practice. In 1977 the ELF harvested 6,000 tons of grain, not far short of their 7,200-ton target that would ensure self-sufficiency in grain for the organization's estimated 12,000 fighters.[60]

One of the most promising elements in the development of a viable Eritrean economy is the prospect for transforming one of the traditional landholding systems, the desa or communal system, into a genuinely democratic cooperative or collective land system. Of the three landholding systems in Eritrea, the tselmi, risti, and desa, the latter predominates in most highland areas. (In the lowlands, where much of the population lived as nomads, previous colonial governments had, until recently, been the principal landowners, controlling some 70 percent of the land.)[61]

The desa system is basically communal, with ownership in the hands of the village and the redistribution of land every three to seven years among the various households. However, the traditional system has often been abused by feudal lords and richer peasants who own better farming implements and, with the political power they possess, have absolute control of the periodic redistribution of the land in which not only do they take more than the average share but also the most fertile pieces of land.[62] The challenge, as the ELF views it, is to make the traditional desa system not only democratic but scientific as well.[63] In other words, the communal basis for agricultural production already exists and, although abused in the past, can serve as an initial basis for cooperative or even collective farming. This would, in theory, be similar to Julius Nyerere's concept of ujamaa in Tanzania. With communalism already in existence as a mode of production, the process of transforming farming to a truly cooperative or collective endeavor would appear to be that much more realistic.

The political consciousness of the peasant population has been undergoing a great transformation, especially since the mass organizing campaign of the EPLF began in earnest in 1975. Agitation and propaganda among the peasants is the staple diet provided the guerrilla forces. Some Eritreans would even maintain that the peasants' consciousness is being raised even more quickly than that of the more urbanized citizenry, as the peasants are in constant contact with the liberation movements. One of the greatest challenges to any Eritrean government would surely be the transformation of previously nomadic people into settled agriculturalists.* Both fronts recognize the necessity of such action and can be expected to try a series of agricultural experiments for the nomads, who, for the most part, have seen their animals destroyed by the heavy fighting and bombing of the past decade.

Another glaring contradiction facing the partisans is the disparity between town and countryside in Eritrea. The thrust of the revolution, at least in the 1970s, has been from the center outward. Both the ELF and EPLF are aware that the gaps between the cities and countryside need to be narrowed. The cities cannot be the only centers for economic or political development. More scientific agricultural methods and development of agro-industries are two good starts in beginning to close the city-country gap. Time will be a crucial factor in the development of such schemes.

Ultimately, all of the above speculation depends heavily on future political and military events in the Eritrean arena. The results of the 1978 Ethiopian counteroffensive certainly postpone all but the narrowest programs for ambitious economic development. Even more important, as repeatedly noted throughout this book, is the course of Eritrean politics: the cooperation or confrontation between the EPLF and the ELF and the question of Osman Saleh Sabbe. The Eritrean revolution is entering another crucial juncture with the long-term military outcome likely to depend on Eritrean cohesion. The other important variable, of course, is the massive amount of assistance that the Ethiopians have reaped from their Soviet and Cuban collaborators. It is with this question in mind that we now turn to the wider ramifications of the revolution in Eritrea.

NOTES

1. Africa, no. 79 (March 1978), p. 15.
2. Ibid., p. 25.
3. Africa Confidential 19 (July 7, 1978): 3.
4. Sudanow 4 (February 1979): 17.
5. New African, no. 126 (February 1978), p. 25.
6. Africa Research Bulletin, September 15, 1977, p. 4531.
7. Ibid.

*The Eritrean population is roughly 20 percent urban and 80 percent rural, with probably no more than 25 percent of the total population classified as nomadic.

8. Eritrean Peoples Liberation Front, Vanguard 2 (February-March 1977): 25.

9. Agence France-Presse, Africa, no. 2537 (December 1, 1978), p. 20.

10. David Lamb, "Critical Moment at Hand in Ethiopia's Eritrea War," Los Angeles Times, May 29, 1978, p. 7. For further discussion of this issue, see Eritreans for Liberation in North America, Eritrea in Struggle, vol. 3 (September-November 1978).

11. Tom J. Farer, War Clouds on the Horn of Africa (Washington, D.C.: Carnegie Endowment for International Peace, 1976), p. 136.

12. Patrick Gilkes, "Eritrea Could Stand Alone," African Development 9 (April 1975): 18.

13. Hailu W. Emmanuel, "Major Ports of Ethiopia: Aseb, Jibuti, Mesewa," Ethiopian Geographical Journal 3 (1965): 41.

14. Gerard Chaliand, "The Horn of Africa's Dilemma," Foreign Policy 30 (Spring 1978): 119.

15. G. K. N. Trevaskis, Eritrea: A Colony in Transition (London: Oxford University Press, 1960), p. 39.

16. Ibid., p. 40.

17. Ibid.

18. Ibid.

19. Hailu W. Emmanuel, "Concession Agriculture in Eritrea," Ethiopian Geographical Journal 2 (1964): 35.

20. Addis Ababa Chamber of Commerce, Agriculture, Industry and Commerce in Ethiopia and Eritrea (Addis Ababa, 1957), p. 35.

21. Eritrea Chamber of Commerce, "Agriculture in Eritrea," Trade and Development Bulletin 2 (March-April 1973): 17.

22. Trevaskis, op. cit., p. 39.

23. Eritrea Chamber of Commerce, op. cit., p. 11.

24. Ibid.

25. Gilkes, op. cit.

26. Addis Ababa Chamber of Commerce, op. cit., pp. 59-69.

27. Trevaskis, op. cit., p. 41.

28. Ibid.

29. Ethiopian Chamber of Commerce, Guide Book of Ethiopia (Addis Ababa, 1954), p. 188.

30. Trevaskis, op. cit.

31. Gilkes, op. cit.

32. Bernd Debusmann, "Eritrean Rebels Set Sights on Big Business," Los Angeles Times, October 7, 1977, pt. 1-B, p. 4.

33. Trevaskis, op. cit.

34. Ethiopian Chamber of Commerce, op. cit., p. 189.

35. Mesfin Woldemariam, An Introductory Geography of Ethiopia (Addis Ababa: Mesfin, 1972), p. 131.

36. Trevaskis, op. cit.

37. Addis Ababa Chamber of Commerce, op. cit., p. 60.

38. Emmanuel, op. cit.

39. Eritrean Liberation Front, The Eritrean Revolution: Sixteen Years of Armed Struggle (Beirut: ELF Foreign Information Center, 1977), p. 27.

40. Interview with Ahmad Muhammed Sayid, ELF Information Bureau, Khartoum, Sudan, December 1977.

41. Eritrean Liberation Front, Political Programme (Beirut: ELF Foreign Information Center, May 28, 1975), pp. 33-34.

42. Ibid.

43. Eritrean Peoples Liberation Front, National Democratic Programme of the Eritrean Peoples Liberation Front (n.p., January 31, 1977).

44. Ibid., pp. 25-26.

45. Ibid., p. 26.

46. Fulvio Grimaldi, "The New Eritrea," Sudanow 2 (December 1977): 24.

47. Eritrean Liberation Front, Eritrean Newsletter 20 (February 1, 1978): 6.

48. Eritreans for Liberation in North America, Eritrea in Struggle 2 (February 1978): 5.

49. Eritreans for Liberation in North America, Liberation 6 (July-August 1977): 14.

50. Eritreans for Liberation in North America, Eritrea in Struggle 11 (November 1977): 3.

51. Ibid., p. 7.

52. Eritreans for Liberation in North America, Liberation 6 (July-August 1977): 12.

53. Ibid.

54. Interview with an EPLF cadre, Khartoum, Sudan, December 1977.

55. New African, no. 124 (December 1977), p. 1184.

56. Weekly Review (Nairobi) 154 (December 19, 1977): 15.

57. Felix Greene, The Enemy (New York: Vintage Books, 1971), p. 187.

58. Ibid., pp. 187-88.

59. Ibid., pp. 188-89.

60. Debusmann, op. cit., p. 5.

61. Eritreans for Liberation in North America, Eritrea in Struggle 2 (November 1977): 2.

62. Ibid.

63. Interview with Ahmad Muhammed Sayid, op. cit.

6
WIDER RAMIFICATIONS OF
THE ERITREAN REVOLUTION

Within the Horn of Africa conflicts of many kinds are taking place, and these cannot be mentally grasped or theo-
retically explained by reference to any single set of actors
or factors. At a very early stage in the analysis, it be-
comes pointless to claim that the conflicts are solely or
even primarily caused by religion, or by great power involvement, or that they primarily involve conflict between
supranational, or national, or sub-national contestants.
The conflict cluster as a whole makes sense only in terms
of all of these and the ways in which they relate to one another.

Christopher Clapham

Although Christopher Clapham penned these words in 1972 in
reference to a more "contained" situation in the Horn of Africa, his
argument takes on much greater meaning today.[1] The Eritrean revolution, in a geopolitical sense, raises many more questions than it
answers. This concluding chapter briefly sketches the struggle in
the context of the Horn of Africa, the African continent, the Middle
East, and the superpower rivalries.

Numerous questions related to the Eritrean revolution are
worthy of exploration. The issue of African territorial sovereignty
and the Organization of African Unity (OAU) Charter are challenged
head-on by the Eritrean movement. The future of the Ethiopian polity
is challenged to no less a degree. The ultimate fate of the states of
Somalia and Djibouti could well be tied into the outcome in Eritrea.

Eritrea's geopolitical position has served as an attraction to
both the USSR and the United States. Because of its location, Eritrea
has sometimes been viewed as a virtual extension of the Middle East
conflict. It is, after all, just across the Red Sea from Saudi Arabia,

the world's largest oil exporter. The Red Sea itself is considered crucial as a sea-lane and as the back door to the Middle East conflict area. The lines of communication and transportation through the Red Sea and Indian Ocean are considered vital to the oil route from the Persian Gulf to the ports of Western Europe. These and other issues are examined in detail below.

AFRICAN TERRITORIAL SOVEREIGNTY

When the OAU was formed in 1963, one of the serious questions facing this body was whether the African national entities composed of diverse ethnic groups were to be permitted to disintegrate after the attainment of independence. The OAU solution to this problem was spelled out in its charter, Article III, paragraph 3, which declares that member states affirm "respect for the sovereignty and territorial integrity of each State and for its inalienable right to independent existence."

The question of colonial boundaries has been of the utmost importance in the Horn of Africa. The Ethio-Somalian border, involved in Somalia's abortive Ogaden campaign of 1977/78, has been a major point of contention between the two countries since before the inception of the OAU Charter. The OAU remained neutral, but with a pro-Ethiopia bent, during the Ogaden war because of the organization's desire not to divide Africa and the recognition of colonial borders in the OAU Charter. The Eritrean question has presented other challenges to the organization. The situation is unique because Eritrea was a self-contained colonial unit

> and therefore can itself rely on the principle of the sanctity of colonial boundaries which is the holy writ in the Third World, above all in Africa.[2]

The irony for Eritreans is that the OAU has repeatedly refused to deal with the question of Eritrean sovereignty, precisely because the OAU does not want to dispute colonial boundaries. For the Eritrean question to even appear on an OAU conference agenda, an OAU member-country must request it as a topic for discussion. So far, this has not occurred, although the Eritreans themselves attempted to bring up the issue at the OAU meeting in Khartoum, Sudan, in July 1978, with no success.

The OAU and its constituent members, in refusing to confront the Eritrean issue, are worried that an independent Eritrea might create a dangerous precedent by encouraging latent secessionist movements across the continent. Yet, as Tom Farer points out, we know very little about the "teaching effects" of particular moments in the stream of history. The chain of assumptions leading from an Eritrean victory . . . to secessionist struggles elsewhere on the continent is long, complicated, and weak. Will many potential dissidents even be aware of what happened in Ethiopia? If aware, will they appreciate the unique characteristics of the Eritrean case which undoubtedly distinguish it from their own?[3]

Farer goes on to argue that an Eritrean victory might even frighten African governing elites into

a more generous, tension-reducing response to the demands of geographically peripheral or ethnically distinct groups for a fairer share of collective goods.[4]

The bad-precedent or "domino" argument is highly conjectural on the part of various regimes throughout Africa. Should insurgent movements occur in other countries, the dissidents hardly need to look toward Eritrea for an example or an excuse. Yet, until the Eritrean issue is resolved, it will continue to remain a unique thorn in the side of the OAU.

ETHIOPIA: A FRAGMENTED FUTURE?

Despite their Soviet- and Cuban-aided victory in the Ogaden war in March 1978, the Ethiopian regime still faces a number of very serious internal problems. The $1 billion worth of military equipment provided by the Soviet Union did not come in the form of aid: it must be paid for in full. Because the USSR has insisted on at least partial cash payment, Ethiopia's foreign reserves have more than halved since their high point of Eth$620 million* in late 1976.[5] The remainder of the military debt is being settled in a series of barter deals. By mid-1978, as much as one-half of Ethiopia's exported coffee was going to Eastern Europe—its value calculated at 15 percent below the world market rate.[6] Swarms of locusts were once again invading the Horn area and could devastate crops in a number of provinces if not quickly eradicated. Parts of Wollo and Tigre provinces are once again being affected by drought. The crops that have grown in Wollo have been infected with a fungus that, when consumed, causes gangrene.

---

*The official exchange rate is Eth$2.07 to U.S.$1.00.

The Dergue, furthermore, has alienated a number of political factions within Ethiopia and, at one point in mid-1977, was facing rebellions in 9 of its 13 provinces in addition to the war with Eritrea. The future of the Dergue is open and can only be dealt with in the most superficial terms here. It is, however, necessary to look at the challenge presented to the Ethiopian regime by the Eritrean revolution in terms of the new opposition groups facing the Ethiopian state.

Contrary to the Eritreans, the opposition movements dealt with here are not interested in independence but, rather, social change within some sort of Ethiopian framework. Within this context the Ethiopian People's Revolutionary Party (EPRP) and the Tigre People's Liberation Front (TPLF) exercise their options inside Ethiopia. It is also in this context that the Eritrean movement has been, and can continue to be, of valuable assistance to the opposition in Ethiopia and a further obstacle to the Dergue.

The EPRP is an underground Marxist-oriented movement that was founded in 1972. Its main strength has been among Ethiopian students, teachers, and some labor unions. The EPRP publishes agitational pamphlets and considers the Dergue a reactionary military clique. The group advocates an immediate return to civilian rule under a proletarian party. Most of the EPRP activities in and around Addis Ababa have centered on assassination of Dergue members and sympathizers.

The EPRP and the Eritrian Peoples Liberation Front (EPLF) have, on a fairly regular basis, maintained a tactical alliance with one another. The two groups issued a joint statement on March 3, 1976, pledging cooperation in their respective struggles against the Dergue. In the joint statement, the EPRP lent unconditional support to the Eritreans' struggle for independence,[7] thus being the only Ethiopian group to have taken such a position at that time. In return, the EPLF gave support to the EPRP in their attempt to implement a national democratic revolution in Ethiopia. The two parties also agreed to cooperate militarily and materially; the EPLF has provided military training as well as political assistance to the EPRP.

The EPRP, however, suffered a number of serious setbacks during the first half of 1978. Splits and countersplits were caused by arguments over military and political strategies. One faction joined the Dergue and exposed clandestine members of the EPRP in Addis Ababa, thus bringing about the very bloody but successful government campaign against the party in February.[8]

It has often been noted that it is difficult to assess the EPRP's overall strength. Support among the peasantry has never been great. However, the

EPRP's real shortcoming is its lack of support inside the army. EPRP slogans have occasionally been adopted by

> units of the 2nd Division in Asmara . . . but they appear
> to have been inspired more by dissatisfaction with Mengistu
> than by a deeper belief in the virtues of EPRP itself. The
> energies of the movement may accelerate the disintegration
> of the Dergue . . . [but] EPRP is unlikely ever to replace
> it.[9]

The TPLF was in a substantially stronger position by mid-
1978 than the EPRP. It operates only in Tigre Province, immedia-
ately south of Eritrea on Ethiopia's northern border. The TPLF had
attained a degree of success in its struggle for self-determination
by conducting classical guerrilla warfare in the rural areas, weakening government positions, and finally, attempting to isolate the towns.
TPLF's 2,000 guerrillas have posed an increasingly effective challenge to the Dergue since the formation of the group in 1975.

Tigre, the present-day location of the city of Axum, shares a
common language with highland Eritrea (Tigrinya), a similar traditional culture, and a common resentment of Amhara domination over
the centuries. The TPLF is modeled in many political, as well as
military, ways after the EPLF. A number of TPLF's fighters went
to the EPLF for training, and other Tigreans already fighting for the
EPLF joined them. The TPLF has engaged in some joint military
operations with both the EPLF and the Eritrean Liberation Front
(ELF), particularly during the "peasant march" of May 1976 and,
more recently, to counter the long-awaited Ethiopian invasion of
Eritrea, which was in part launched from Tigre.

Much to the delight of the Dergue, the TPLF has been in open
warfare with two other antigovernment groups that conduct some of
their operations in Tigre. The Ethiopian People's Revolutionary
Army (the armed wing of the EPRP) and the Ethiopian Democratic
Union (EDU) had, in the first half of 1978, suffered decisive defeats
at the hands of the TPLF, leaving the TPLF in its strongest position
in Tigre since its inception.

Three other significant movements (not counting the ethnic
Somalis) are also posing challenges to the Dergue at present. Two
have had no real direct bearing on the Eritrean struggle: the Oromo
Liberation Front, in the south and southeastern regions of Ethiopia,
and the Afar Liberation Front in the east, in the area adjacent to
Djibouti. The third, the pro-Western EDU, under the leadership of
the former governor of Tigre, Ras Mengesha Seyoum, has been in a
pattern of rapid decline since mid-1977. The royalist EDU has operated primarily in Tigre and Begemdir provinces and, with ELF help
in early 1977, captured the strategic town of Humera, on the Ethio-
pian(Begemdir)-Eritrean border. The Dergue retook Humera in
June 1977, and the EDU was expelled from Tigre by TPLF forces in

January 1978. Consequently, the EDU has undergone a fragmentation process, and what forces remain are divided between the old, monarchist EDU and the recently formed Ethiopian People's Democratic Revolutionary party.[10]

It is evident from the above discussion that the Dergue is faced with a number of serious challenges to its control of a substantial portion of territory. The Eritrean challenge is considered the most serious to the regime, yet there is a systematic pattern of serious opposition throughout Ethiopia itself. Much of this pattern can be attributed to the fact that in spite of the heavy-handed efforts (or maybe in part because of them) of Menelik and Haile Selassie to consolidate power in a centralized government, centralization never effectively took hold in much of Ethiopia. Regional, decentralized power zones were the basis for Ethiopian politics for centuries.[11] What strong leaders like Menelik and Haile Selassie could not effect in their lifetimes is going to be difficult for the Mengistu regime to accomplish in a relatively short period of time. While the Dergue's Eritrean policy has been an essentially more intensified continuation of the emperor's approach, their internal policies have brought to the fore a number of very serious historical problems.

THE HORN OF AFRICA

The war between Ethiopia and Somalia in the Ogaden, which ended in defeat for Somalia in March 1978, had important implications for the success of the Eritrean independence struggle. Without going into a very detailed explanation of the Ethio-Somalian issue, we can still evaluate the effect of the Ogaden campaign on Eritrea. In brief, the ethnic Somalis living in Ethiopia's Ogaden region—represented by the Western Somali Liberation Front (WSLF), in conjunction with the Somalian Army—attempted to make good the long-standing claim to the Ogaden as part and parcel of the Somalian nation. Somalian occupation of parts of the Ogaden in July 1977 led to an eventual, if brief, occupation of nearly one-third of Ethiopia's territory.

It took the combined efforts of Soviet and Cuban forces backing a freshly equipped Ethiopian Army and militia to drive the regular Somalian forces and much of the WSLF from the Ogaden in March 1978. The Soviet support of Mengistu's regime has led to a drastic realignment of forces in the Horn of Africa. The major Somalian defeat at Jijiga has been described as

> a textbook-perfect assault that employed massive airlifts
> and bombing raids along with pinpoint barrages of artillery
> to clear the way for columns of tanks backed by battalions
> of Cuban troops in armored personnel carriers.[12]

Only a relatively small part of the Somalian Army is thought to have escaped intact from Jijiga.

The Somalian invasion of the Ogaden prompted massive Soviet and Cuban support in the form of both men and matériel. It is likely that much of the Soviet and Cuban buildup would not have taken place had the Somalis not attempted to conquer the Ogaden during this period of time. Much of the new Soviet weaponry has, however, been turned against the Eritreans. Although the Ogaden campaign did create a temporary Ethiopian diversion away from Eritrea, allowing the liberation fronts to consolidate some important gains, the broader effect of the massive foreign assistance has meant an increased number of Eritrean casualties, both military and civilian.

It appeared to many casual observers that Somalian separation was well crushed at Jijiga. Nothing could be further from the truth: not only is the WSLF operating in rural areas of the Ogaden but the Mogadishu government has not given up its dream of reuniting all Somalis under a single flag.[13] The ethnic Somalian problem in the Ogaden will continue to plague this as well as future Ethiopian governments:

> The guerrilla war drags on, as it has for 400 years. The Ethiopians are again garrisoned in the towns. The Somali guerrillas . . . control the countryside and have forced Ethiopia to resupply some towns by air.[14]

For both the Somalis and Ethiopians, the Ogaden campaign of 1977/78 may have turned out to be another in a series of battles in a long, drawn-out war.

Djibouti also found the Ogaden campaign to be costly. By early 1978, port activity had decreased by more than one-third because the Addis Ababa-Djibouti railway had stopped operating.[15] The port and the railway are the small ex-French colony's only sources of income. The questions of viability and control in Djibouti are crucial for Ethiopia, especially in light of the uncertainty surrounding control of the Eritrean ports of Massawa and Assab.

The issue of Djibouti's viability poses some interesting questions about future cooperation in the Horn of Africa. A number of observers have proposed some form of confederal arrangement for the entire Horn area, which might go so far as incorporating an Eritrean entity as well. Both the Soviet Union and Cuba's Fidel Castro have advocated a federated solution to the Horn's many problems.[16]

Tom Farer has presented a good discussion of this concept in his book, War Clouds on the Horn of Africa.[17] While he outlined some interesting prospects for development of resources through mutual cooperation, Farer was nevertheless pessimistic about the future of accommodation in the area. Since the publication of Farer's book in 1976, the Ogaden campaign has come and gone, Djibouti has gained a very tenuous independence, and the Eritrean liberation struggle has accelerated immensely, to say nothing of the Dergue's response and the international realignment on the Horn. None of these events would tend to encourage more optimism about confederal arrangements in the near future.

In the final analysis, the question of resurgent nationalism itself may postpone any sort of federal arrangement far beyond the foreseeable future. None of the Eritreans interviewed in the course of researching this book seemed to want to confront such an issue at this particular point in time. In the attempt to address themselves to the very pressing problems of their respective countries, the people of the Horn area may be overlooking the optimum solution to their own problems as well as those of their neighbors.

THE UNITED STATES—WHAT ROLE NOW?

Before evaluating the contemporary role of the U.S. government in the Ethio-Eritrean conflict, it is necessary to present a brief overview of the past U.S. role in Ethiopia vis-à-vis Eritrea. During the years of the current struggle, until 1977, the United States has played a significant role in the conflict. Through its extensive aid program over a 24-year period, the United States inevitably became involved in the structure and activities of numerous Ethiopian institutions, particularly those of the Ethiopian Army.

The U.S. interests in the Horn area have been numerous and varied over the years. Most of these have been strategic in nature. High on the list, until very recently, was "the unhampered use of Kagnew Station," in the words of one former U.S. ambassador to Ethiopia. [18] This communications facility was "strategically vital" to the United States for many years, being the only such military installation in Africa. [19] A second strategic interest is in the maritime rights of passage through the Red Sea, including the Suez Canal in the north and the Bab el Mandeb to the south. The free flow of traffic in the Red Sea is an essential component in maintaining Western Europe's industrial lifeline; that is, its uninterrupted supply of Middle Eastern oil. Furthermore, the United States is concerned about the ongoing Arab-Israeli hostilities; both Kagnew Station and the Red Sea are (or were) connected to the Middle East conflict.

Although the United States played no direct role in liberating Eritrea from Italian occupation, it did move into Eritrea shortly after the successful British campaign. The U.S. support of the Allied cause was translated into military projects "provided at first, by the firm of Johnson Drake & Piper, Inc., working under the control of American military and civil aviation authorities."[20] Upon U.S. entry into the war, as noted previously, the U.S. Army began using Eritrea as a supply depot and its ports as passageways for U.S. ships. The United States constructed an aircraft assembly plant at the airport of Gura and established a naval base at Massawa, as well as modernized the commercial harbor there. It converted workshops in Asmara into a repair base and an Italian military store at Ghinda into a major ammunition depot for the British Navy.[21]

During this same period, the United States began to make use of the British Radio Marina communications facilities in Asmara. Shortly after Averell Harriman's visit to Eritrea in 1942—where he met, among others, Ethiopian officials—the possibility of a U.S. communications center at Asmara came closer to being a reality.[22] However, for the duration of British Military Administration in Eritrea, there was little the United States could do to secure its own base in Eritrea. Yet the desire for a strategically located communications base in Asmara would help to guide U.S. actions in the subsequent "disposal" of Eritrea.

As one of the Four Powers, the United States was involved in the three-year unsuccessful attempt to determine Eritrea's future. The Four Powers shifted their respective positions on Eritrea's fate according to whatever seemed politically advantageous at a given point in time. The United States, at different points, supported Eritrean independence after a collective trusteeship, opted for an Italian trusteeship, and favored dividing Eritrea, with a large portion going to Ethiopia.

Once the issue of Eritrea's fate was referred to the UN General Assembly, the United States was able to be of considerable assistance to Ethiopia in devising the formula that was subsequently adopted in Resolution 390A (V), in December of 1950. The two U.S. lawyers advising the United States and Ethiopia in the five-member commission (United States, United Kingdom, Mexico, Brazil, and Ethiopia) reached agreement on the legal complexities involved, and U.S. constitutional concepts entered directly into the language of the UN resolution.[23]

Kagnew Station and the arms-assistance agreements between the United States and Ethiopia grew out of the Eritrean discussions at the United Nations. The United States had indicated to the Ethiopian government in advance of the December 1950 resolution adopted by the General Assembly that once Ethiopia reassumed sovereignty over Eritrea, it (the United States) would want to conclude an agreement by which the United States would take over the large communications center there, just outside Asmara.[24] For some time, Ethiopia had been pressing the United States for arms and a military mission.

The British government, in 1952, decided that it could no longer continue providing military aid to Ethiopia, thereby opening up a perfect opportunity for the Americans and Ethiopians to begin a new series of military agreements.

The United States and Ethiopia signed two agreements on May 22, 1953. The first permitted the use by the United States until 1978 of the communications facilities at Asmara. This base was subsequently named "Kagnew" in honor of the Ethiopian contingent that fought in Korea. The second agreement governed the provision of granting military assistance and training to the Ethiopian armed forces.

The United States wanted the communications base at Asmara because

> it was located in the tropics far from the north and south magnetic poles, the "aurora borealis" and magnetic storms, in a zone where the limited degree of seasonal variations between sunrise and sunset reduced the need for numerous frequency changes.[25]

Its mile-and-a-half-high altitude and location near the equator made Kagnew an excellent primary relay station in the U.S. worldwide defense communications system.

Kagnew Station became, over the years, a $60 million complex and the largest high-frequency station for the United States. Kagnew's function has been variously described as that of an eavesdropping operation, a space-tracking station, and a naval communications facility. The station's activities involved "various types of intelligence, electronic countermeasures such as jamming, target exploitation, and transmission of coded material."[26] It no doubt served as an electronic listening post, monitoring both Arab and Soviet communications.

By the mid-1960s, Kagnew Station was staffed by 1,800 military and civilian personnel, who were accompanied by almost 1,400 dependents at an annual operating cost of nearly $13 million. The de facto price the United States paid in "rent" for Kagnew was $10-$12 million a year in the form of military aid to the Ethiopian government.

Due to a variety of factors, the United States began to phase out Kagnew Station as a major communications facility. Concern for the station's security, in light of the Eritrean revolution, was one factor. The fall of the Haile Selassie government was another. The advance of satellite technology in facilitating more sophisticated communications also played a role in the decision to demote the importance of Kagnew. Finally, the development of an alternative site on Diego Garcia, an isolated British-controlled island in the Indian Ocean, spelled the end for the Asmara facility.

The price of maintaining Kagnew Station for a 25-year period was a tremendous amount of economic and military assistance going to Ethiopia from the United States (see Appendix C). It is not unfair to characterize this aid package as rent for Kagnew. Ethiopia's military assistance regularly consisted of two-thirds of the total U.S. military aid to Africa. Total military assistance, in the form of both loans and grants, for the years 1946-75 inclusive, was $286.1 million (see Appendix C).

In addition to having been Ethiopia's major military ally for 24 years, the United States was also its principal economic partner. The United States took about 40 percent of Ethiopia's exports—including 70 percent of its primary crop, coffee—while it provided less than 20 percent of Ethiopia's imports. Total economic assistance to Ethiopia in the form of loans and grants—from 1946 to 1976, inclusive—was $350.8 million. This figure takes into account such programs as Food for Peace, the Peace Corps, and the U.S. Agency for International Development programs (see Appendix C). U.S. economic aid has been supplemented by limited private investment and by projects assisted by U.S.-based private foundations.

In 1960 a formal, secret agreement was concluded between the U.S. Department of State and the Ethiopian government that, in essence, committed the United States to train and equip a 40,000-man Ethiopian military force (see Appendix G). The U.S. Congress was not informed of this commitment, which was only revealed in a 1970 Senate subcommittee investigation through testimony by David Newsom, the then assistant secretary for African affairs.[27] In a crucial segment of this agreement, the United States "reaffirmed its continuing interest in the security of Ethiopia and its opposition to any activities threatening the territorial integrity of Ethiopia." This section was included to reassure Ethiopia in regard to the threat of Somalian "irredentist" claims coming from the newly independent Republic of Somalia.

In implementing the 1960 agreement, the United States became involved in the military structure and activities of the Ethiopian Army. Inevitably this gave the United States a role in helping Ethiopia to suppress the ensuing Eritrean liberation struggle. The 1960 agreement was soon supplemented by further extensions of military aid in 1962, 1963, and 1964 (see Appendix D).

Besides supplying a substantial amount of weaponry to the Ethiopians, the United States supplied critical military personnel to aid the Ethiopian Army. The Military Assistance Advisory Group (MAAG) maintained a large (107 men in 1970)[28] contingent in Ethiopia, some of whom allegedly specialized in counterinsurgency training. There was also a U.S. mapping mission in Ethiopia producing an extensive geographical survey of the country. U.S. pilots on mapping missions over Eritrea were accused of working in collusion with Ethiopian commandos to pinpoint Eritrean guerrilla camps and movements.

By 1970, 6,000 U.S. citizens were working in some capacity in Ethiopia and Eritrea, a great majority of them in direct support of the Haile Selassie government.[29] Of these, 3,200 were stationed at Kagnew; 925 were in the Peace Corps; 250 were with the mapping mission, MAAG, and NAMRU (a naval medical research unit); and 1,500 private U.S. citizens were in business, missionary, or other related employment.

U.S. policy toward the Horn of Africa has been inconsistent, at best, and in a state of confusion, at worst, since the Dergue took power in Ethiopia in September 1974, and particularly since Jimmy Carter became president in January 1977. During the Ford administration (August 1974 to January 1977) there was a tentative move away from the wholehearted support that the U.S. government had extended to Ethiopia under Haile Selassie. The United States began to hesitate about continuing military aid to the Dergue: it never acquiesced to an Ethiopian request for $30 million worth of ammunition in February 1975.[30] By June 1976, the United States was applying pressure on the Dergue to halt the so-called peasant march against Eritrea. Yet, as Assistant Secretary for African Affairs William E. Schaufele told a Senate subcommittee two months later,

> Our emphasis of the Eritrean question has been on the need for internal negotiations to resolve the status of Eritrea within Ethiopia. . . . The movement to establish an independent Eritrea is not something we either acknowledge or recognize.[31]

For the Carter administration to form any kind of comprehensive policy toward Ethiopia and the Horn, the goals and objectives of the United States in the area would have to be clearly understood. This may, in fact, be where the present problem arises. A still-classified document, Presidential Review Memorandum 21 (PRM 21), apparently outlines Carter's early policies toward the Horn area, but it is not known whether a series of coherent objectives was spelled out.[32]

U.S. objectives in the area would seem to fall into four categories: strategic, political, economic, and moral (read "human rights"). The strategic objectives would be concerned with keeping the sea routes, especially the Red Sea corridor connecting the Mediterranean and Indian oceans, open; effectively countering the growing Soviet naval presence in the area; and maintaining adequate base facilities for communication and related functions.

These strategic objectives would form some sort of basis for U.S. political and economic goals. The political questions center on Soviet and Cuban involvement in the Horn and some conceivable extension of the Middle East conflict to the Horn region. Economically, the United States would be most concerned with the free flow of oil and other commerce through the Red Sea to Israel and Western Europe.

All of the aforementioned points were no doubt discussed to some degree in PRM 21. The major disagreements within the Carter administration seem to center on which approach, if any, to take toward the massive Soviet and Cuban presence in the Horn, particularly in Ethiopia. President Carter, himself, certainly helped to create the conditions leading up to the influx of Soviet arms and personnel when he cut off military assistance and sales credits to Ethiopia in May 1977. The cuts came in response to gross human rights violations in Ethiopia, in addition to the fact that the Dergue had just concluded a large arms transaction with the Soviet Union and had closed down a series of U.S. installations, including Kagnew Station. In effect, the Dergue was only preempting the Carter administration on actions that were certain to be taken in the near future.

Despite the Carter administration's concern over Soviet involvement in Ethiopia, the United States rejected the Somalis' requests for arms and other material in January 1978. The U.S. position on the Ogaden conflict at this juncture was that it would do nothing to help either side until the situation had been "resolved."[33] This cautionary policy was a retreat of sorts from an earlier Carter decision to supply Somalia with defensive weapons "to help pry the strategically placed East African nation from the Soviet orbit."[34]

Why was U.S. policy toward the Horn so muddled and indecisive? To answer this question, we must look more closely at the African policy makers in the Carter administration. The main protagonists are UN Ambassador Andrew Young, National Security Adviser Zbigniew Brzezinski, and Secretary of State Cyrus Vance. Previously, Vice-President Walter Mondale had been coordinating the administration's African policy but gave up those chores late in 1977.[35]

Throughout 1977, Andrew Young, with the assistance of Africanists in the State Department and the UN Mission in New York, set the style and tone of Carter's U.S. African policy. Young's emphasis is a gradual, low-profile approach, stressing the need for Africans to define and cope with their own problems, with economic aid from the United States.

Zbigniew Brzezinski, on the other hand, tends to link African issues, such as the conflict in the Horn, to wider U.S.-Soviet problems, such as the Strategic Arms Limitation Treaty (SALT). His attitude is similar to Henry Kissinger's concept of "linkage." It has been suggested that Brzezinski might even sacrifice an early SALT agreement, if necessary, to put pressure on the Soviets to behave in a way he considers more consistent with détente.[36]

Secretary of State Vance appears to be in a position somewhere in between Young and Brzezinski. Vance is sometimes described as moderate, or pragmatic, in relation to his African policy-making colleagues.

Carter has vacillated between listening to one, then another of his African advisers. This has not made for a clear or systematic policy in relation to the Horn. During the first half of 1978, Carter clearly moved away from the Andrew Young approach and toward the harder-line Brzezinski mode of viewing Soviet activity in the Horn in terms of confrontation. While Brzezinski continues to opt for a host of pressure tactics in dealing with Soviet actions, Young remains convinced "that in any peaceful competition with the Soviets and the Cubans, we win hands down and lose nothing." Young believes that promoting human rights and U.S. economic interests should be the main U.S. objectives in Africa and that Soviet/Cuban-related questions should be only number three on the list of priorities.[37]

As long as President Carter continues to be of many minds regarding Africa, and in particular the Horn, no clear policy will emerge. Africa Confidential believes that because of the diverse input, "U.S. policy often appears confused, leading many observers to question just exactly who is in charge."[38]

One more element in the formation of U.S. policy toward the Horn of Africa warrants mention here: the congressional input toward policy making in the Horn. This can be summarized by noting the recommendations made by U.S. Representatives Don Bonker (D-Wash.) and Paul Tsongas (D-Mass.) upon the completion of their fact-finding mission to the Horn from December 12 to December 22, 1977. The list of recommendations is fairly noncommital and only includes a few sentences on Eritrea.[39] It can be summarized as follows:

1. The United States should make clear its position of total neutrality between the disputing states in the Horn of Africa.

2. At this time, the United States should not provide direct or indirect military assistance to Somalia.

3. The United States must get involved politically in the Horn to ameliorate existing problems through negotiation.

4. The United States should voice deep concern for human rights in Ethiopia and object to the Soviet Union's complicity and support of what is happening there.

5. The United States should continue and even accelerate economic humanitarian assistance to all countries in the Horn.

6. The United States should strongly denounce Soviet motives and activities in the Horn of Africa.

7. The U.S. government should do more to educate its people, and particularly the Congress, on the political situation in the Horn.

Only in point five is Eritrea given any mention and, true to form, this brief note is as indecisive as overall U.S. policy in the area. Section 5f states that,

> As for Eritrea, the United States should not be indifferent to the suffering occurring in that territory as a result of its efforts to regain an autonomous relationship with Ethiopia. Options such as providing greater assistance to Eritrean refugees should be pursued. [40]

While Bonker and Tsongas confuse autonomy with independence, they, at least, appear cognizant of the abrogation of the Ethio-Eritrean federal arrangement, which the State Department has never publicly recognized.

Based on the information available, one could only speculate in which direction U.S. policy in the Horn is headed and that might be more like a shot in the dark. One thing, however, does seem clear: the Horn of Africa is probably not the key to the future of U.S.-Soviet naval competition in the Indian Ocean, nor is it immensely important in the de-escalation of hostilities in the Middle East. The Horn area can only lead to exacerbated superpower rivalries if either the USSR or the United States sees the importance of the area in a larger-than-life perspective.

SOVIETS AND CUBANS IN THE HORN OF AFRICA

The Soviet Union and Cuba have been active participants in the politicomilitary realignment of the Horn of Africa. From 1969 until their switch to Ethiopia in 1977, the Soviet Union had been Somalia's strongest patron, while conversely, Somalia had been one of the strongest Soviet supporters in Africa. The Soviets and Cubans, by their support of the Mengistu regime, by their intervention in the Ogaden war, and by their actions in Eritrea, are recording a series of gains and losses that is significant not only for their own regimes but for the entire Red Sea littoral as well.

What were Soviet motives in this area? The Soviet Union has been particularly concerned about the strength of its military and strategic position in the Red Sea-Indian Ocean area for some time. For years, there was a virtual Western naval monopoly in the Indian Ocean. The U.S. concentration on Diego Garcia made this situation even more pronounced. The Soviets are very likely seeking to lay the foundation for an active defense against the U.S. missile-bearing submarines that could be used to patrol the Indian Ocean.[41] In overall Soviet naval strategy, dependable bases are a necessity, from the southern tip of the Red Sea and into the Indian Ocean itself. Their only reliable access to a base in this area now is at Aden, in the People's Democratic Republic of Yemen (PDRY). In switching their support from Somalia to Ethiopia in mid-1977, the Soviets sacrificed their well-outfitted base at the port of Berbera, hopefully in exchange for the nominally Ethiopian ports of Massawa and Assab.

The seas and sea routes hold other keys to explaining Soviet objectives in the area. The Indian Ocean could be important to the Soviets as a link in the sea route to the USSR's Pacific coast and to countries such as India and Vietnam. Almost 50 percent of Soviet military and economic assistance now goes to Indian Ocean littoral states.[42] Furthermore, the area could produce economic benefits for the Soviets:

> The area's abundant mineral and sea-protein resources are the envy of [the] Russians, who depend heavily on the sea as a source of protein, running in short supply these days. The Indian Ocean is an important operating area for Soviet trawlers.[43]

Soviet motives in the Horn of Africa are not limited to naval strategy. In coming to Ethiopia's side with such massive aid in both the Ogaden and in Eritrea, the Soviets seemed to be demonstrating to all of Africa "that the Soviet Union has world power, air and naval, to carry out its intentions anywhere."[44] The airlift of arms to Ethiopia in December 1977 illustrated that the Soviets could mount a large offensive far from their own borders in a quick period of time. In addition, the Soviets used the Ogaden campaign

> to test out new weapons and to coordinate their battlefield tactics, just as America did in Vietnam. . . . The Russian army introduced at least one weapon never before seen in the west. This is the BMP-one, a highly mobile armoured vehicle mounted with a 73mm gun, an anti-tank missile and a heat-seeking anti-aircraft missile.[45]

Other Soviet motives have also been suggested for Moscow's actions backing Ethiopia in the Ogaden war. Ethiopia has a much larger population than does Somalia (25 million versus 3 million), more economic potential, and what must have seemed to the Soviets as a more viable socialist revolution. By involving itself with the

Mengistu regime, the USSR also figured to greatly reduce U.S. influence in the Horn area and possibly preclude Chinese influence in the Horn's most populous state.

At the conclusion of the Ogaden campaign, much of the Soviet logistical support and many of the advisers moved north, to Eritrea. Ethiopia, without the ports of Massawa and Assab, is hardly the prize the Soviets have been competing for. The Soviets probably had nearly 1,000 men in Eritrea in early 1978, and it seems likely that Soviet ships fired rockets in support of the Ethiopians during the battle for Massawa in December 1977.[46] In addition, there are indications that the Soviets are building naval facilities on the strategically important Dahlak Islands, some 20 miles off Massawa.[47] Meanwhile, some of the Soviets' 1,500 East German allies in Ethiopia will be spending the next three years expanding the port of Assab as well as carrying out a feasibility study for a new Assab-Addis Ababa railway.[48]

In its continuing effort to consolidate its strength in the Red Sea area, the Soviet Union signed a 20-year treaty of friendship with Ethiopia in November 1978. Of particular importance, vis-à-vis Eritrea, was Article 10 of the 15-point treaty, which said that the signatories would "continue to cooperate in the military field" in the interest of ensuring their defense capabilities.[49]

While the balance sheet is not yet complete for the Soviets' activities in the Horn, some preliminary evaluations are possible. Nationalism has been an exceptionally strong force in the Horn, as it has been for the whole of Africa. It would seem that the Soviets neglected the importance of nationalism in Somalia and are doing the same in Ethiopia. It has been said that Somalian President Siad Barre is "a nationalist first, a Moslem second, and a Marxist third."[50] The Soviets have tended to superimpose questions of socialism onto essentially nationalistic issues and, by doing so, have obscured the reality in dealing with African countries. It appears that the Soviets have a great deal of difficulty viewing African politics in primarily nationalistic or ethnic terms, without a socialist ideology attached. Particularly in the Horn, nationalism exists as an ideology itself, regardless of any relationship to socialism.

The Soviets, and to a lesser degree the Cubans, misjudged the causes of the Somalian-Ethiopian Ogaden dispute very badly. They deluded themselves into thinking that some measure of "socialist brotherhood" could lend itself to overcome essential national differences. In the same manner, they have misjudged the Ethio-Eritrean conflict. The USSR has ostensibly pushed Mengistu for a negotiated settlement with Eritrea. Yet, ultimately, Soviet lack of understanding of the Eritrean question as a colonial one will doom Soviet moves for accommodation to failure. Had the Soviets correctly assessed the Eritrean revolution, and the chances for the use of port facilities at Massawa and Assab over the long run, they would have never embraced Mengistu's regime so vigorously.

The Cuban involvement in the Horn certainly overlaps with that of the Soviets, yet needs to be viewed separately, as their motives are quite different. Motives for the large Cuban presence in Ethiopia, estimated at 17,000 men in April 1978,[51] are really twofold: on the one hand, the Cubans owe a considerable debt to the Soviet Union; on the other, Cuba views itself as being in the revolutionary forefront of the Third World.

As for the debt owed to the USSR, Cuba's economic dependence on Soviet aid probably totals between $3 billion and $4 billion.[52] It is convenient for the Soviets to utilize surrogate fighters such as the Cubans for a number of reasons. First, many Cubans have died in battle in Ethiopia; very few Soviets actually see combat. Second, the Soviets tend to be socially awkward, bordering on the heavy handed, in their dealing with Africans, whereas the Cubans seem more at ease in the African environment. Third, Cuban presence in Ethiopia, and other African countries, is less provocative because Cuba is a small, ostensibly nonaligned country and many Cubans are black.

However, Cuban indebtedness to the Soviet Union, whether economic or moral, is not in itself a satisfactory answer for Cuban actions in Ethiopia, particularly in regard to Eritrea. Fidel Castro has never really veered away from the concept of exporting the Cuban revolution to other Third World countries. While this element of Cuban foreign policy has essentially failed in Latin America, Cuba's assistance has been much more readily accepted in African countries —such as Angola, under the Neto regime.

The Cuban role in the Ogaden, particularly at Jijiga, mentioned above, was fairly clear: without Cuban personnel backed by Soviet logistics, the Ethiopians could not have administered such a resounding defeat to the Somalis. Their role in Eritrea has been less clear. The best estimates put their numbers at 3,500 in Eritrea, mostly in Asmara. They appear to be lending logistical support to Mengistu's troops and have been flying combat missions against the Eritrean forces as well.[53]

The Cubans, until mid-1978, were not altogether unsympathetic toward the Eritrean movement. Eritreans had trained in Cuba in the past, and Castro had generally viewed the guerrillas as a part of the larger African liberation movement. This explained, in part, why Castro appeared hesitant about lending all-out support to Mengistu in Eritrea. Furthermore, Castro seemed to be aware of the ideological and tactical considerations between the WSLF and the more sophisticated Eritrean movement.

However, by September 1978, the Cubans publicly sided with the Dergue against the Eritreans:[54]

> Castro rationalized this turnabout by declaring the Dergue a "genuinely progressive force" and claiming that the Eritreans were not acting for an "international reactionary conspiracy" of conservative Arab states.[55]

In addition to combat roles in Eritrea, the Cubans are fulfilling a reinforcement function in the Ogaden. As Ethiopian troops have been moved from Jijiga to Eritrea, their place has been taken by Cubans.[56] For Ethiopia it is crucial to have the assistance of Cuban combat units. Mengistu seems determined to find a military solution in Eritrea; and, as the Ethiopians have illustrated during the past two years, without substantial outside personnel in a fighting capacity, the Ethiopian forces are incapable of delivering a mortal blow to the Eritrean guerrillas.

THE MIDDLE EAST

A number of countries in the Middle East region have involved themselves, to one degree or another, in the Eritrean conflict. Israel, Syria, Iraq, Saudi Arabia, the Sudan, the PDRY, and Libya all believe that there are potential losses or gains to emerge from the course of Eritrea's future. It is accurate to say that although the Eritrean revolution will have little impact on the overall future of the Middle East, it has been regularly used as a pawn in the power struggles of the area.

Israel has been one of the most active states involved in the Eritrean arena. As far back as the early 1960s, the Israelis began assisting the Ethiopian government in its counterinsurgency efforts against the ELF. The Israelis were clearly concerned with the Red Sea becoming an "Arab lake," should an independent Eritrea emerge. Israeli defense analysts have argued—erroneously, this author believes—that an independent Eritrea would enhance the capacity of Arab states to blockade or harass (Israeli) commerce passing through the Red Sea and the Gulf of Aden to and from the port of Eilat.[57] Of particular concern, before the shah was ousted from power, was the flow of Iranian oil on which Israel so heavily depended. Yet, the suspension of Iranian oil shipments—in this case, from the source—has had little effect upon Israel as the United States has guaranteed the Israelis oil supplied until 1984. In addition, aspects of the Israeli assistance program (particularly the counterinsurgency efforts) might be viewed as surrogate assistance for the United States.[58] In cases considered politically or militarily sensitive, it is not unusual for a regional ally of the United States to act on the latter's behalf.

Israel's assistance to the Mengistu regime has been strange, if one allows for Israel's relations with Ethiopia's other patrons: the Soviet Union, Cuba, Libya, and the PDRY. For the most part, Israeli assistance to the Dergue ended in February 1978, when Israeli Foreign Minister Moshe Dayan publicly acknowledged Israel's role in Ethiopia. Until that time, however, the Israelis continued to supply spare parts and ammunition for U.S.-made weapons, service U.S.-made F-5 jet fighters, and maintain a small contingent of military advisers in Addis Ababa. Although accused of constructing naval bases on the Dahlak Islands off Massawa, no evidence of Israeli-occupied facilities has been found there.

Most of the Israeli fears about an independent Eritrea appear to be without sound basis. It is virtually impossible for a non-Arab Eritrea to help create an Arab lake of the Red Sea. Even if one were to be concerned about the Eritrean movement's anti-Israeli position, an independent Eritrean state hardly changes the fundamental realities of Middle Eastern politics. Tom Farer sums up this argument well when he says that,

> Most of the thinking I have seen about Eritrea constitutes what I call the geometer's approach to strategy. You take a compass; you stick a point in the territory. You draw progressively larger concentric circles. Then you say: "My God! It is so close to Israel, the Persian Gulf, the whole Middle East; it must be important." Geometers are inclined to forget that military technology has changed fundamentally from the 18th century.[59]

Other implausible arguments regarding an independent Eritrea and its relationships to Israel are often put forward. These deal with the strangulation of Israeli shipping in the Red Sea, Israeli vessels being attacked in the straits of Bab el Mandeb, and the prospect of certain Palestinian groups being given a free hand to operate from Eritrean shores against Israeli commerce. Although these arguments will not be explored here, I believe that their validity tends to fade in the light of objective analysis.

Syria and Iraq have been the ELF's strongest supporters over the years. In supporting the Eritrean struggle, the two nominally socialist countries have been competing for regional power in those few places where they can hope to exert influence. Iraq initially began aiding the ELF in 1968 to undermine any Syrian influence in the organization.[60] Today, the Iraqi Ba'th probably has the greatest influence upon the ELF; neither Iraq nor Syria carry much weight with the EPLF. In spite of all of the Eritrean, particularly ELF, propaganda in praise of the respective Ba'thist parties, neither Syria nor Iraq can seriously hope to have much influence on an independent Eritrean government. The Pan-Arab ideology is hardly significant inside Arab League member Somalia, where the entire population is Muslim; multiethnic Eritrea is a far less likely success for any sort of Pan-Arab ideology.

If one wished to make the argument that Islam is essentially a conservative force in the politics of the Middle East and the Horn, one would have to look no further than Saudi Arabia. The Saudis, in search for traditional stability in the region, are implementing an active pro-Muslim and anticommunist policy in the Horn. The Saudis view with alarm the presence of a radical regime in Ethiopia. The Eritrean revolution is no less a threat, as an independent, socialist Eritrea would lie directly across the Red Sea from the Arab bastion of conservatism. In keeping with its ideological bent, Saudi Arabia supported Somalia in the Ogaden campaign and gives a good deal of assistance to Osman Saleh Sabbe in Eritrea. Since the Soviet departure from Somalia, relations between Mogadishu and Riyadh have warmed up considerably. With Sabbe in Arabia to carry the Pan-Islamic banner, the Saudis are capable, at least, of fanning the flames of religious rivalries. Saudi Arabian actions merit close attention in relation to the future of the Eritrean revolution.

The Sudan, under President Numeiri, has also invested a great deal of time and energy in the Eritrean issue. In fact, the EPLF's numerous successes in 1977 were tremendously aided by Numeiri's tacit support for the Eritreans. On January 30, 1977, Numeiri announced his assistance to the Eritreans in their fight for independence from Ethiopia. Numeiri claimed to have evidence that the Dergue had been actively aiding certain Sudanese politicians who attempted an earlier coup d'etat in Khartoum. [61]

In spite of these circumstances, the Eritrean liberation movements do not entirely trust the Numeiri government in backing them until independence. By mid-1977 the Sudanese president was pushing "a more prudent scheme for autonomy," similar to the arrangement that exists between the southern Sudan and the rest of the country. [62] The Eritreans tend to view Numeiri's Sudan as prone to blow with the wind, especially in light of the U.S. and Saudi Arabian assistance that has been discussed for the Khartoum government.

Libya had been a supporter of the EPLF for some time, on the basis of Colonel Qaddafi's stand aiding revolutionary movements in the region. Yet, this commitment proved to be even thinner than that of the Sudanese government. Precisely because of Numeiri's problems with the Ethiopians in 1977, Libya switched its support to the Dergue, in the hope that this action might facilitate the downfall of Ńumeiri, whom Qaddafi despises.[63] It is believed that Libya agreed not only to provide economic assistance to the Dergue but also to finance the whole program for equipping the peasant militia and for purchasing many heavy weapons.[64]

The PDRY has maintained an even less consistent policy than has Libya. The Aden government, a long-time supporter of the Eritrean movement, particularly the EPLF, also switched sides in mid-1977. When Ethiopia turned to the Soviet Union for military aid, the South Yemenis decided that it was best to follow the lead of their Soviet patrons. From that time, the PDRY has publicly supported the Dergue, yet nevertheless allowed the Eritreans to continue to operate from Aden.[65] By early 1978, the South Yemeni combat role in Eritrea had come to include piloting MiG-21s and -23s, flying reconnaisance helicopters, and operating tanks and heavy artillery.[66]

In June 1978 the political situation in the PDRY underwent tremendous upheaval. PDRY President Salim Rubay-Ali was ousted in a power struggle that centered on relations with the Yemen Arab Republic and—more important, in this instance—the growing PDRY involvement in the Horn under Soviet and Cuban pressure. Rubay's downfall may have, in part, been brought about by his decision to order the estimated 1,000 South Yemeni pilots and soldiers in Eritrea to take no further part in military actions.[67] It had been reported earlier in the month that Rubay promised to openly extend facilities to the Eritreans again.[68]

In summary, it would be difficult to make any conclusive judgments about the impact of the Eritrean revolution on the Middle East region. The revolution has certainly been used as a pawn in the various power struggles and personality clashes that exist in the area, yet in terms of overall strategic implications between the United States and the USSR, and between the Israelis and the Arabs, the Eritrean revolution has far less impact than we are often led to believe. The outcome of the Eritrean struggle has much more significant impact for the Horn area itself.

CONCLUSION

The power shifts and changing alignments in the Horn of Africa are events that virtually no observer would have predicted a few years ago. Somalia was believed to be one of the Soviet Union's staunchest friends on the African continent; the United States had been the most important Ethiopian patron for more than a quarter of a century. Imagining the Soviet Union, Cuba, the PDRY, Libya, and Israel lined up with the Ethiopian regime to fight a two-front war seems impossible. Yet, these shifts did take place and have severely altered the geopolitical landscape of the Horn. The factors that continue to steer, or alter, the unfolding drama in the area will no doubt be based much more on a given country's perspective and what it wants to see rather than on any notion of objective reality. As Tom Farer so aptly notes, "Crises, like beauty, exist not in the nature of things but in the minds of men."

One nation that has not been discussed previously warrants brief mention here. So far the People's Republic of China has played a very small part in the great power rivalries in the Horn. In August 1977 China declared its support for Somalia in the Ogaden conflict, [69] but this can easily be seen as their predictable reaction in taking the opposite side from the USSR. Somalian President Siad Barre did visit China early in 1978, and the Chinese may be looking toward a more active role in the politics of the Horn, now that the Soviets seem firmly entrenched in neighboring Ethiopia.

The question might arise as to why the Chinese have not played a larger role in the Eritrean conflict. After all, there exists an ideological affinity between the Chinese and Eritreans, and the situation would seem to be ideal to counter Soviet influence in the area. There are several explanations available, none of them compelling; but, taken as a whole, they shed some light on the answer.

First, it was not until 1978 that the USSR illustrated such a large and firm commitment to Ethiopia; it did attempt to play both sides against the middle in dealing with Somalia and Ethiopia all throughout 1977. Second, the Chinese are going through serious internal upheaval of their own, and African foreign policy may not be seen as a priority to be dealt with immediately. Third—and with this the EPLF would have no argument—Mao's doctrine of a self-reliant people's war compels China to insist that guerrilla movements do their own fighting. Finally, China lacks the modern weapons to intervene, as the Soviets have, in the Horn. Bearing these conditions in mind, Chinese involvement in the Horn may be slow and tentative in the near future.

At the end of the 1970s, Eritrea's future remains very much in question. It seems that in spite of the success of the 1978/79 Ethiopian counteroffensive, the Eritrean liberation forces are committed to the existence of a radically altered independent state. It appears no less certain that the Ethiopian regime of Mengistu Haile Mariam will use all of the force he can muster to prevent Eritrea's rebirth. While time might ultimately favor the Eritrean movement, there are various factors that could either speed or retard the present course of events.

The first possibility is a change in leadership of the Dergue. Should a new person, or party, emerge with power in Ethiopia, conditions for talks between Eritrea and Ethiopia might improve. It should be noted, however, that it is difficult to envision any Ethiopian government granting Eritrea outright independence unless Addis Ababa has been militarily brought to its knees. For a while, it was common in the Western press to see mention of a right-wing military takeover in Ethiopia, with an accompanying turnaway from the Soviet Union and back toward the United States. Considering the vacillating nature of U.S. policy today, a turn toward the United States might be a boon to the Eritrean movement.

The second possibility, which would deal a severe blow to the Eritrean forces, is a cutoff of Sudanese aid in the form of prohibition of passage across the Sudanese-Eritrean border. Should President Numeiri establish substantially better relations with Mengistu or any future Ethiopian government, he could attempt to impose an autonomous solution similar to the southern Sudan on the Eritrean movement. While the Eritrean forces receive little or no material help from Numeiri, the large number of Eritreans living in the Sudan and the freedom of movement that the guerrillas have in the border area are important in keeping the pressure on the Ethiopian troops in Eritrea. The Eritreans would need another friend in the area quickly; the only other help, such as the Sudan's, that they have received in the past has come from the PDRY, and there is substantial doubt as to whether they can depend on Aden for anything at this point.

Third, there is the question of continued Soviet and Cuban support: for how long and to what degree? This question may be more appropriate in regard to Fidel Castro, who was hesitant to fully support Mengistu with Cuban ground forces in Eritrea as he did in the Ogaden. The Cubans, at one time, were pushing hard for a negotiated settlement in Eritrea. Now that the Cubans and Soviets have aided the Dergue in recapturing all of the cities and major towns in Eritrea, to what degree are they committed to acting as counterinsurgents against the Eritrean movement in the countryside?

Last, the tensions that have impeded the Eritrean movement from within continue to do so. Losing the towns they had occupied from 1977/78 has served to exacerbate existing tensions between the ELF and the EPLF. Whether or not these personal and ideological conflicts can be resolved is the key variable in the future of the revolution. For as long as the competing Eritrean groups continue fighting among themselves, it is certain that they will make little progress toward their goal of national independence.

In conclusion, it is hoped that this book has served to illustrate the following points:

1. Eritrean nationalism was forged as a result of Italian colonialism followed by Ethiopian repression of the Eritrean population.

2. The Eritrean movement is not simply one of secession or independence, but a revolution in a broad sense.

3. Real socioeconomic changes have taken place in Eritrean-controlled parts of Eritrea.

4. Economic viability for Eritrea can, if political factors permit, become a reality.

5. Continuing disunity within the Eritrean movement in addition to substantial external assistance to the Ethiopians indicate that no lasting solution to the Ethio-Eritrean conflict will be found in the near future.

The Horn of Africa has consistently been the graveyard of numerous predictions. Beyond acknowledging that the Eritreans still have a long, arduous road to travel toward their goal of independence, the only certainty is that events in Eritrea and the Horn merit the closest attention in the near future.

NOTES

1. Christopher Clapham, "Ethiopia and Somalia," in U.S., Congress, House Subcommittee on International and Political and Military Affairs of the Committee on Foreign Affairs, U.S. Policy and Request for Sale of Arms to Ethiopia, Hearings, 94th Cong., 1st sess., March 5, 1975, p. 27.

2. Tom J. Farer, War Clouds on the Horn of Africa (Washington, D.C.: Carnegie Endowment for International Peace, 1976), p. 137.

3. Ibid., p. 139.

4. Ibid.

5. Mesfin Gabriel, "The War Effort Takes Too Much," New African 130 (June 1978): 33.

6. Ibid.

7. Eritreans for Liberation in North America, "Joint Statement of the EPLF and EPRP," Liberation 5 (July–August 1976): 21.

8. Africa Confidential 19 (June 23, 1978): 4.

9. Ibid. 19 (January 6, 1978): 6.

10. Ibid., p. 4.

11. For further discussion of this theme, see Ronald J. Horvath, "The Wandering Capitals of Ethiopia," Journal of African History, vol. 1 (1969).

12. "The Ogaden Debacle," Newsweek, March 20, 1978, p. 46.

13. David Lamb, "Somalia Continues to Eye Ogaden Region," Los Angeles Times, June 7, 1978, pt. 1-A, p. 1.

14. Ibid., p. 9.

15. Gerard Chaliand, "The Horn of Africa's Dilemma," Foreign Policy 30 (Spring 1978): 129.

16. Africa Research Bulletin, May 15, 1978, p. 4808.

17. Farer, op. cit., pp. 147-51.

18. U.S., Congress, Senate, Subcommittee on African Affairs of the Committee on Foreign Relations, Ethiopia and the Horn of Africa, Hearings, 94th Cong., 2d sess., August 4, 5, and 6, 1976, p. 35.

19. Ibid.

20. G. K. N. Trevaskis, Eritrea: A Colony in Transition (London: Oxford University Press, 1960), p. 37.

21. Ibid.

22. U.S., Congress, Senate, Subcommittee on United States Security Agreements and Commitments Abroad, United States Security Agreements and Commitments Abroad: Ethiopia, Hearings, 91st Cong., 2d sess., June 1, 1970, p. 1882.

23. U.S., Congress, Senate, Subcommittee on African Affairs of the Committee on Foreign Relations, op. cit., p. 26.

24. Ibid.

25. Ibid.

26. R. A. Diamond and David Fouquet, "American Military Aid to Ethiopia—and Eritrean Insurgency," Africa Today 19 (1972): 42.

27. U.S., Congress, Senate, Subcommittee on United States Security Agreements and Commitments Abroad of the Committee on Foreign Relations, op. cit.

28. Ibid., p. 1913.

29. Ibid., p. 1947.

30. Herrick Warren and Anita Warren, "The U.S. Role in the Eritrean Conflict," Africa Today 23 (April-June 1976): 49.

31. U.S., Congress, Senate, Subcommittee on African Affairs of the Committee on Foreign Relations, op. cit., p. 119.

32. "The Horn: Will Carter Exploit the Soviet Gamble?" New African 122 (October 1977): 986.

33. Oswald Johnston, "U.S. Rejects Somali Bid for Arms, Troops," Los Angeles Times, January 18, 1978.

34. Ibid.

35. Bernard Gwertzman, "U.S. Remains of Two Minds (At Least) on Africa," New York Times, June 4, 1978, pt. 4, p. 1.

36. Ibid.

37. "Young Details U.S. Priorities in Africa," Los Angeles Times, June 9, 1978, p. 5.

38. Africa Confidential 19 (May 12, 1978): 5.

39. U.S., Congress, House, War in the Horn of Africa: A Firsthand Report on the Challenges for United States Policy, Report to the Committee on International Relations, 95th Cong., 2d sess., December 12-22, 1977, pp. 49-51.

40. Ibid., p. 51.

41. Ibid., p. 45.

42. Ibid.

43. Ibid.

44. Africa Research Bulletin, February 15, 1978, p. 4703.

45. Ibid., April 15, 1978, p. 4774.

46. "Russia's Dangerous Game," Sudanow 3 (February 1978): 18.

47. Michael Wells, "Russians Shelling Massawa?" Manchester Guardian Weekly, January 29, 1978, p. 7.

48. Fred Halliday, "Soviet Union's Precarious Ethiopian Foothold," New African 127 (March 1978): 19.

49. Agence France-Presse, Africa, no. 2535 (November 24, 1978), p. 22.

50. David Lamb, "Russ Isolated in a Somalia They Helped to Develop," Los Angeles Times, October 3, 1977, p. 6.

51. Graham Hovey, "Tough Job for Cuba in Eritrea Is Seen," New York Times, April 2, 1978, p. 7.

52. "The Game Cubans Play," Los Angeles Times, May 17, 1978, pt. 2, p. 6.

53. "The Cubans in Africa," Newsweek, March 13, 1978, p. 37.

54. Agence France-Presse, Africa, no. 2517 (September 22, 1978), p. 21.

55. Daniel S. Papp, "The Soviet Union and Cuba in Ethiopia," Current History 76 (March 1979): 113.

56. Africa Research Bulletin, December 15, 1978, p. 5065.

57. Farer, op. cit., p. 125.

58. For further discussion of this point, see Richard Sherman, "Israeli Aid to East and Northeast Africa," Davka, vol. 2 (June 1972).

59. U.S., Congress, Senate, Subcommittee on African Affairs of the Committee on Foreign Relations, op. cit., p. 102.

60. Mordechai Abir, "The Contentious Horn of Africa," Conflict Studies 24 (June 1972): 7.

61. Africa Research Bulletin, February 15, 1977, p. 4282.

62. Jonathan Randal, "Long Struggle Shows Eritreans They Have Few Friends," Washington Post, April 9, 1978, p. A29.

63. Colin Legum, "Realities of the Ethiopian Revolution," World Today 33 (August 1977): 310.

64. Africa Confidential 18 (August 5, 1977): 6.

65. Legum, op. cit.

66. "South Yemen's Role," Weekly Review (Nairobi) 156 (February 13, 1978): 11-12.

67. Los Angeles Times, June 27, 1978, p. 15.

68. Ibid., June 7, 1978, p. 31.

69. Africa Research Bulletin, September 15, 1977, p. 4527.

Appendix A

RESOLUTION 390 (V), "ERITREA: REPORT OF THE UNITED NA-
  TIONS COMMISSION FOR ERITREA; REPORT OF THE INTERIM
  COMMITTEE OF THE GENERAL ASSEMBLY ON THE REPORT
  OF THE UNITED NATIONS COMMISSION FOR ERITREA," FROM
  THE FIFTH UNITED NATIONS GENERAL ASSEMBLY, 316TH
  PLENARY MEETING, 1950

A

Whereas by paragraph 3 of Annex XI to the Treaty of Peace with
Italy, 1947, the Powers concerned have agreed to accept the recom-
mendation of the General Assembly on the disposal of the former
Italian colonies in Africa and to take appropriate measures for giving
effect to it,

Whereas by paragraph 2 of the aforesaid Annex XI such disposal
is to be made in the light of the wishes and welfare of the inhabitants
and the interests of peace and security, taking into consideration the
views of interested governments,

Now therefore

The General Assembly, in the light of the reports* of the United
Nations Commission for Eritrea and of the Interim Committee, and

Taking into consideration

(a) The wishes and welfare of the inhabitants of Eritrea, including the views of the various racial, religious and political groups of
the provinces of the territory and the capacity of the people for self-
government,

(b) The interests of peace and security in East Africa,

(c) The rights and claims of Ethiopia based on geographical, historical, ethnic or economic reasons, including in particular Ethiopia's
legitimate need for adequate access to the sea,

Taking into account the importance of assuring the continuing
collaboration of the foreign communities in the economic development
of Eritrea,

Recognizing that the disposal of Eritrea should be based on its
close political and economic association with Ethiopia, and

---

*See Official Records of the General Assembly, Fifth Session,
Supplements, nos. 8 and 14.

161

Desiring that this association assure the inhabitants of Eritrea the fullest respect and safeguards for their institutions, traditions, religions and languages, as well as the widest possible measure of self-government, while at the same time respecting the Constitution, institutions, traditions and the international status and identity of the Empire of Ethiopia,

A. Recommends that:

1. Eritrea shall constitute an autonomous unit federated with Ethiopia under the sovereignty of the Ethiopian Crown.

2. The Eritrean Government shall possess legislative, executive and judicial powers in the field of domestic affairs.

3. The jurisdiction of the Federal Government shall extend to the following matters: defence, foreign affairs, currency and finance, foreign and interstate commerce and external and interstate communications, including ports. The Federal Government shall have the power to maintain the integrity of the Federation, and shall have the right to impose uniform taxes throughout the Federation to meet the expenses of federal functions and services, it being understood that the assessment and the collection of such taxes in Eritrea are to be delegated to the Eritrean Government, and provided that Eritrea shall bear only its just and equitable share of these expenses. The jurisdiction of the Eritrean Government shall extend to all matters not vested in the Federal Government, including the power to maintain the internal police, to levy taxes to meet the expenses of domestic functions and services, and to adopt its own budget.

4. The area of the Federation shall constitute a single area for customs purposes, and there shall be no barriers to the free movement of goods and persons within the area. Customs duties on goods entering or leaving the Federation which have their final destination or origin in Eritrea shall be assigned to Eritrea.

5. An Imperial Federal Council composed of equal numbers of Ethiopian and Eritrean representatives shall meet at least once a year and shall advise upon the common affairs of the Federation referred to in paragraph 3 above. The citizens of Eritrea shall participate in the executive and judicial branches, and shall be represented in the legislative branch, of the Federal Government, in accordance with law and in the proportion that the population of Eritrea bears to the population of the Federation.

6. A single nationality shall prevail throughout the Federation:

(a) All inhabitants of Eritrea, except persons possessing foreign nationality, shall be nationals of the Federation;

(b) All inhabitants born in Eritrea and having at least one indigenous parent or grandparent shall also be nationals of the Federation. Such persons, if in possession of a foreign nationality, shall, within six months of the coming into force of the Eritrean Constitution, be free to opt to renounce the nationality of the Federation and retain such foreign nationality. In the event that they do not so opt, they shall thereupon lose such foreign nationality;

(c) The qualifications of persons acquiring the nationality of the Federation under sub-paragraphs (a) and (b) above for exercising their rights as citizens of Eritrea shall be determined by the Constitution and laws of Eritrea;

(d) All persons possessing foreign nationality who have resided in Eritrea for ten years prior to the date of the adoption of the present resolution shall have the right, without further requirements of residence, to apply for the nationality of the Federation in accordance with federal laws. Such persons who do not thus acquire the nationality of the Federation shall be permitted to reside in and engage in peaceful and lawful pursuits in Eritrea;

The rights and interests of foreign nationals resident in Eritrea shall be guaranteed in accordance with the provisions of paragraph 7.

7. The Federal Government, as well as Eritrea, shall ensure to residents in Eritrea, without distinction of nationality, race, sex, language or religion, the enjoyment of human rights and fundamental liberties, including the following:

(a) The right to equality before the law. No discrimination shall be made against foreign enterprises in existence in Eritrea engaged in industrial, commercial, agricultural, artisan, educational or charitable activities, nor against banking institutions and insurance companies operating in Eritrea;

(b) The right to life, liberty and security of person;

(c) The right to own and dispose of property. No one shall be deprived of property, including contractual rights, without due process of law and without payment of just and effective compensation;

(d) The right to freedom of opinion and expression and the right of adopting and practicing any creed or religion;

(e) The right to education;

(f) The right to freedom of peaceful assembly and association;

(g) The right to inviolability of correspondence and domicile, subject to the requirements of the law;

(h) The right to exercise any profession subject to the requirements of the law;

(i) No one shall be subject to arrest or detention without an order of a competent authority, except in case of flagrant and serious violation of the law in force. No one shall be deported except in accordance with the law;

(j) The right to a fair and equitable trial, the right of petition to the Emperor and the right of appeal to the Emperor for commutation of death sentences;

(k) Retroactivity of penal law shall be excluded;

The respect for the rights and freedoms of others and the requirements of public order and the general welfare alone will justify any limitations to the above rights.

8. Paragraphs 1 to 7 inclusive of the present resolution shall constitute the Federal Act which shall be submitted to the Emperor of Ethiopia for ratification.

9. There shall be a transition period which shall not extend beyond 15 September 1952, during which the Eritrean Government will be organized and the Eritrean Constitution prepared and put into effect.

10. There shall be a United Nations Commissioner in Eritrea appointed by the General Assembly. The Commissioner will be assisted by experts appointed by the Secretary-General of the United Nations.

11. During the transition period, the present administering Power shall continue to conduct the affairs of Eritrea. It shall, in consultation with the United Nations Commissioner, prepare as rapidly as possible the organization of an Eritrean administration, induct Eritreans into all levels of the administration, and make arrangements for and convoke a representative assembly of Eritreans chosen by the people. It may, in agreement with the Commissioner, negotiate on behalf of the Eritreans a temporary customs union with Ethiopia to be put into effect as soon as practicable.

12. The United Nations Commissioner shall, in consultation with the administering Power, the Government of Ethiopia, and the inhabitants of Eritrea, prepare a draft of the Eritrean Constitution to be submitted to the Eritrean Assembly and shall advise and assist the Eritrean Assembly in its consideration of the Constitution. The Constitution of Eritrea shall be based on the principles of democratic government, shall include the guarantees contained in paragraph 7 of the Federal Act, shall be consistent with the provisions of the Federal Act and shall contain provisions adopting and ratifying the Federal Act on behalf of the people of Eritrea.

13. The Federal Act and the Constitution of Eritrea shall enter into effect following ratification of the Federal Act by the Emperor of Ethiopia, and following approval by the Commissioner, adoption by the Eritrean Assembly and ratification by the Emperor of Ethiopia of the Eritrean Constitution.

14. Arrangements shall be made by the Government of the United Kingdom of Great Britain and Northern Ireland as the administering Power for the transfer of power to the appropriate authorities. The transfer of power shall take place as soon as the Eritrean Constitution and the Federal Act enter into effect, in accordance with the provisions of paragraph 13 above.

15. The United Nations Commissioner shall maintain his headquarters in Eritrea until the transfer of power has been completed, and shall make appropriate reports to the General Assembly of the

United Nations concerning the discharge of his functions. The Commissioner may consult with the Interim Committee of the General Assembly with respect to the discharge of his functions in the light of developments and within the terms of the present resolution. When the transfer of authority has been completed, he shall so report to the General Assembly and submit to it the text of the Eritrean Constitution;

B. Authorizes the Secretary-General, in accordance with established practice:

1. To arrange for the payment of an appropriate remuneration to the United Nations Commissioner;

2. To provide the United Nations Commissioner with such experts, staff and facilities as the Secretary-General may consider necessary to carry out the terms of the present resolution.

316th plenary meeting,
2 December 1950.

B

The General Assembly, to assist it in making the appointment of the United Nations Commissioner in Eritrea.

Decides that a Committee composed of the President of the General Assembly, two of the Vice-Presidents (Australia and Venezuela), the Chairman of the Fourth Committee and the Chairman of the Ad Hoc Political Committee shall nominate a candidate or, if no agreement can be reached, two or three candidates, for the post of United Nations Commissioner in Eritrea.

316th plenary meeting,
2 December 1950.

The Committee established by the General Assembly under the above resolution to nominate a candidate or candidates for the office of United Nations Commissioner in Eritrea agreed to nominate the following candidates:

Mr. Victor Hoo (Assistant Secretary-General);
Justice Aung Khine (Burma);
Mr. Eduardo Anze Matienzo (Bolivia).

The General Assembly, at its 325th plenary meeting on 14 December 1950, elected by secret ballot Mr. Eduardo Anze Matienzo to the office of United Nations Commissioner in Eritrea.

Source: Middle East Journal 5 (1951): 89-91.

Appendix B

1. Establish a People's Democratic State

    A. Abolish the Ethiopian colonial administrative organs and all antinational and undemocratic laws as well as nullify the military, economic, and political treaties affecting Eritrea signed between colonial Ethiopia and other governments.
    B. Safeguard the interests of the masses of workers, peasants, and other democratic forces.
    C. Set up a People's Assembly constituted of people's representatives democratically and freely elected from antifeudal and antiimperialistic patriotic forces. The People's Assembly shall draw the constitution, promulgate laws, elect the people's administration, and ratify national economic plans and new treaties.
    D. Protect the people's democratic rights—freedom of speech, the press, assembly, worship, and peaceful demonstration; develop antifeudal and antiimperialist worker, peasant, women, student, and youth organizations.
    E. Assure all Eritrean citizens equality before the law without distinction as to nationality, tribe, region, sex, cultural level, occupation, position, wealth, faith, etc.
    F. Severely punish Eritrean lackeys of Ethiopian colonialism who have committed crimes against the nation and the people.

2. Build an Independent, Self-Reliant, and Planned National Economy

    A. Agriculture

        (1) Confiscate all land in the hands of the aggressor Ethiopian regime, the imperialists, Zionists, and Eritrean lackeys and put it in the service of the Eritrean masses.
        (2) Make big nationalized farms and extensive farms requiring modern techniques state-farms, and use their produce for the benefit of the masses.
        (3) Abolish feudal land relations and carry out an equitable distribution of land. Strive to introduce cooperative

farms by creating conditions of cooperation and mutual assistance so as to develop a modern and advanced system of agriculture and animal husbandry capable of increasing the income and improving the lot of the peasantry.

(4) Induce the peasants to adopt modern agricultural techniques, introduce them to advanced agricultural implements, and provide them with advisors, experts, veterinary services, fertilizers, wells, dams, transportation, finance, etc., in order to alleviate their problems and improve their livelihood and working conditions.

(5) Provide the nomads with veterinary services, livestock breeding experts, agricultural advisors, and financial assistance in order to enable them to lead settled lives, adopt modern techniques of agriculture and animal husbandry, and improve their livelihood.

(6) Provide for the peaceful and amicable settlement of land disputes and inequality among individuals and villages in such a way as to harmonize the interest of the aggrieved party with that of the national economic interest.

(7) Advance the economic and living conditions in, and bridge the gap between, the cities and the countryside.

(8) Make pastures and forests state property, preserve wild life and forestry, and fight soil erosion.

(9) Maintain a proper balance between agriculture and industry in the context of the planned economy.

(10) Promote an association that will organize, politicize, and arm the peasants with a clear revolutionary outlook so they can fully participate in the anticolonial and antifeudal struggle, defend the gains of the revolution, free themselves from oppression and economic exploitation, and manage their own affairs.

B. Industry

(1) Nationalize all industries in the hands of the imperialists, Zionists, and Ethiopian colonialists and their Eritrean lackeys as well as resident aliens opposed to Eritrean independence.

(2) Nationalize big industries, ports, mines, public transport, communications, power plants, and other basic economic resources.

(3) Exploit marine resources, expand the production of salt and other minerals, develop the fishing industry, and explore oil and other minerals.

(4) Allow nationals who were not opposed to the independence of Eritrea to participate in national construction by own-

ing small factories and workshops compatible with national development and the system of administration.

(5) Strive to develop heavy industry so as to promote light industry, advance agriculture, and combat industrial dependence.

C. Finance

(1) Nationalize all insurance companies and banks, so as to centralize banking operations, regulate economic activitives, and accelerate economic development.

(2) Establish a government-owned central national bank and issue an independent national currency.

(3) Prohibit usury in all its forms and extend credit at the lowest interest in order to eliminate the attendant exploitation of the masses.

D. Trade

(1) Construct essential land, air, and sea transportation and communications to develop the nation's trade.

(2) Handle all import and export trade.

(3) Nationalize the big trading companies and regulate the small ones.

(4) Prohibit the export of essential commodities and limit the import of luxury goods.

(5) Regulate the exchange and pricing of the various domestic products.

(6) Strictly prohibit contraband trade.

(7) Establish trade relations with all countries that respect Eritrean sovereignty irrespective of political systems.

E. Urban Land and Housing

(1) Make urban land state property.

(2) Nationalize all excess urban houses in order to abolish exploitation through rent and improve the livelihood of the masses.

(3) Set, taking the standard of living into account, a rational rent price in order to improve the living conditions of the masses.

(4) Compensate citizens for nationalized property in accordance with a procedure based on personal income and the condition of the national economy.

(5) Build appropriate modern houses to alleviate the shortage of housing for the masses.

3. Develop Culture, Education, Technology, and Public Health

A. Culture

    (1) Obliterate the decadent culture and disgraceful social habits that Ethiopian colonialism, world imperialism, and Zionism have spread in order to subjugate and exploit the Eritrean people and destroy their identity.

    (2) In the new educational curriculum, provide for the proper dissemination of, respect for, and development of the history of Eritrea and its people, the struggle against colonialism and oppression and for national independence, and the experience, sacrifices, and heroism, as well as the national folklore, traditions, and culture of the Eritrean people.

    (3) Destroy the bad aspects of the culture and traditions of Eritrean society and develop its good and progressive content.

    (4) Ensure that the Eritrean people glorify and eternally cherish the memory of the heroic martyrs of the struggle for independence who, guided by revolutionary principles, gave their lives for the salvation of their people and country.

B. Education

    (1) Combat illiteracy to free the Eritrean people from the darkness of ignorance.

    (2) Provide for universal compulsory education up to the middle school.

    (3) Establish institutions of higher education in the various fields of science, arts, technology, agriculture, etc.

    (4) Grant students scholarships to pursue studies in the various fields of learning.

    (5) Establish schools in the various regions of Eritrea in accordance with the need.

    (6) Separate education from religion.

    (7) Make the state run all the schools and provide free education at all levels.

    (8) Integrate education with production and put it in the service of the masses.

    (9) Enable nationals, especially the students and youth, to train and develop themselves in the sciences, literature, handicrafts, and technology through the formation of their own organizations.

(10) Provide favorable work conditions for experts and the skilled to enable them to utilize their skills and knowledge in the service of the masses.

(11) Engage in educational, cultural, and technological exchange with other countries on the basis of mutual benefit and equality.

C. Public Health

(1) Render medical services freely to the people.

(2) Eradicate contagious diseases and promote public health by building the necessary hospitals and health centers all over Eritrea.

(3) Scientifically develop traditional medicine.

(4) Establish sports and athletic facilities and popularize them among the masses.

4. Safeguard Social Rights

A. Workers' Rights

(1) Politicize and organize the workers, whose participation in the struggle had been hindered by the reactionary line and leaderships, and enable them, in a higher and more organized form, to play their vanguard role in the revolution.

(2) Abolish the system of labor laws and sham trade unions set up by Ethiopian colonialism and its imperialistic masters to exploit and oppress Eritrean workers.

(3) Enforce an eight-hour working day and protect the right of workers to rest one day a week and twenty-five days a year.

(4) Promulgate a special labor code that properly protects the rights of workers and enables them to form unions.

(5) Assure workers comfortable housing and decent living conditions.

(6) Devise a social security program to care for and assist workers who, because of illness, disability, or age, are unable to work.

(7) Prohibit unjustified dismissals and undue pay-cuts.

(8) Protect the right of workers to participate in the management and administration of enterprises and industries.

B. Women's Rights

(1) Develop an association through which women can participate in the struggle against colonial aggression and for social transformation.

(2) Outline a broad program to free women from domestic confinement, develop their participation in social production, and raise their political, cultural, and technical levels.

(3) Assure women full rights of equality with men in politics, economy, and social life as well as equal pay for equal work.

(4) Promulgate progressive marriage and family laws.

(5) Protect the right of women workers to two months maternity leave with full pay.

(6) Protect the right of mothers and children, provide delivery, nursery, and kindergarten services.

(7) Fight to eradicate prostitution.

(8) Respect the right of women not to engage in work harmful to their health.

(9) Design programs to increase the number and upgrade the quality of women leaders and public servants.

C. Families of Martyrs, Disabled Fighters, and Others Needing Social Assistance

(1) Provide necessary care and assistance to all fighters and other citizens who, in the course of the struggle against Ethiopian colonialism and for national salvation, have suffered disability in jails or in armed combat.

(2) Provide assistance and relief to the victims of Ethiopian colonial aggression, orphans, the old, and the disabled as well as those harmed by natural causes.

(3) Render necessary assistance and care for the families of martyrs.

5. Ensure the Equality and Consolidate the Unity of Nationalities

A. Abolish the system and laws instituted by imperialism, Ethiopian colonialism, and their lackeys in order to divide, oppress, and exploit the Eritrean people.

B. Rectify all errors committed by opportunists in the course of the struggle.

C. Combat national chauvinism as well as narrow nationalism.

D. Nurture and strengthen the unity and fraternity of Eritrean nationalities.

E. Accord all nationalities equal rights and responsibilities in leading them toward national progress and salvation.

F. Train cadres from all nationalities in various fields to ensure common progress.

G. Safeguard the right of all nationalities to preserve and develop their spoken or written language.

H. Safeguard the right of all nationalities to preserve and develop their progressive culture and traditions.

I. Forcefully oppose those who, in the pursuit of their own interests, create cliques on the basis of nationality, tribe, region, etc., and obstruct the unity of the revolution and the people.

6. Build a Strong People's Army

A. Liberate the land and the people step by step through the strategy of people's war. Build a strong land, air, and naval force capable of defending the country's borders, territorial waters, air space, and territorial integrity as well as the full independence, progress, and dignity of its people in order to attain prosperity and reach the highest economic stage. The people's army shall be:

—politically conscious, imbued with comradely relations, and steeled through revolutionary discipline;
—full of resoluteness, imbued with a spirit of self-sacrifice, participating in production; and
—equipped with modern tactics, weapons, and skills.

Being the defender of the interests of the workers and peasants, it serves the entire people of Eritrea irrespective of religion, nationality, or sex. The basis of this army is the revolutionary force presently fighting for national independence and liberation.

B. Establish a people's militia to safeguard the gains of the revolution and support the People's Army in the liberated and semi-liberated areas.

C. Establish a progressive and advanced military academy.

7. Respect Freedom of Religion and Faith

A. Safeguard every citizen's freedom of religion and belief.

B. Completely separate religion from the state and politics.

C. Separate religion from education and allow no compulsory religious education.

D. Strictly oppose all the imperialist-created new counterrevolutionary faiths, such as Jehovah's Witnesses, Pentecostalism, Bahaism, etc.

E. Legally punish those who try to sow discord in the struggle and undermine the progress of the Eritrean people on the basis of religion whether in the course of the armed struggle or in a people's democratic Eritrea.

8. Provide Humane Treatment to Prisoners of War and Encourage the Desertion of Eritrean Soldiers Serving the Enemy

   A. Oppose the efforts of Ethiopian colonialism to conscript duped soldiers to serve as tools of aggression for the oppression and slaughter of the Eritrean people.
   B. Encourage Eritrean soldiers and plainclothesmen who have been duped into serving in the Ethiopian colonial army to return to the just cause and join their people in the struggle against Ethiopian aggression and welcome them to its ranks with full right of equality.
   C. Provide humane treatment and care for Ethiopian war prisoners.
   D. Severely punish the die-hard, criminal, and atrocious henchmen and lackeys of Ethiopian colonialism.

9. Protect the Rights of Eritreans Residing Abroad

   A. Struggle to organize Eritreans residing abroad in the already formed mass organizations so they can participate in the patriotic anticolonial struggle.
   B. Strive to secure the rights of Eritrean refugees in the neighboring countries, win them the assistance of international organizations, and work for the improvement of their living conditions.
   C. Welcome nationals who want to return to their country and participate in their people's daily struggles and advances.
   D. Encourage the return and create the means for the rehabilitation of Eritreans forced to flee their country and land by the vicious aggression and oppression of Ethiopian colonialism.

10. Respect the Rights of Foreigners Residing in Eritrea

   A. Grant full rights of residence and work to aliens who have openly or covertly supported the Eritrean people's struggle against Ethiopian colonial oppression and for national salvation and are willing to live in harmony with the legal system to be established.
   B. Mercilessly punish aliens who, as lackeys and followers of Ethiopian colonialism, imperialism, and Zionism, spy on or become obstacles to the Eritrean people.

11. Pursue a Foreign Policy of Peace and Nonalignment

   A. Welcome the assistance of any country or organization which recognizes and supports the just struggle of the Eritrean people without interference in its internal affairs.

B. Establish diplomatic relations with all countries irrespective of political and economic system on the basis of the following five principles:

—Respect for each other's independence, territorial integrity, and national sovereignty;
—Mutual nonaggression;
—Noninterference in internal affairs;
—Equality and mutual benefit; and
—Peaceful coexistence.

C. Establish good friendly relations with all neighbors.

D. Expand cultural, economic, and technological ties with all countries of the world compatible with national sovereignty and independence and based on equality. Do not align with any world military bloc or allow the establishment of any foreign military bases on Eritrean soil.

E. Support all just and revolutionary movements, as our struggle is an integral part of the international revolutionary movement in general, and the struggle of the African, Asian, and Latin American peoples against colonialism, imperialism, Zionism, and racial discrimination in particular.

Adopted by the First Congress
of the EPLF on
January 31st, 1977

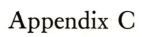

Appendix C

TABLE C.1

U.S. Economic and Military Assistance to Ethiopia, 1946–76
(U.S. fiscal years, millions of dollars)

Program	Postwar Relief Period, 1946–48	Marshall Plan Period, 1949–52	Mutual Security Act Period, 1953–61	1962–69	1970	1971	1972	1973	1974	1975	1976	TQ	Total FAA Period, 1962–76[a]	Total Loans and Grants, 1946–76[a]	Repayments and Interest, 1946–76[a]	Total, Less Repayments and Interest
									Foreign Assistance Act Period							
Economic Assistance, Total	0.8	1.3	84.5	141.9	18.9	23.4	33.0	12.0	36.4	23.8	13.5	0.5	303.4	350.8	40.8	310.0
Loans	0.4	—	29.6	63.6	10.6	14.9	26.7	4.8	15.0	7.2	3.4	—	146.1	145.2	40.8	104.4
Grants	0.4	1.3	54.9	78.3	8.3	8.5	6.3	7.2	21.4	16.6	10.1	0.5	157.2	205.6	—	205.6
AID and predecessor agencies	—	1.2	75.7	104.1	15.6	20.4	31.1	8.8	20.7	17.2	5.6	b	223.5	261.1	36.2	224.9
Loans	—	—	29.6	57.4	10.6	14.9	26.7	4.8	15.0	7.2	—	—	136.6	135.3	36.2	99.1
Grants	—	1.2	46.1	46.6	5.0	5.5	4.4	4.0	5.7	10.0	5.6	b	86.8	125.7	—	125.7
(Security supporting assistance)	(—)	(—)	(—)	(3.3)	(—)	(—)	(—)	(—)	(—)	(—)	(—)	(—)	(3.3)	(3.3)	(—)	(—)
Food for Peace (PL 480)	—	b	8.8	15.5	1.3	0.9	0.8	1.0	13.9	5.2	7.2	0.4	46.2	55.1	4.1	51.0
Loans	—	—	—	6.1	—	—	—	—	—	—	3.4	—	9.5	9.5	4.1	5.4
Grants	—	—	8.8	9.4	1.3	0.9	0.8	1.0	13.9	5.2	3.8	0.4	36.7	45.6	—	45.6
Title I, total	—	—	—	6.1	—	—	—	—	—	—	3.4	—	9.5	9.5	4.1	5.4
Repayable in U.S. dollars, loans	—	—	—	5.6	—	—	—	—	—	—	3.4	—	9.0	9.0	4.0	5.0
Payable in foreign currency, planned for country use	—	—	—	0.5	—	—	—	—	—	—	—	—	0.5	0.5	0.1	0.4
Title II, total grants	—	b	8.8	9.4	1.3	0.9	0.8	1.0	13.9	5.2	3.8	0.4	36.7	45.6	—	45.6
Emergency relief, economic development, and world food program	—	—	8.1	6.5	1.1	0.8	0.7	0.9	13.9 b	5.2	3.2	0.4	32.7	40.8	—	40.8
Voluntary relief agencies	—	b	0.8	2.9	0.2	0.1	0.1	0.1	—	—	0.6	—	4.0	4.8	—	4.8

(US $ millions)															
Other economic assistance	0.8	—	—	—	—	—	—	—	—	—	—	33.7	34.7	0.5	34.2
Loans	0.4	—	—	—	—	—	—	—	—	—	—	—	0.4	0.5	-0.1
Grants	0.4	—	—	—	—	—	—	—	—	—	—	33.7	34.3	—	34.3
Peace Corps	—	—	22.3	2.0	2.1	1.1	2.2	1.8	1.4	0.7	0.1	33.7	33.8	—	33.8
Other	—	—	—	—	—	—	—	—	—	—	—	—	0.9[c]	0.5	0.4
Military Assistance, Total	—	47.7	119.1	12.0	13.2	11.0	12.1	24.1	37.6	7.4	—	238.8	286.1	1.4	284.7
Credits or loans	—	—	—	—	—	—	—	11.0	25.0	—	—	36.0	36.0	1.4	34.6
Grants	—	47.7	119.1	12.0	13.2	11.0	12.1	13.1	12.6	7.4	—	202.8	250.1	—	250.1
MAP grants	—	40.5	98.8	10.6	11.8	11.0	9.4	12.3	12.5	7.4	—	174.6	214.6	—	214.6
Credit sales under FMS	—	—	—	—	—	—	—	11.0	25.0	—	—	36.0	36.0	1.4	34.6
Military Assistance Service Funded grants	—	—	—	—	—	—	—	—	—	—	—	—	—	—	—
Transfers from excess stocks	—	7.2	14.8	1.4	1.4	—	2.7	0.8	0.1	—	—	22.7	30.0	—	30.0
Other grants	—	—	5.5	—	—	—	—	—	—	—	—	5.5	5.5	—	5.5
Total Economic and Military Assistance	0.8	132.2	261.0	30.9	36.6	45.5	24.1	60.5	61.4	20.9	1.3	542.2	636.9	42.2	594.7
Loans	0.4	29.6	63.5	10.6	14.9	26.7	4.8	26.0	32.2	3.4	—	182.1	181.2	42.2	139.0
Grants	0.4	102.6	197.4	20.3	21.7	18.8	19.3	34.5	29.2	17.5	1.3	360.0	455.7	—	455.7
Other U.S. Government Loans and Grants	2.7	9.4	13.1	d	d	d	d	d	d	d	d	13.1	25.2	25.9	-0.7
Export-Import Bank loans	2.7	9.4	13.1	d	d	d	d	d	d	d	d	13.1	25.2	25.9	-0.7
All other loans	—	—	—	d	d	d	d	d	d	d	d	—	—	—	—

TQ = transition quarter

[a] As of September 30, 1976.
[b] Less than $50,000.
[c] Principal fully repaid on loan portion.
[d] No programs subsequent to fiscal year 1966.

Source: U.S., Agency for International Development, Statistics and Reports Division, U.S. Overseas Loans and Grants, July 1, 1945–September 30, 1976, p. 96.

Appendix D

U.S.-ETHIOPIAN AGREEMENTS

The 1962, 1963, and 1964 agreements between the U.S. and Ethiopia concerned deliveries of equipment to the extent funds would be available under the on-going U.S. military assistance program to Ethiopia. Deliveries to Ethiopia of equipment identified under these three agreements have all been completed. The substance of these agreements is as follows:

1962 Agreement—In a memorandum signed in 1962, the U.S. Government agreed to provide certain items of equipment for the Ethiopian Army, Air Force, and Navy. The Army items generally were contained in the 1960 commitment and hence this agreement was simply to speed up delivery of these items. The Army items provided were ammunition, armored personnel carriers, and corrugated roofing material. The Air Force portion of the agreement was to provide T-28D, F-86, and T-33 aircraft and to continue support of the T-28A and F-86 squadrons. The Navy portion of the commitment was to provide one LCM.

1963 Agreement—In a memorandum signed in 1963, the U.S. Government agreed to provide various items of civic action equipment, e.g., woodworking shop equipment, road graders, D-7 bulldozers, road scrapers, scoop loaders, and well-drilling equipment. For the Navy, armed 40-foot Coast Guard utility boats (Sewart Cruisers) were provided. It was also agreed to discuss the organization of the Ethiopian Air Force and Navy.

1964 Agreement—In a message dated 18 June 1964, the U.S. Government authorized the Ambassador to inform the Emperor of Ethiopia that we would provide a squadron of 12 F-5 aircraft to the Ethiopian Air Force. Deliveries of the aircraft were conditioned upon the preparedness of the Ethiopian Air Force to receive them.

Source: U.S., Congress, Senate, Subcommittee on United States Security Agreements and Commitments Abroad of the Committee on Foreign Relations, United States Security Agreements and Commitments Abroad: Ethiopia, Hearings, 91st Cong., 2d sess., June 1, 1970.

Appendix E

ETHIOPIAN ARMED FORCES, 1975-76

Army: 41,000

1 mech div with 1 mech, 2 inf bdes.
3 inf divs, each of 3 inf bdes.
1 tank battalion.
1 airborne infantry battalion.
4 armoured car squadrons.
4 artillery battalions.
2 engineer battalions.
12 M-60 med, 50 M-41 lt tks; about 50 M-113 APC; 56 AML-245/60 armd cars; 36 75mm pack, 52 105mm and 12 155mm how; 146 M-2 107mm and M-20 4.2-in. mor. (36 M-60; M-113 on order.)

Navy: 1,500

1 coastal minesweeper.
1 training ship (ex-US seaplane tender).
5 large patrol craft (ex-US PGM type).
4 coastal patrol craft (less than 50 tons).
4 landing craft (ex-US LCM, less than 100 tons).

Air Force: 2,300; 37 combat aircraft

1 lt bomber squadron with 4 Canberra B-2.
1 fighter-bomber squadron with 10 F-86F.
1 fighter-bomber squadron with 9 F-5A.
1 recce squadron with 6 T-28A.
1 COIN squadron with 8 Saab-MFI 17.
1 tpt sqn with 6 C-47, 2 C-54, 5 C-119G and 3 Dove.
3 trg sqns with 20 Safir, 19 T-28A/D, 20 T-33A, 5 F-5B.
1 hel sqn with 10 AB-204B and 2 UH-IH.
(12 F-5E, 12 A-37B and 15 Cessna 310 on order).

Para-Military Forces: 19,200; Territorial Army active strength 8,000; mobile emergency police force 6,800; frontier guards 1,200; commando force 3,200.

Source: International Institute for Strategic Studies, The Military Balance, 1975-1976.

Appendix F

1. The anomalies which had existed before will be done away with and the people of the Eritrean Administrative Region will, in a new spirit and in cooperation and collaboration with the rest of the Ethiopian people, have full participation in the political, economic and social life of the country. They will, in particular, play their full role in the struggle to establish the people's democratic republic in accordance with the program of the Ethiopian National Democratic Revolution.

2. The program of the Ethiopian National Democratic Revolution has affirmed that the right of self-determination of nationalities can be guaranteed through regional autonomy which takes due account of objective realities prevailing in Ethiopia, its surroundings and in the world at large. To translate this into deeds, the government will study each of the regions of the country, the history and interactions of the nationalities inhabiting them, their geographic positions, economic structures, and their suitability for development and administration. After taking this into consideration, the government will, at an appropriate time present to the people the format of the regions that can exist in the future. The entire Ethiopian people will then democratically discuss the issue at various levels and decide upon it themselves.

3. Having realized the difficulties existing in the Administrative Region of Eritrea and the urgency of overcoming them, and in order to apply in practice the right of self-determination of nationalities on a priority basis, the Provisional Military Government is prepared to discuss and exchange views with the progressive groups and organizations in Eritrea which are not in collusion with feudalist reactionary forces in the neighborhood, and imperialists.

4. The government will give full support to progressives in the Eritrean Administrative Region who will, in collaboration with progressives in the rest of Ethiopia and on the basis of the program of the Ethiopian National Democratic Revolution, endeavor to arouse, organize, and lead the working masses of the region in the struggle against the three enemies of the Ethiopian people—feudalism, bureaucratic capitalism, and imperialism—and thereby promote the unity of the oppressed classes of Ethiopia.

5. The government will give all necessary assistance to those Ethiopians who, because of the long lack of peace in the Eritrean Administrative Region, have been in exile in neighboring countries and

in far-off alien lands so that they may, as of today, return to their own country.

6. The government will make a special effort in rehabilitating those Ethiopians who might have lost their property because of the adverse conditions that had existed. All those who have been dislocated from jobs and their education as a result of the existing problem will be enabled to avail themselves of their employment and educational opportunities which Ethiopia can offer in any of the regions.

7. People who have been in prison as a result of the existing problem will be released. The cases of those who have been sentenced to life imprisonment or death will be carefully examined and reviewed as soon as peaceful conditions are restored and, on the basis of their offenses, they will either receive reduced prison terms or be all together released.

8. The state of emergency will be lifted as soon as the major decisions begin to be implemented and peace is guaranteed in the Eritrean Administrative Region.

9. A special commission entrusted with the task of ensuring the implementation of decisions 5 to 7 above will be established by proclamation.

The Provisional Military Government of Ethiopia believes that the problem in the Eritrean Administrative Region can be peacefully solved along the lines outlined above.

Appendix G

The precise substance of the 1960 commitment is as follows:

Indicative of the deep and continuing interest of the United States in the welfare and progress of Ethiopia, the following are the responses of the United States Government to certain requests previously made by the Ethiopian Government, subject of course in each case to the action of the United States Congress in making available to the Executive Department the funds involved, and upon the mutual development of the usual detailed arrangements for implementation of the proposed projects:

1. The United States agrees to provide in the current fiscal year, certain training, equipment and support for a fourth division of the Imperial Ethiopian Army.

2. The United States agrees to commence discussions with a view to reaching mutual agreement regarding modification of the existing Military Assistance Program to take into account the training and equipment of the fourth division and of such support units as may be mutually agreed upon.

3. The United States will provide to the Imperial Ethiopian Navy, on a loan basis, a seaplane tender (AVP) for use as a training ship and will provide training in the United States for the necessary officers and crew.

4. The United States agrees to study the needs of the Imperial Ethiopian Police with a view to seeing whether the United States is in a position to meet a part of them.

5. The United States is prepared to implement immediately the first stage in the establishment of the Haile Selassie I University, in general accordance with the recommendations of the University of Utah team headed by Dr. Bentley.

6. The United States is prepared to provide, through the Development Loan Fund acting in cooperation with the International Bank for Reconstruction and Development and subject to agreement on loan terms, financing for two road sectors of the Third Highway Program plus additional highway equipment.

7. The United States is prepared to provide up to U.S. $1.5 million in special assistance and to continue technical assistance in the current U.S. fiscal year at approximately the present level for agreed projects and programs.

The United States Government also reaffirmed its continuing interest in the security of Ethiopia and its opposition to any activities threatening the territorial integrity of Ethiopia.

The United States Government announced its great interest in obtaining agreement to the extension of the facilities presently operated by the United States Government at Kagnew Station in Asmara.

Source: U.S., Congress, Senate, Subcommittee on United States Security Agreements and Commitments Abroad of the Committee on Foreign Relations, United States Security Agreements and Commitments Abroad: Ethiopia, Hearings, 91st Cong., 2d sess., June 1, 1970.

BIBLIOGRAPHY

Abir, Mordechai. "The Contentious Horn of Africa." Conflict Studies, vol. 24 (June 1972).

_____. Oil, Power and Politics. London: Frank Cass, 1974.

Addis Ababa Chamber of Commerce. Agriculture, Industry and Commerce in Ethiopia and Eritrea. Addis Ababa, 1957.

Africa, no. 79 (March 1978), pp. 14-15, 25.

Africa Confidential, 1970-79.

Africa Research Bulletin, 1971-79.

Agence France-Presse. Africa, 1977-79.

Araia Tseggai. "The Case for Eritrean National Independence." Black Scholar 7 (June 1976): 20-27.

Association of Eritrean Students in North America. Selected Articles from "Vanguard," October 1977.

Association of Eritrean Students in North America and Association of Eritrean Women in North America. In Defense of the Eritrean Revolution. New York, February 1978.

Barker, Arthur J. Eritrea 1941. London: Faber, 1966.

Bell, J. Bowyer. "Endemic Insurgency and International Order: The Eritrean Experience." Orbis 18 (Summer 1974): 427-50.

Berhane Woldegabriel. "The Refugee Problem." Sudanow 2 (July 1977): 7-14.

Binder, David. "Ethiopia Said to Prepare Attack on Eritrean Rebels." New York Times, May 12, 1976.

Bruce, James. Travels to Discover the Source of the Nile. Edinburgh: G. G. J. & J. Robinson, 1790.

Cabral, Amilear. Revolution in Guinea: Selected Texts by Amilear Cabral. New York: Monthly Review Press, 1969.

Campbell, John Franklin. "Background to the Eritrean Conflict." Africa Report, May 1971, pp. 19-20.

_____. "The Red Sea and Suez." In The Indian Ocean: Its Political, Economic and Military Importance, edited by A. J. Cottrell and R. M. Burrell, pp. 129-53. New York: Praeger, 1972.

Chaliand, Gerard. Armed Struggle in Africa. New York: Monthly Review Press, 1969.

_____. "The Horn of Africa's Dilemma." Foreign Policy 30 (Spring 1978): 116-31.

Conti-Rossini, Carlo. Storia d'Ethiopia. Milan: Officina D'Arte Grafica A. Lucini, 1929.

Davidson, Basil. The Liberation of Guine. Baltimore: Penguin, 1969.

Debusmann, Bernd. "Eritrean Rebels Set Sights on Big Business." Los Angeles Times, October 7, 1977, pt. I-B, p. 4.

Diamond, R. A., and David Fouquet. "American Military Aid to Ethiopia—And Eritrean Insurgency." Africa Today 19 (1972): 37-43.

Eritrea Chamber of Commerce. "Agriculture in Eritrea." Trade and Development Bulletin 2 (March-April 1973): 7-17.

Eritrean Liberation Front. ELF: The National Revolutionary Vanguard of the Eritrean People. N.p., 1978.

_____. Eritrean Newsletter, 1977-78.

_____. Eritrean Revolution, 1975-78. (Bimonthly journal.)

_____. The Eritrean Revolution. Beirut: ELF Foreign Information Center, 1977-78.

_____. The Eritrean Revolution: Sixteen Years of Armed Struggle. Beirut: ELF Foreign Information Center, 1977.

_____. Political Programme. Beirut: ELF Foreign Information Center, May 28, 1975.

Eritrean Peoples Liberation Front. EPLF: Serving the Masses on the Medical Front. New York, October 1976.

_____. National Democratic Programme of the Eritrean People's Liberation Front. N.p., 1977.

_____. Vanguard, vol. 2 (February-March, 1977).

_____. Vanguard, vol. 13 (January 1976).

_____. Vanguard, vol. 1 (January 1973).

Eritreans for Liberation in North America. Eritrea in Struggle, 1976-78. (Bimonthly newsletter.)

_____. Liberation, vol. 6 (July-August 1977).

_____. Liberation, vol. 6 (March-June 1977).

_____. Liberation, vol. 6 (January-February 1977).

_____. Liberation, vol. 6 (November-December 1976).

_____. Liberation, vol. 5 (July-August 1976).

_____. Liberation, vol. 5 (January-February 1976).

_____. Liberation, vol. 5 (September-October 1975).

_____. "Notes on Eritrean History (Part I)." Liberation, vol. 5 (1976).

_____. Reactionary Clique Forced Out of EPLF. N.p., 1976.

_____. Revolution in Eritrea. New York: EFLNA, 1975.

Ethiopian Chamber of Commerce. Guide Book of Ethiopia. Addis Ababa, 1954.

Farer, Tom J. War Clouds on the Horn of Africa. Washington, D.C.: Carnegie Endowment for International Peace, 1976.

Foreign Report 1547 (August 16, 1978): 1-3.

Getahun Dilebo. "Historical Origins and Development of the Eritrean Problem, 1889-1962." Current Bibliography on African Affairs 7 (1974): 221-44.

Gilkes, Patrick. The Dying Lion: Feudalism and Modernization in Ethiopia. New York: St. Martin's Press, 1975.

_____. "Eritrea Could Stand Alone." African Development 9 (April 1975): 18–19.

Great Britain, Ministry of Information. The Abyssinian Campaigns. London: H.M. Stationery Office, 1942.

_____. The First to Be Freed. London: H.M. Stationery Office, 1944.

Greene, Felix. The Enemy. New York: Vintage Books, 1971.

Grimaldi, Fulvio. "The Eritrean Road to Unity?" Middle East, no. 38 (December 1977), pp. 57–59.

_____. "The New Eritrea." Sudanow 2 (December 1977): 23–26.

Gwertzman, Bernard. "U.S. Remains of Two Minds (At Least) on Africa." New York Times, June 4, 1978, pt. 4, p. 1.

Hailu W. Emmanuel. "Concession Agriculture in Eritrea." Ethiopian Geographical Journal 2 (1964): 35–44.

_____. "Major Ports of Ethiopia: Aseb, Jibuti, Mesewa." Ethiopian Geographical Journal 3 (1965): 35–42.

Halliday, Fred. "Soviet Union's Precarious Ethiopian Foothold." New African 127 (March 1978): 19.

Hamilton, David. "Ethiopia's Embattled Revolutionaries." Conflict Studies 82 (April): 16–18.

Hanson, Mary. "Eritrea: The Hidden War in East Africa." Pacific Research and World Empire Telegram, vol. 1 (September 1969).

Hess, Robert L. Ethiopia: The Modernization of Autocracy. Ithaca, N.Y.: Cornell University Press, 1970.

Johnston, Oswald. "U.S. Rejects Somali Bid for Arms, Troops." Los Angeles Times, January 18, 1978.

Lamb, David. "Critical Moment at Hand in Ethiopia's Eritrea War." Los Angeles Times, May 29, 1978.

_____. "Rebellions Erupt in Ten of Ethiopia's Provinces." Los Angeles *Times*, June 19, 1977.

_____. "Russ Isolated in a Somalia They Helped to Develop." Los Angeles *Times*, October 3, 1977, p. 6.

_____. "Somalia Continues to Eye Ogaden Region." Los Angeles *Times*, June 7, 1978, pt. I-A, p. 1.

Legum, Colin. "Realities of the Ethiopian Revolution." *World Today* 33 (August 1977): 305-12.

Levine, Donald. *Greater Ethiopia*. Chicago: University of Chicago Press, 1974.

_____. *Wax and Gold*. Chicago: University of Chicago Press, 1965.

Lobban, Richard. "Eritrean Liberation Front: A Close-up View." *Munger Africana Library Notes*, no. 13. Pasadena: California Institute of Technology, September 1972.

_____. "The Eritrean War: Issues and Implications." *Canadian Journal of African Studies* 10 (1976): 335-46.

Longrigg, Stephen H. *A Short History of Eritrea*. Oxford: Clarendon Press, 1945.

Los Angeles *Times*, May-June 1978.

_____, November 1978.

Marcum, John A. *The Anatomy of an Explosion (1950-1962)*. The Angolan Revolution, vol. 1. Cambridge: Massachusetts Institute of Technology Press, 1969.

_____. *Exile Politics and Guerrilla Warfare (1962-1976)*. The Angolan Revolution, vol. 2. Cambridge: Massachusetts Institute of Technology Press, 1978.

Markakis, John. *Ethiopia: Anatomy of a Traditional Polity*. Oxford: Clarendon Press, 1974.

Markakis, John, and Nega Ayele. *Class and Revolution in Ethiopia*. Nottingham: Spokesman, 1978.

Mesfin Gabriel. "Ethiopia Promises 'the Year of the Offensive.'" New African 126 (February 1978): 23-24.

_____. "The War Effort Takes Too Much." New African 130 (June 1978): 33.

Mesfin Woldemariam. "Ethiopia and the Indian Ocean." In The Indian Ocean: Its Political, Economic and Military Importance, edited by A. J. Cottrell and R. M. Burrell, pp. 181-95. New York: Praeger, 1972.

_____. An Introductory Geography of Ethiopia. Addis Ababa: Mesfin, 1972.

Morrison, Godfrey. "The Southern Sudan and Eritrea," n.p., n.d.

New African, no. 126 (February 1978), p. 25.

_____, no. 124 (December 1977), pp. 1183-85.

_____, no. 122 (October 1977), pp. 986-87.

New York Times, 1978-79.

Newsweek, March 20, 1978, p. 46.

_____, March 13, 1978, pp. 36-42.

_____, January 23, 1978, pp. 35-36.

_____, July 25, 1977, p. 14.

Ottaway, David. "Eritrean Rebel Front Gains Support." Washington Post, October 18, 1974.

Oudes, Bruce. "The Lion of Judah and the Lambs of Washington." Africa Report, May 1971, pp. 21-23.

Pankhurst, Estelle Sylvia. Eritrea on the Eve. Woodford Green, Essex: New Times and Ethiopia News Books, 1952.

_____. Ethiopia and Eritrea. Woodford Green, Essex: Lalibela House, 1953.

Pankhurst, Richard. Economic History of Ethiopia, 1800-1935. Addis Ababa: HSIU Press, 1968.

Papp, Daniel S. "The Soviet Union and Cuba in Ethiopia." Current History 76 (March 1979): 110-14, 129-30.

Peninou, Jean Louis. Eritrea: The Guerrillas of the Red Sea. N.p., 1975.

Randal, Jonathan. "Long Struggle Shows Eritreans They Have Few Friends." Washington Post, April 9, 1978, p. A29.

Robinson, David. "War in Eritrea." Contemporary Review 219 (1971): 1270.

Schoff, Wilfred H., trans. The Periplus of the Erythraean Sea. New York: Longmans, Green, 1912.

Sudanow, 4 (February 1979): 16-17.

_____, 3 (November 1978): 26-27.

_____, vol. 3 (April 1978).

_____, 3 (February 1978): 18.

Tamene Asmara. "Ethiopia Pulls Back, Cites Signs of Peace." Washington Post, June 21, 1976.

Tekle Amare. The Creation of the Ethio-Eritrean Federation. Ann Arbor, Mich.: University Microfilms, 1964.

Time, February 6, 1978.

_____, July 25, 1977, pp. 34-36.

Trevaskis, G. K. N. Eritrea: A Colony in Transition. London: Oxford University Press, 1960.

Trimingham, Spencer J. Islam in Ethiopia. London: Oxford University Press, 1952.

U.S., Congress, House. United States Arms Policies in the Persian Gulf and Red Sea Areas: Past, Present and Future. Report of a Staff Survey Mission to Ethiopia, Iran, and the Arabian Peninsula, Pursuant to H. Res. 313, 95th Cong., 1st sess., 1977.

_____. War in the Horn of Africa: A Firsthand Report on the Challenges for United States Policy. Report to the Committee on

International Relations, 95th Cong., 2d sess., December 12-22, 1977.

U.S. Congress, House. Subcommittee on International and Political and Military Affairs of the Committee on Foreign Affairs. U.S. Policy and Request for Sale of Arms to Ethiopia. Hearings, 94th Cong., 1st sess., March 5, 1975.

U.S., Congress, Senate. The International Security Assistance and Arms Export Control Act of 1977: Report No. 95-195 to Accompany S. 1160, 95th Cong., 1st sess., May 1977.

U.S., Congress, Senate. Subcommittee on African Affairs of the Committee on Foreign Relations. Ethiopia and the Horn of Africa. Hearings, 94th Cong., 2d sess., August 4, 5, and 6, 1976.

U.S., Congress, Senate. Subcommittee on United States Security Agreements and Commitments Abroad of the Committee on Foreign Relations. United States Security Agreements and Commitments Abroad: Ethiopia. Hearings, 91st Cong., 2d sess., June 1, 1970.

Warren, Herrick, and Anita Warren. "The U.S. Role in the Eritrean Conflict." Africa Today 23 (April-June 1976): 49.

Weekly Review (Nairobi) 156 (February 13, 1978): 11-13.

_____, 154 (December 19, 1977): 13-15.

Wells, Michael. "Russians Shelling Massawa?" Manchester Guardian Weekly, January 29, 1978, p. 7.

Yordanos, Gebre Medhin. "Eritrea: Background to Revolution." Monthly Review 28 (September 1976): 52-61.

Zekarios, Ambaye. Land Tenure in Eritrea. Addis Ababa: Addis Ababa Press, 1966.

INDEX

193

About the Author

RICHARD SHERMAN holds a B.A. from the University of California, Los Angeles, and a Phd. in Politics from Brandeis University.

Dr. Sherman has published a number of articles about politics in northeast Africa. His most recent articles have appeared in <u>Horn of Africa</u>.

Dr. Sherman is a consultant on African and Middle Eastern affairs. From 1968-70 he lived in northern Ethiopia as a Peace Corps Volunteer.